the Art of

PLEASE NOTE

The Art of Natural Family Planning is an excellent source of information on the sympto-thermal method of natural family planning. Many couples have learned how to practice this method solely from this book and with complete satisfaction.

Numerous couples are also using this book as part of a comprehensive instructional program. The Couple to Couple League offers these couples two means of obtaining formal instruction.

The League holds **natural family planning classes** in communities across the United States and in several other countries. These courses are taught by certified instructor-couples and normally consist of four two-hour sessions scheduled one month apart. Private counseling is available to those who have attended classes.

A **Home Study Course** is available through the League for those who prefer comprehensive self-instruction because they cannot attend Couple to Couple League classes. Individualized counseling is also available to couples who learn through this course.

For more information on League classes or the **Home Study Course,** contact The Couple to Couple League, P.O. Box 111184, Cincinnati, Ohio 45211.

Natural Family Planning

The Art of
Natural Family Planning

by

John and Sheila Kippley

Foreword by Konald A. Prem, M.D.

Published by
The Couple to Couple League
International, Inc.
P.O. Box 111184
Cincinnati, OH 45211-1184

Third edition, third printing

Third Edition
    Third printing: 20,000 August, 1987
    Previous editions and printings: 200,000

Cataloging Data
L.C. RG 136.K574
    Dewey 613.9434

Kippley, John F. and Sheila K.
The Art of Natural Family Planning
Includes bibliography.
Foreword by Konald A. Prem, M.D.

1. Natural Family Planning   2. Birth Control
3. Sexual Morality   4. Breast-feeding

ISBN 0-9601036-6-X

How to Use This Book

This book is divided into two parts. Part One explains the "why" of natural family planning. Part Two explains the "how to" of the sympto-thermal method of natural family planning.

For most couples the practice of natural family planning is more than just another form of birth control. Because it involves abstinence during the fertile time, most couples have various motivations which lead to the conclusion that natural family planning (NFP) is the best form of conception regulation. In other words to choose NFP is to make and to keep making a reasoned choice, and some of these reasons are examined in Part One.

To learn the practice of natural family planning is similar to learning to tie your shoes. At first it looks extremely simple, then it looks complicated, and then it becomes simple for you. In explaining the how-to-do-it of natural family planning in Part Two, we have chosen to be complete without getting into the detail of a college anatomy class. If this approach makes things appear a bit complicated at first, remember the shoelace example. Imagine what it would be like for you to explain to us in words and diagrams how to tie your shoes—something we do everyday without thinking.

In its broad outlines, nothing could be much simpler to understand than natural family planning. A woman learns to observe a few simple female bodily signs which indicate when she is fertile or infertile, and the couple govern their sexual conduct according to whether they are trying to achieve or avoid conceiving a baby. The details get into an explanation of the fertility symptoms, what causes each one, and how to observe, chart and interpret them. The typical situation is very simple but there are exceptions; and in this manual we analyze a number of out-of-the-ordinary situations so that you can practice NFP more easily. For a quick look at what NFP is like in practice, you might want to turn to Chapter 11. After a few pages of review, there are several examples. We think that most experienced couples will have an experience somewhat like that of Couple A in those examples.

Chapter 11 contains references to some of the key pages dealing with the details of the method. If you are nursing a baby or are pregnant, we suggest that you read Chapter 10 right away. An index, a detailed table of contents, and a glossary of terms also help make this book usable.

Welcome to the growing number of those who have used this manual to discover and use the best methods of birth regulation the world has ever known.

All net proceeds from the sale of this book go to the Couple to Couple League International, Inc., a non-profit organization to assist couples with the successful practice of natural family planning.

For further information:
   The Couple to Couple League
   P.O. Box 111184
   Cincinnati, OH 45211-1184
   Telephone: (513) 661-7612

Note: The national office cannot accept collect phone calls from anyone, nor can it provide counseling to non-members. Please see the next page for information about maintaining membership.

Addresses of other organizations referred to in the text:
   La Leche League International (LLLI)
   9616 Minneapolis Avenue
   Franklin Park, IL 60131
   Counseling telephone number at any time: (312) 455-7730

   ICEA Bookcenter
   Box 20048
   Minneapolis, MN 55420
   U.S.A.
   Telephone: (612) 854-8660

The Art of
Natural Family Planning

This page is for use by couples who are learning natural family planning by self instruction rather than through attendance at Couple to Couple League classes.

In this manual there are several references to additional samples in the CCL *Practical Applications Workbook*. This workbook contains 20 different charts plus an answer sheet, and it is helpful for learning and for building confidence in your ability to interpret charts correctly.

The Couple to Couple League is a non-profit organization supported primarily by contributions from its members, and it publishes a newsletter every other month to keep couples up-to-date about natural family planning. The modest annual membership contribution brings this newsletter to your home.

The most complete manual available, a workbook for gaining experience, and periodic updating and important reminders in the newsletter all form important parts of the overall program of the Couple to Couple League to assist you with natural family planning.

TO: CCL, P.O. Box 111184
Cincinnati, Ohio 45211-1184

Here's our membership contribution. Please send us *The CCL News* six times a year so we can keep up-to-date on natural family planning.

Also send us the Practical Applications Workbook.

Annual Membership Contribution	$15.00
Workbook	2.00

Please make checks payable to the Couple to Couple League. Contributions to CCL are tax deductible. Ohio residents: please add 5-1/2% sales tax to the cost of the workbook.

Please print your name and address as you want *The CCL News* addressed to you.

Name _____Date_____

Address _____

City_____State _____Zip _____

Other materials: Basal temperature thermometers, daily observation charts and other books related to parenting can also be purchased from the CCL National Office. Just ask for a complete materials list.

Acknowledgments

First and foremost, a special note of thanks must be given to Konald A. Prem, M.D. Without his expertise and experience this manual would not be the same and might not exist at all. Dr. Prem was one of the few who kept the light of natural family planning switched on when most of his medical colleagues had opted for the contraceptive approach. He helped us in starting the Couple to Couple League, has given unstintingly of his time to the Twin Cities CCL chapter, and has provided us with what seems to be most of what we have learned about natural family planning. Furthermore, he reviewed the biologically oriented chapters of this book in great detail and suggested numerous alterations to make it both more accurate and more readable.

Secondly, we want to express our indebtedness to the pioneers whose work made this manual possible — to Dr. W. Tyler Smith who in 1855 first described cervical mucus and its relationship to sperm migration, to Dr. Mary Putnam Jacobi who in 1876 was the first to provide an exact description of basal temperature changes during the menstrual cycle; to Drs. Kyusaku Ogino and Hermann Knaus for their discoveries about ovulation in the 1920s; to Dr. T.H. van de Velde, a Dutch gynecologist who in 1926 was the first to recognize the relationship of ovulation and the temperature rise; to Fr. Wilhelm Hillebrand, a German Catholic priest who in 1935 was the first to combine the temperature shift with calendar rhythm; to Dr. Edward F. Keefe of New York for his use in 1953 of the mucus symptom in union with the temperatures and for his discovery in 1962 of the cervical changes throughout the fertility cycle; to Dr. John Marshall of England for his writings on temperature theory; to Drs. Evelyn and John Billings for their work in developing rules of thumb to make the observation of cervical mucus more useful as an indicator of fertility; to Dr. Claude Lanctot, who early recognized and promoted the value of having trained couples instruct others about natural family planning; to the pioneer organizations of couples who have helped so many others during the last decade; to La Leche League for its educational work

vii

about the benefits of breast-feeding.

Thirdly, we want to acknowledge the help we have received from those who reviewed our preliminary edition and sent us their comments and suggestions: Dr. Paul Busam, Rev. Marc Calegari, S.J., Roger and Peggy Carter, Bill and Joan Cossette, Rose Gioiosa, Barbara Gross, Gretchen Healy, Dr. Tom Hilgers, Terry and Nancy Hornback, Dr. Claude and Anne Lanctot, Dr. John McCarthy, Fr. John Mucharski, Dr. Tom Nabors, Rev. Stephen Schneider, O.F.M., Frank and Connie Sheehan, Dr. Pierre Slightam, Paul and Carol Vitek, and Pat Yearian. We also give special thanks to the CCL teaching couples who have made suggestions for making this manual more usable. All of these contributions have made the task of writing this manual much easier, but the final responsibility for the present book must remain with us.

We also acknowledge the kind permission to quote from the following copyrighted sources: Max Levin, "Sexual Fulfillment with Rhythm" *Marriage,* June 1966; Fr. Paul Marx, O.S.B., *The Death Peddlers: War on the Unborn,* Collegeville, Minn.: St. John's University Press, 1971; and Michael F. Valente, *Sex: The Radical View of a Catholic Theologian,* New York: The Bruce Publishing Company, 1970.

Finally, we thank all those couples who have indicated in one way or another their satisfaction with and successful use of the previous editions of this book. Such comments have been helpful indeed in providing the stimulus to complete the present edition in the hopes of making adequate information about natural family planning available to all who desire it.

John and Sheila Kippley
The Couple to Couple League International, Inc.

Table of Contents

sion—Expanded ideas about love—Expanded meanings of the marital embrace—Be positive about the difference—Authentic notions about freedom

Foreword

Natural family planning has come of age. It is therefore with great pleasure that I introduce this book to its readers.

Throughout the history of man, a natural but limited form of child spacing has been available through long term breast-feeding. However, the introduction of bottle feeding with cow's milk and milk substitutes deprived mothers of the natural infertility derived from successful long term lactation. Today only two groups of women still enjoy that period of prolonged postpartum relative infertility: 1) those in cultures in which the practice of nursing described in this book as "ecological breast-feeding" continues and 2) those who have learned this practice despite the lack of cultural support. Since it is scientifically established that maternal breast milk is the best infant food and that the breast-feeding pattern described in this manual definitely provides an extended period of infertility, it is of distinct value that this form of breast-feeding is described and recommended to those interested in natural family planning. On the average, such a nursing pattern may provide 18 to 30 months spacing between births without supplemental spacing methods.

However, most couples today seek to regulate conception beyond the possibilities offered by breast-feeding and many are interested in natural methods. The first real help for those interested in natural family planning became available in the 1930's through the independent research of Doctors Kyusaku Ogino in Japan and Hermann Knaus in Austria. These pioneers in reproductive physiology discovered that ovulation occurs approximately two weeks prior to the following menstruation. From their observations they formulated certain rules of thumb for periodic coital abstinence that became known as "rhythm." Because their systems did not sufficiently consider the various forms of menstrual irregularity experienced by many women, many couples were disillusioned by repeated failures. Although the reasons for these failures are now better understood, rhythm is no longer recommended by natural family planners. It is still recognized, however, for what it was: the first natural family planning system in the history of mankind based upon scientific study and oriented toward an educated awareness of fertility.

The efficiency of natural family planning systems was aided immensely by the discovery that the hormone progesterone, produced by the ovary after ovulation, caused an easily measured elevation of the basal body temperature which persisted until menstruation. Observations of signs and symptoms of ovulation such as ovulation pain (Mittelschmerz), pelvic pressure, changes in the amount and physical characteristics of cervical mucus and changes in cervical os dilatation led to the development of the sympto-thermal method of natural family planning. During the 1950's and 1960's, while studying the reasons for rhythm failures by application of the basal body temperatures graph, I assisted many couples to develop a high degree of proficiency using the sympto-thermal methods for family limitation. Published studies referred to in this manual have shown that a sophisticated practice of the sympto-thermal method can achieve a use-effectiveness rate comparable to or better than most artificial contraceptive methods except sterilization and the original high dose combined oral contraceptive pills.

Although there is no scientific justification for negative comments about the effectiveness of the sympto-thermal method of natural family planning, it is obvious that its effectiveness for any given couple will depend upon several factors: the couple must learn it, understand it, and above all be motivated to make it work. Many couples so motivated have asked in the past and are asking with increasing frequency today this question: "Where can we learn about natural family planning?"

In 1962 the late Doctor Carl Hartman, an eminent reproductive physiologist, wrote in his compendium of human reproduction, *Science and the Safe Period*—"no physician should refuse to teach the best methods of calculating the fertile period to patients requesting the instruction." Unfortunately, the majority of my medical colleagues have ignored this advice: only a few have remained informed and are knowledgeable about the scientific developments in natural family planning. Because of their apathy and lack of information, some physicians attempt to persuade patients to abandon natural family planning in favor of sterilization or the artificial methods.

This widespread physician apathy toward natural family planning provided the stimulus to interested married couples and physicians to organize teaching teams to instruct other interested couples outside the traditional medical setting. A few such groups began to function in the 1960's in certain areas of the country. In 1971 John and Sheila Kippley approached me and with my cooperation established the Couple to Couple League, a volunteer organization to provide the effective teaching of natural family planning on a nationwide basis. In addition, they saw the need for an authoritative instruction manual. I was pleased to cooperate in both of these projects and allowed them to use many of the informative fertility graphs I had collected over more than 20 years of interest and experience in the sympto-thermal method.

The normal instructional format for the interested couple combines formal classes such as those taught by the Couple to Couple League and the personal study of an authoritative manual. However, such an opportunity is not available to all today. While a book is no substitute for adequate personalized instruction, this manual can be used for self-instruction in geographic areas where formal classes are not yet available. Serving as a reliable source of information for married couples and physicians alike, it is an indispensable aid to the successful practice of the art of natural family planning.

Konald A. Prem, M.D.
Professor and Head
Department of Obstetrics and Gynecology
University of Minnesota

Introduction

The title of this manual, *The Art of Natural Family Planning,* was chosen very deliberately. In practice, natural family planning is an art. It involves a certain amount of skill in observing and interpreting the monthly signs. It is relatively simple, but still it has to be learned. It involves the use of reason in the learning process and in making decisions about whether to express mutual marital affection in the coital embrace or in some other way.

As in any art, one's practice of natural family planning improves through experience. It doesn't require any genius to become skilled in this art, but it does require a little practice in the observation and interpretation of signs in order for the couple to feel really comfortable with it. In a way it is like swimming. The person who says "I can't swim and I can't learn and therefore I won't try" will never develop the art of swimming with those attitudes. The person who has an open attitude, follows directions, and practices soon feels comfortable swimming: an art has been learned. So also with natural family planning.

Purpose

The primary purpose of this manual is to help people to develop the art of natural family planning. It can also be used by those, such as doctors, who simply want more information, but it is designed especially for typical couples with common, ordinary concerns about family planning. This manual is intended to help those couples in two ways.

First of all, the manual is as complete a handbook on the various methods of natural family planning as the average couple can buy or can understand.

Secondly, the manual is more than a convenient handbook on the biological aspects of natural family planning. It was not our intention simply to produce a book about the anatomy and physiology of the female reproduction system. We felt that it was necessary to spend some time examining attitudes toward natural family planning. The day is fortunately

1

past when scientists were supposed to inform others about fact after fact without ever making any moral evaluations; and if there is any area of human concern where the use of scientific facts is related to morality, it is in sexual behavior and the transmission of life. The reader should thus realize that every book about sex or birth control expresses the convictions of its author, even if that conviction is that sex is without moral consequence. It is our experience that some writers on this subject cloak their values and their real reasons for writing; we have decided on a policy of openness, even if that means that some readers will reject us.

Our comments about attitudes and morality are intended first of all to help the people who share our convictions. Frequently, such people feel rather lonely today, and they are looking for a way to express their own convictions. Secondly, these comments are intended to raise some questions for others who are open to serious thought about these matters. In our present society, it is difficult to hear these questions raised, and we are convinced that many couples will come to agree with us after further reflection on the values involved. Lastly, a discussion of attitudes is important because in a great many human efforts the key to success is attitude. When the coach of a winning team is asked for the reasons, he almost always names a "can do" attitude as one of his most important ingredients. In this manual, we have assembled accurate information about the scientific facts and explained the attitudes that make for success. We think that with this combination every couple can have a winning effort.

However, the manual is not intended to encourage people to stop having babies. Even though the methods of natural family planning are themselves in accord with the order of God's creation, they can be used selfishly. The advertising industry has subtly developed rather expensive tastes in many of us, and it can be a real temptation to postpone pregnancy or limit our family size more in the interests of materialism than anything else.

At the same time, it is recognized that many couples have what they think are sufficiently serious reasons for wanting to space out or to avoid another pregnancy. Such couples will find in this manual the ways of family planning that are in accord with God's design for human sexuality.

Fertility Awareness

The form of natural family planning that is described in this manual is called the sympto-thermal method. It is essentially a system of observing, recording, and interpreting facts about what is happening within a woman's body during her monthly cycle. As such, the information can be used by couples who want a baby and by others who desire to avoid pregnancy. Those whose natural family planning takes the form of complete abstinence from sexual intercourse rather obviously do not need this information for family planning purposes. However, we know of a group of women in a religious order who became skilled in making some of these observations for the purpose of greater self-knowledge. They found it quite helpful to be able to relate changes of mood to the phases within their menstrual cycles. The same would certainly hold true for married women as well.

Every woman has a periodic cycle, usually about a month long, during which she becomes fertile* and then becomes naturally infertile*. There are certain bodily signs that occur just before, during and after the fertile phase of her cycle. The couple using natural family planning observe and interpret these signs to know when the wife is fertile and when she is infertile. If they want a pregnancy, they have sexual intercourse at the most fertile time; and if they wish to avoid pregnancy, they avoid genital contact during the fertile phase. As we shall explain more fully in later chapters, this does not mean that they shun all show of affection, but it does exclude contact of the sexual organs.

Another aspect of natural family planning is the relationship between ecological breast-feeding and an extended period of natural infertility (the term "ecological breast-feeding" is fully explained in Chapter 10). This manual differs from most books on family planning because it goes into some detail about the proper kind of breast-feeding that provides this form of natural infertility. It also describes various cultural practices that can upset this ecological relationship between mother and baby.

The sympto-thermal method that is described and recommended in this manual differs significantly from the system that was known for years as the "calendar rhythm method" or simply "rhythm." The older calendar rhythm made insufficient allowances for irregularity in the woman's monthly cycle and the woman's own individual ovulation pattern. As a method it had a failure rate that was high enough to be very discouraging to a good number of married couples. The old rhythm system was based on the research reported by Dr. Kyusaku Ogino (1924, Japan) and Dr. Hermann Knaus (1929, Austria), who discovered that a woman ovulates about two weeks before the beginning of her next menstrual cycle. In the fifty-odd years since then, much additional information has been discovered about the changes that take place in a woman's body during the fertile part of her monthly cycle. No one seriously involved in natural family planning today recommends the use of the Ogino-Knaus rhythm, and the criticisms of it should not be made about the methods described in this manual. At the same time, it should be recognized that the Ogino-Knaus rhythm could be effective for about 80 percent of married couples if they were willing to abide by its rules; properly used, it could be about as effective as the mechanical contraceptives available during the years before the Pill.

*See the Glossary of Terms for meanings of words.

The Couple to Couple League

The Couple to Couple League is an interfaith, nonprofit organization dedicated to helping couples develop the art of natural family planning. It began in the fall of 1971 when the authors of this manual secured the assistance of Dr. Konald Prem and began offering what they hoped would be a regularly recurring series of four meetings on natural family planning. At the prescribed time for the beginning of the first meeting in a school library in Shoreview, a suburb north of St. Paul, Minnesota, exactly one person, a lone man, was in attendance. The decision to start promptly at eight o'clock was reconsidered on queasy stomachs,—and within ten minutes or so about thirty people filled the room. Thus, the League was born, and since then we have seen an ever increasing interest in natural family planning.

The Religious Question

From the preliminary edition we received several questions about the inclusion of religious values in this manual. We think that these are valid questions and deserve an answer. Our discussion of this issue is found in Chapter 2.

Mutual Support

Still, a book is no substitute for people. In a society that is increasingly oriented toward contraception and abortion, many believers in natural family planning find themselves in a somewhat embattled position. Thus the League also exists to provide an opportunity for couples to share friendship, concerns, and values in an atmosphere of love and support.

Principles

As an organization the Couple to Couple League has certain principles that guide its operation. These can be stated rather briefly with a short comment on some.

—Natural family planning is an art, and like the arts of natural childbirth or breast-feeding or swimming, it needs to be learned. In animals, for example, swimming is guided by instincts; but among men and women, the natural capacities need to be developed through learning and practicing proper techniques.

—Natural family planning is a truly humanizing art because it utilizes the human powers of observation, analysis, and interpretation. It also develops the same human strengths that are necessary for monogamous marriage and marital fidelity.

—Natural family planning is the best approach in every respect—health, morality, and in the development of married love. Natural family planning can be a marriage-building art because it requires continuous working together, cooperative decision making and in-depth communication. On the other hand, birth control by abortion, sterilization and contraception is contrary to God's order of creation.

—Every couple can learn the various methods involved in natural family planning. Widespread experiments have shown that lack of education is no barrier; even the illiterate have learned to use natural family planning successfully. Present techniques are known as the "sympto-thermal" method, and scientific developments may bring about further additions to the art of natural family planning. The Couple to Couple League does not limit itself to recommending any one technique; instead, it teaches all the available techniques so that each couple can make their own decision about which ones they will use.

—Present methods can determine fertile periods accurately enough so that couples can achieve an efficiency of self-regulation that ranks with the most effective means of contraception.

—"Natural" means that which is in accord with the very being of man and woman as creatures made in the image and likeness of God.

—"Natural" does not mean "doing what comes naturally" in the sense of the easiest or most convenient. In sexual matters, associating "natural" and "easy" has unhappy results including the contemporary acceptance of non-marital relations and contraception.

—Couples need the help of God in placing the sexual drive at the service of authentic married love—both in respect to other men and women and in their own interpersonal relations.

—Because sexual activity is habit-forming, couples benefit from self-control and the resulting freedom that should be a part of a healthy marriage. Such self-control forms a realistic aspect of natural family planning.

—Children are a gift from God, whether asked for or not. If parents are working at becoming lovers, unplanned children will not be unwanted children but will be accepted and loved for their own sake.

—The best instruments for transmitting adequate information on natural family planning are groups of informed couples dedicated to helping other couples. Clinics staffed by professionals have been tried in various places and have not proved to be the answer. Even where successful, clinics are too limited geographically and are expensive to operate. Nor is the individual physician the general answer. Doctors are not only busy, but all too many of them simply don't know much about current natural family planning—and many of them aren't interested. Books such as this one are quite helpful to some, but they are even more helpful in conjunction with group support and discussion.

Thus, it is part of the CCL philosophy to inform interested couples through groups that have regularly scheduled meetings. Leader couples are encouraged to keep meetings small enough so that adequate discussion can take place. A series of four meetings held at monthly intervals forms the core of CCL training, and couples are requested to attend all four meetings for adequate instruction.

If you would like more information about membership in the Couple to Couple League or about starting a chapter where you live, contact CCL at the address given at the end of the next paragraph.

Keeping Up-to-Date

The Couple to Couple League strongly encourages interested couples and other persons to keep up-to-date in natural family planning by becoming members of the League. A small annual membership contribution provides much needed financial support to this non-profit organization. (Contributions are tax-deductible.) It also brings the *The CCL News* 6 times a year. Through this newsletter, the national office informs its members of any and all new developments in natural family planning as well as providing other information and articles of continuing interest. Please send checks and your complete name, address and zip code to CCL, P.O. Box 111184, Cincinnati, Ohio 45211-1184.

Part One

Decision Making

The "Why" of

Natural Family Planning

1
Why Natural Family Planning?
—Some Tangible Values

Introduction

It is difficult to read the newspaper for much more than a week without seeing an article on birth control. Sometimes attention is drawn to the size of the population; at other times, there is an analysis of the birth rates which at the time of this writing have decreased to below the level of zero population growth in the United States and some other countries. Such interest in population is nothing new whether one looks at the big world and national picture or at the small picture of the individual family size. The Reverend Thomas R. Malthus became the father of population studies with his gloomy predictions of overpopulation and starvation in *An Essay on the Principle of Population* published in 1798, and population studies continue to be very much a part of the contemporary scene.

While many couples are concerned with the global population problems, most couples have a more urgent interest in the size of their own family. Studies have indicated that the American and Canadian family in which there is ecological breast-feeding but which practices no conscious form of family planning will have about seven or eight children.[1] That is a far cry from the dozen to fifteen children that some young couples fear they will have if they don't practice contraception from the first day of their marriage, but it is also more than many families feel they would like to manage.

In addition to the statistics that have been developed from cultures unaffected by contemporary cultural trends, the modern Western woman has encountered something that was rarely encountered by her older sisters in a culture such as rural Quebec at the turn of the century; namely, the birth of one child only ten to fourteen months after the birth of another. The fact that this is due almost entirely to the absence of ecological breast-feeding in our culture (as will be seen in Chapter 10) is unknown to most couples, and the prospect of having a baby every year is just plain scary to a great many of them.

9

This ecological imbalance was brought about by cultural pressures ("be free from your baby") and by pediatricians who led Western women to abandon breast-feeding or to become token breast-feeders at best. To attempt to deal with this situation, the obstetricians and gynecologists countered with everything that the drug companies could provide—condoms, diaphragms, foams, jellies, the Pill, the intrauterine device (IUD), and more efficient tools and techniques for abortions.

To be sure, the preceding generalizations do not apply to all doctors, and certainly the development of contraception is due to more than the absence of breast-feeding. Our point is that the emphasis by the medical practitioners concerned with the care of mothers and infants has been oriented in the recent past toward a pharmaceutical rather than a natural approach; the woman who found both a pediatrician and a gynecologist who would teach her what is recommended in this book has been a fairly rare exception to the general rule. Today, some women are fortunate enough to be able to shop around for doctors who either advocate or at least go along with the natural ways of doing things, and when they find their desired combination of pediatrician and gynecologist they consider themselves lucky indeed.

There is no denying the success of the medical-industrial complex in aiding and influencing the Western public to adopt artificial practices in both baby care and birth control. This has been costly as we will indicate later. However, the higher the cost, whether it be in terms of dollars of health or other values, the more evident it is that any knowledgeable person today is aware that all sorts of things and services are being sold for birth control. With all these products and medical services, and with the promise of more drugs to come, why is there a growing interest in natural family planning?

We have found that there are a number of reasons that people give for their new or renewed interest in natural family planning; these reasons tend to be of several somewhat different types. One grouping is concerned with values that are more or less tangible, material or measurable. This includes such values as ecology, esthetics, cost, effectiveness, achieving a pregnancy, physical health, reversibility, life itself, sterilization, and personal freedom. The second group centers around values that are more or less intangible or spiritual such as self-awareness, attitudes toward a baby, personal development, personal moral authority, and religion. A third group of values is concerned with the morality of contraception and its consequences. A fourth group of values places emphasis on marriage building. All in all, a very impressive list of values is involved in family planning. We think an analysis of these values shows that the natural ways of conception regulation are the most advantageous to the person, the couple, and to society.

In reviewing these values, it may seem to some that we are too negative toward contraception. (In this text the word "contraception" and phrases such as "contraceptive approach" include sterilization and the abortifacient methods of birth control as well as those that are temporary means of preventing conception.) It has been suggested that we stress only the positive values of natural family planning while not emphasizing the negative aspects of contraception. Although we are not following that suggestion, we think enough of the feeling behind it to take a few lines to explain why the subject is treated as it is. For one thing, we have found many people very concerned to learn the truth about the health and life aspects of popular birth control practices. Since their experience has been that the Couple to Couple League was the first place they found out some of these things, we feel it useful and perhaps necessary to provide that information, unpleasant as it may be, in this book.

Secondly, we think that some people may be reading these pages in order to get more facts for making a decision. If so, they know already that at first glance the contraceptive approach seems attractive: it is the "in" thing with most doctors, thus making it appear scientific; it looks easy; and it has the obvious feature of maximizing the possible amount of coitus whether such maximization is a real marriage builder or not. On the other hand, they know that natural family planning requires some amount of personal self-discipline and control. However, many people, perhaps even most people, would like to know more about the various bases for comparison between the contraceptive and the natural approaches to family planning—beyond the fact that one may be easier than the other.

Thirdly, some people are interested in the philosophy behind a particular pattern of behavior. While in these few pages we cannot pursue this aspect of the question in the depth we would like to, we can at least point out some significant—and sometimes rather startling—comments made by advocates of the contraceptive approach. We assume also that this book will be read by at least a few people who are not in sympathy with the conviction that natural family planning is both the best and the only morally sound way of family planning. We would hope that as they follow some of the ideas about the philosophical and long-range implications of the contraceptive approach, they will at least come to understand that a negative stand toward contraceptive, technological birth control is not a form of longing for the past but is rather a concern that man should respond to the challenges of life in ways that are not destructive of authentic human values. It is the conviction of many that these human values are supported by the approach of natural family planning but not by the contraceptive one. Readers will have to decide for themselves whether they agree with that conviction after they have read the discussions dealing with the values that are involved in this issue.

Ecology

Some of the renewed interest in natural family planning stems from a growing realization that it is wise to live in accord with nature. Many people are appalled by the harm that has been done by men when they applied their scientific knowledge without sufficient regard for the way it would upset the balance of nature. Others are just as concerned about the bodily pollution that is caused by contraceptive drugs and intrauterine devices. As a result, there is increased concern today for doing things the natural way, whether it involves growing vegetables, feeding a baby or family planning. It would be highly inconsistent for someone to be interested in organic foods and then to take a powerful birth control drug. It should be unthinkable that someone concerned about the life of trees or birds could be unconcerned about the life of human beings still in the womb.

We know that some people are interested in natural family planning because of their interest in the delicate ecological relationship between a mother and her nursing baby, but we don't know how much of it comes from an interest in the wider ecology movement. All we can say is that it would be consistent for ecology-minded people to be interested in natural family planning, and it would be highly inconsistent for them to criticize it.

It is also worth noting that the solutions to basic ecological problems are dependent upon the exercise of a certain amount of self-control by the human race. The acceptance of self-control as a key to the solution of the problems of physical ecology helps prepare people for the self-control that plays a part in natural family planning.

Esthetics

Esthetics has to do with the beauty or "pleasingness" of something. Natural family planning leaves the sexual embrace in its natural beauty. On the other hand, contraceptive condoms, diaphragms, foams, and jellies all have definite esthetic disadvantages. Such methods make it extremely obvious to the couple that they are interfering with the natural character of the act; they also interrupt a certain spontaneity in the couple's sexual activity. Thus, the Pill was greeted with great enthusiasm because it was a form of birth control that did away with the messiness of the applied, on-the-scene, mechanical contraceptives, and it likewise was more effective even though much more dangerous.

Cost

A quite tangible value that should not be overlooked is the almost total lack of expense connected with natural family planning. Drugs, medically prescribed devices, surgical operations, and repeated visits to the doctor are simply not part of natural family planning; the only expenses are for a thermometer, this manual, and a supply of charts. The contraceptive practice has much higher costs, and the couple who suffer some of the side effects from the drugs, devices, or surgery learn how very expensive it can be for the individual family. On a national basis, who could estimate with any accuracy the amount of money spent on the contraceptive approach — regular medical consultations, prescriptions, surgery, drugs, and devices? Could we talk in less than a billion-dollar-a-year figure?

Further financial savings are available to the couples who adopt the practice of ecological breast-feeding described in Chapter 10.

Effectiveness

A rather tangible value that everyone engaged in any form of family planning is looking for is its effectiveness. Since it is rather widely thought that only the contraceptive approaches are effective, let us state emphatically that the natural family planning system recommended in this manual is highly effective. Couples who were skeptical at first, sometimes very skeptical, keep telling us, "It works!"

At this point we must be a bit technical. It is standard procedure in birth control literature to express the effectiveness of any method in terms of the formula devised by Raymond Pearl in the 1930's: "x" pregnancies per 100 woman-years. The number of pregnancies is known as the "failure rate," a rather unhappy way to describe a new baby. A woman-year refers to one year in a fertile woman's life. Thus, one year for 100 women is known as 100 woman-years. Briefly, the formula is as follows:

$$\frac{\text{Number of Pregnancies x 1200}}{\text{Number of Cycles}} = \text{Rate per 100 Woman Years}$$

If 100 fertile age women had regular intercourse for one year without any form of birth regulation or breast-feeding, the statistics indicate that 80 would become pregnant by the end of the year. The conception rate would be 80 per 100 woman-years. Methods of birth control seek to reduce the figure from 80 to something much less.

How do the various methods of birth control compare? Only three methods have a 100% effectiveness: 100% abstinence, male castration (not vasectomy), and what we might call female castration — the removal of both ovaries (not tubal ligations). Every other method results in some pregnancies (or live births, if abortion be called a birth control method).

Two figures are associated with every method. "Method-effectiveness" refers to the effectiveness of the method when it is used according to the rules. "User-effectiveness" refers to the use of that method in actual practice by couples of various levels of motivation and carefulness. For example, if a Pill user forgets to take her Pill one day and becomes pregnant, it is not regarded as a method failure but as a user failure. Similarly, if a couple do not follow the rules of a natural family planning method or make an error of judgment, and the woman becomes pregnant, it is likewise called a user failure instead of a method failure. On the other hand, if a woman on the Pill follows the rules and still becomes pregnant, it is a method failure. Likewise, if a couple follow the rules of natural family planning and the woman still becomes pregnant, it is called a method failure.

Having described the usual technical terminology, we will now make a substitution, and instead of writing "failure rates," we will refer to "surprise pregnancy rate," because when a birth regulation method fails, the result is not a failure but a new human being.

Effectiveness of the Natural Methods

One of the highest effectiveness rates reported with any method including sterilization comes from a French study published in 1967 in which the couples followed a conservative temperature-only system.[2] They did not have coitus from the start of menstruation until the temperature graph clearly indicated the beginning of postovulation infertility. If the temperature rise was ambiguous, they waited, sometimes for the entire cycle. With such a conservative approach there was only 1 surprise pregnancy in 17,500 cycles yielding a Pearl index of .07 per 100 woman years or 7 per 10,000 woman-years.

● **Doctor Josef Roetzer** of Austria has twice published the results of his work with the sympto-thermal method. In 1978, [3] he reported three pregnancy rates:

1) from coitus in the first six days of the cycle; 2) from coitus in postovulation infertility by his rules; 3) an overall user rate including those who went beyond day 6 and/or did not follow the rules for determining postovulation infertility.

1) Coitus in the first 6 days yielded 1 pregnancy in 8,532 cycles, a Pearl index of less than 0.2 per 100 woman-years.

2) Coitus in postovulation infertility resulted in zero pregnancies in over 17,000 cycles.

3) The overall user rate was a Pearl index of 0.8 (12 surprise pregnancies in 17,026 cycles).

Dr. Roetzer's previous publication reported essentially the same very low surprise pregnancy rates but with fewer cycles.[4] His basic rule of thumb for determining the start of postovulation infertility is explained in Chapter 8 of this manual.

● **Doctor G. K. Doring** of Germany used a different method of determining the fertile and infertile phases. Among 307 couples having coitus only in postovulation infertility and using a temperature-only method, there were 8 pregnancies in 11,352 cycles yielding a Pearl user surprise pregnancy rate of 0.8 per 100 woman-years. Of those 8, "1 was due to a misinterpretation of a temperature rise caused by a cold, 5 were pure patient errors, i.e., intercourse during the fertile phase and 2 had incomplete records . . . Conception never occurred on the 3rd day of hyperthermia," i.e., the post-ovulation upward shift in temperatures.[5]

Another 689 couples in the Doring study had coitus in the time of pre-ovulation infertility according to the calculation "first day of thermal shift minus 7 yields the last day of pre-ovulation infertility," and there were 13 surprise pregnancies from that practice. The overall user rate among the 996 couples was 3.1 per 100 woman-years, 125 surprise pregnancies in approximately 48,387 cycles. Of these, 119 pregnancies were as follows: "12 had misinterpreted temperature rises from colds, 13 conceived toward the end of the 'safe' postmenstrual period, 56 were pure patient errors and 38 had kept incomplete records."[6] We do not have all the data, but a rough analysis indicates that there was a surprise pregnancy rate of less than 1 per 100 woman years among the group who tried to follow the rules — including those who made erroneous interpretations — but excluding those who had coitus at an obviously fertile time or didn't keep adequate records.

● Another study shows the importance of motivation and proper instruction. **Professor Frank Rice** of Fairfield University has reported the results of a sympto-thermal study conducted simultaneously in five countries: Canada, Colombia, France, Mauritius and the United States.[7] The rules used were more liberal than those of Dr. Roetzer or the standard CCL guidelines. There were 128 unplanned pregnancies among the 1,022 couples who contributed a total of 21,936 cycles, yielding a Pearl pregnancy user rate of 7.47 per 100 woman-years. That figure is a bit high for two reasons: one country, Colombia, had a much higher rate than the others due to some initial instruction problems; secondly, for purposes of analysis pregnancy was considered unplanned if the couple did not indicate in the *previous* cycle that they intended to achieve pregnancy in the next cycle. Thus at least 16 last minute "planned" pregnancies were counted as "unplanned."[8]

When the method surprise pregnancies were analyzed as a separate group, there were only 16 cases where following the instructions still resulted in pregnancy, yielding a method effectiveness Pearl rate of .93 per 100 woman-years.

The importance of motivation is illustrated by the Canadian sample. Among couples simply seeking to *delay* another pregnancy the Pearl unplanned user pregnancy rate was 16.09. However, among those trying to *prevent* future pregnancies, the user rate was 1.09 per 100 woman-years. The overall user rate averages in this study were 14.83 for the delayers and 4.13 for the limiters.[9]

METHOD EFFECTIVENESS
Pregnancies to be expected in the first year among 100 fertile
women when the methods are used properly at all times.

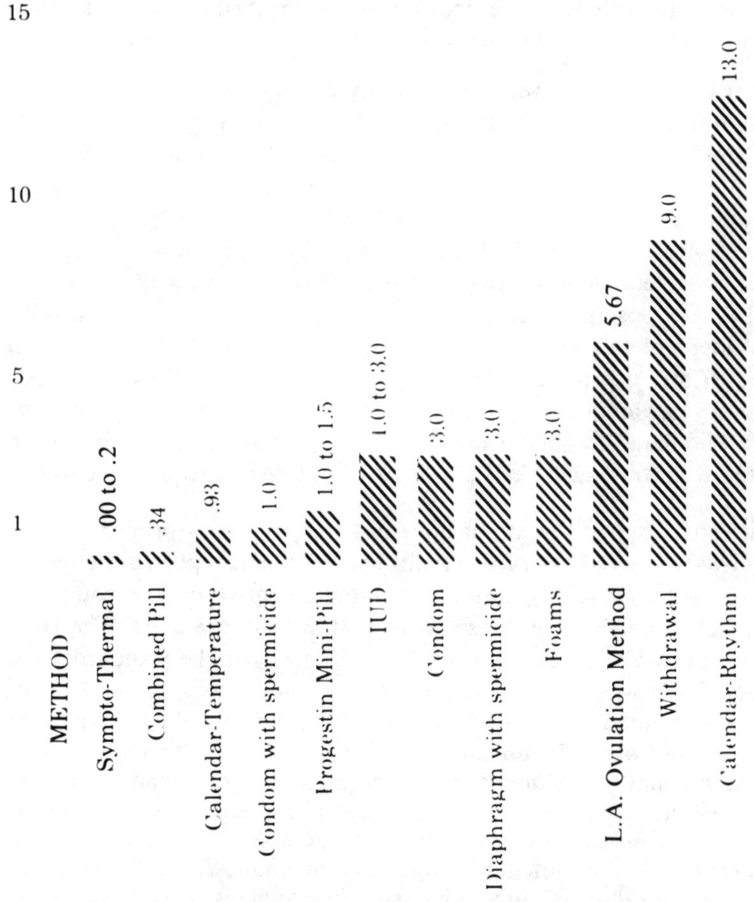

Data base: Sympto-Thermal: J. Roetzer, B. Vincent, M. Wade;
Ovulation Method: M. Wade;
Calendar-Temperature: F.J. Rice;
Other methods: R.H. Hatcher.

**Figure 1.1 Method Effectiveness of Natural and Non-natural
Methods of Birth Control**

●From 1976 to 1978, the U.S. Department of Health, Education and
Welfare sponsored a study to determine the **relative** user effectiveness of
the Sympto-Thermal Method and the Billings Ovulation Method. Couples
with a serious reason to avoid pregnancy were not allowed in the study,
and the resulting group can fairly be called a spacer group by reason of
young age, small family size, and lack of a serious reason for avoiding
pregnancy. At the pure method rate, both sides showed excellent results:
zero method pregnancies with the Sympto-Thermal Method (STM) and

only six with the Ovulation Method (OM) for a Pearl rate of 5.67 per 100 woman years. At the level of user effectiveness, **Dr. Maclyn Wade** and others found that the OM group had an unplanned pregnancy rate approximately two and one-half times higher than that of the STM group.[10] The higher unplanned pregnancy rate in the OM group occurred despite the fact that the OM teachers spent 50% more counseling time with the OM group. The STM Pearl rate of 15.15 per 100 woman years is in the same effectiveness ball park with the spacer group of the Rice-Fairfield study above; the OM Pearl rate of 37.3 is in the same range as spacers using calendar rhythm.[11] It must be noted that the only purpose of the study was to determine the user effectiveness of the two methods relative to each other under the same conditions of instruction and with a randomized sample. Considering the very high *method* effectiveness of both systems, the big difference in *user* effectiveness rates has raised some still unanswered questions.

Effectiveness of the Non-natural Methods

Many studies have been reported, and no two are exactly the same. Doctor Robert Hatcher of Emory University has converted some of these studies into a table showing the approximate number of pregnancies during the first year of use.[12] He gives two rates: one for the method when "used correctly and consistently" and the other as the "average U.S. experience among 100 women who wanted no more children." These correspond closely to the terminology of method effectiveness and user effectiveness except that his user effectiveness includes only the "limiters" but not the "delayers."

● The Various Methods

Sterilization has the lowest surprise pregnancy rates: .04 for tubal ligation (both method and user) and .15 for vasectomy (both method and user). The combined Pill had a pure method rate of .34 but a user rate of 4.0 to 10.0. The low dose progestin-only Pill had a higher method rate (1.0-1.5) but almost the same user rate (5.0-10.0). The IUD had a method rate of 1.0 to 3.0 and a user rate of 5.0. The condom had a method rate of 3.0 and user rate of 10.0. Used with a spermicide the respective rates were less than 1.0 and 5.0. The diaphragm used with a spermicide had a method rate of 3.0 and a user rate of 17.0 while foams by themselves had a method rate of 3.0 and a user rate of 22.0. According to Hatcher, coitus interruptus (withdrawal before ejaculation) has a method rate of 9.0 and a user rate of 20.0 to 25.0.

The Hatcher figures for a method when used correctly and consistently are practically identical to those listed in a client brochure published by HEW.[13] However, the HEW brochure, instead of giving the actual use rates which include carelessness, etc., uses the phrase "but much less effective if used carelessly" for most of the methods listed.

USER EFFECTIVENESS: LIMITERS / SPACERS

Pregnancies in the first year among 100 fertile women classified according to intention to limit family size or to have children later.

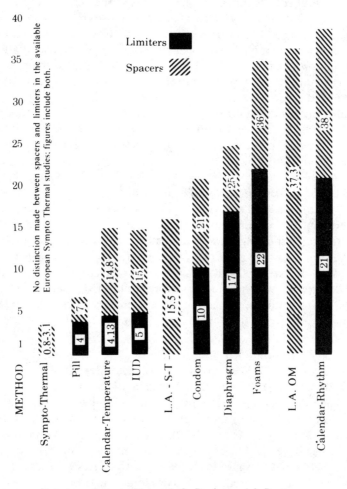

Data base: Sympto-Thermal: G. Doring and J. Roetzer;
Los Angeles STM and OM: M. Wade
Calendar Temperature: F.J. Rice;
Other Methods: N.Ryder and F.Jaffe
See references in text.

Our sources for Limiters/Spacers User Effectiveness did not provide separate categories for "condom with spermicide" and "withdrawal."

Figure 1.2 User Effectiveness of Natural and Non-natural Methods of Birth Control

● **A comparison between spacers and limiters** has been provided by Frederick S. Jaffe,[14] summarizing some work of Norman B. Ryder.[15] This comparison claims to show the percent of women who will become pregnant on a specific method during the first 12 months of use, and it shows significant differences between those using a method only to delay pregnancy and those wanting no more pregnancies. Thus according to Jaffe, each method had the following unplanned pregnancy rates. The figures are given in the percent of women who would become pregnant in the first 12 months. The first figure is for those seeking to delay (d) a pregnancy; the second figure represents those seeking to prevent (p) a pregnancy. Users of the Pill: 7% d and 4% p; the IUD: 15d and 5p; condoms: 21d and 10p; diaphragms: 25d and 17p; foam: 36d and 22p; douche: 47d and 40p.

Obviously, as with modern NFP, motivation makes a difference.

Several things should be noted about these statistics. The figures for the birth control pill and IUD come only from those women whose bodies can tolerate them. That is, the statistics do not take into account those women who stopped these practices because of adverse reactions. Secondly, the IUD is not a method of conception regulation but of postconception abortion, and it is quite possible that the oral "contraceptives" do likewise (see section "Life Itself"). For the person who respects human life from its beginning, these two methods of "birth control" are ruled out, regardless of morality of contraception itself.

There is firmly documented evidence to show that the modern symptothermal method can be used with the same effectiveness as anything else that is currently available with the possible exception of sterilization. Still, it is part of the philosophy of the Couple to Couple League to stress that some pregnancies are going to occur even with a pregnancy rate of less than 1 per 100 woman-years of use.

The adoption of abortion as a backstop to contraception is directly related to the absolutizing of birth control by some advocates of contraception. We believe in absolutizing only God, human life itself, and then the natural way that the Creator has given us for fertility awareness and control.

Achieving a Pregnancy

Many couples who have borne children cannot appreciate the frustration childless couples experience in their desire to bear even one child. Such couples are dismayed even more by the fact that adoption is a very slow process. Due to the vast number of abortions, couples are now waiting two or even three years before they can adopt an infant and their chances of adopting a second infant are slim. In addition, these couples can spend a great deal of money visiting specialists and going through a battery of tests due to their fertility problem.

The fertility awareness developed through the Couple to Couple League natural family planning program can be of great help to couples who have experienced difficulty or unusual delay in achieving pregnancy. In an informal survey, it was found that upwards of 80 percent of the couples attending CCL meetings to achieve a pregnancy had accomplished their objective during the course of instruction or shortly after completion of the series. To those acquainted with fertility awareness, the advice given to some couples by their medical specialists seems as futile as it is costly, and the values of natural family planning are all the more evident.

Physical Health

Physical health is an important tangible value that is respected by natural family planning. In all fairness, it can be said that it is also respected by users of the older forms of contraception, namely the condom and the diaphragm. However, such statements cannot be made about the three most popular forms of birth control today: the Pill, the IUD, and sterilization. For risks of spermicidal foams, see note at end of chapter.

● The Pill

The same newspapers that help to promote the current contraceptive techniques also carry news about their drawbacks. Congressional hearings have been held on the medical hazards of the Pill and entire books have been written about its dangers to health. One author, Morton Mintz, in his book *The Pill*, calls it the most dangerous drug ever unleashed among the general public.[16] Although he is an advocate of contraception, Mr. Mintz condemns the Pill because it subjects women to the risk of blood clots, paralysis, and death when such risk is unnecessary. The older methods may have been less pleasing and less esthetic, but they carried no risk to the woman's health. The long term risks to health from continuous use of the Pill have yet to be determined. Not too long ago, a case of vaginal cancer was traced to the use of a drug by the patient's mother during her pregnancy about 20 years previously. Such long-term results raise all sorts of questions about the ultimate effects of using the Pill.

The short term effects are already apparent. In 1976, a book titled *First Do No Harm* related the personal story of a young woman who died of cancer induced by the Pill.[17] What was unique in her case is that she fought the drug companies and won a settlement that still allowed her to tell her story while most settlements call for silence.

On December 7, 1976, the *Federal Register* carried the revised patient and physician labeling proposed by the Food and Drug Administration,[18] and the new labeling became effective April 3, 1978. Thus the woman who receives a box of birth control pills now also receives a patient insert warning her about the potential risks of taking the Pill. She is warned about increased risks of blood clots which can cause strokes, heart attacks or a pulmonary embolism, all of which can be fatal. She is warned that a clot can cause blindness or impaired vision. She is also warned about a possibility of cancer, liver tumors whose rupture can be fatal, and an increased risk of birth defects in children conceived while her body is still affected by the Pill. In addition, the risk of a developing girl contracting cancer of the cervix or vagina if her mother had DES (diethylstilbestrol), an estrogen, during the pregnancy is estimated at about 1 chance in 1,000 exposures or less. And the list goes on. You can get it from anyone taking the Pill. However, the method used to whitewash all of these alarming warnings is a chart purporting to show that the risks of death are even greater from pregnancy. This is misleading in at least three respects. First of all, many of the problems of the Pill are serious but not necessarily fatal. A woman can live for years with a stroke or impaired vision or blindness. Secondly, most of the mortality risk of pregnancy is concentrated in an identifiable high risk group of women who should never be given the Pill. Thirdly, the relative mortality rates are contradicted by the following British study.

On October 8, 1977 an article titled "Mortality among Oral-contraceptive Users" appeared in *The Lancet*, an English medical journal. The authors reported on a large study in the United Kingdom. Women on the Pill had a death rate from diseases of the circulatory system 5 times greater than the controls, and this death rate became 10 times greater than the controls if the women had been on the Pill continuously for five years or more. The overall total mortality rate among the women who had *ever* used the Pill was increased by 40%. This excess mortality rate "was substantially greater than the death rate from complications of pregnancy in the controls," and it increased with age, cigarette smoking, and duration of oral contraceptive use.[19]

People die from the consequences of overweight, but is it imaginable that the Food and Drug Administration would allow the drug companies to market a weight control pill that carried such risks to life and health?

● The IUD

The intrauterine device likewise has its share of disadvantages to the health of the mother. It can cause irritation, bleeding, cramping, perforation of the uterus, and even death. It also seems to damage the Fallopian tubes, and it has been responsible for pelvic inflammatory disease (PID).

Damage to the uterus from the IUD itself and from PID sometimes leaves a woman permanently sterile — perhaps capable of conceiving but not capable of carrying the baby in the damaged uterus. The FDA notes that the use of the IUD "clearly carries with it some risk of pelvic inflammatory disease and possibly infertility." Thus, "it is essential that physicians discuss the desire for further pregnancy with all women prior to IUD insertion."[20] An increased risk of ectopic pregnancy has also been noted.[21]

The booklet that the FDA now requires patients to be given before insertion warns the woman of the following possible adverse reactions: anemia, backache, blood poisoning (septicemia), bowel obstruction, cervical infection, complete or partial expulsion, cysts on ovaries and tubes, delayed menstruation, difficult removal, embedment, fainting at the time of insertion or removal, fragmentation of the IUD, intermenstrual spotting, internal abdominal adhesions, pain and cramps, painful intercourse, pelvic infection, perforation of the uterus or cervix, pregnancy, pregnancy outside the uterus (tubal or ovarian), prolonged or heavy menstrual flow, septic abortion (infected miscarriage) followed in some cases by blood poisoning (septicemia) which can lead to death, spontaneous abortion (miscarriage), vaginal discharge and infection.

Some of the warnings border on the tragi-comical. For example the booklet for the Cu-7 (Searle Laboratories' IUD) warns that there may be some complications with removal if the retrieval thread isn't visible or breaks. Then the doctor might have to use an instrument or X-ray. Or the woman may have to be hospitalized where a D & C might have to be performed. If some of these procedures become necessary, says the booklet, "you may have to wait a little while for a new Cu-7 to be inserted, until your doctor determines that the uterus has returned to normal" (1977 Cu-7 booklet). As if a woman would want another one after all of that!

Faced with these rather obvious disadvantages to health, many couples have turned to sterilization of either the man or the woman. Female sterilization involves various methods of cutting or blocking the Fallopian tubes, while male sterilization consists of cutting or blocking the vas deferens (vasectomy).

● **Female Sterilization**

The operations are commonly thought to have small risks, but that is not the same as no risk. H.P. Dunn, M.D., notes that "every operation carries the risk of hemorrhage or infection. Sterilization by laparoscopy involves blowing up the abdominal cavity with nitrous oxide gas, introducing a small telescope, and dividing the tubes with diathermy. Some patients have died from cardiac failure during the inflation procedure. Others have suffered wounds of the bowel, bladder, and large blood vessels. Even intra-abdominal explosions have occurred.[22] He also notes that "the 14 days after childbirth are the worst, not the best, time to have any operation."[23]

Complications following a tubal ligation are fairly common. "If pregnancy does occur, there is an increased risk that the embryo will lodge in the divided tube."[24] This is known as an ectopic pregnancy; it is always fatal to the new life and can be fatal to the mother. A death rate from the coagulation technique was reported to be 8 per 100,000 women in 1973-74 compared to 3 per 100,000 for the Pill and 4 to 5 per 100,000 for the IUD.[25]

Subsequent gynecological ills and treatment have been reported in a number of articles. M.V. Muldoon reported that of 374 patients who were followed for at least 10 years after tubal ligation, 43% needed further gynecological treatment and 25% required major gynecological surgery.[26] J.R. Neil and others followed 454 patients for up to 28 months and found that from 22% to 39% of sterilized women had subsequent menstrual problems such as much heavier periods and increased menstrual pain.[27]

● **Vasectomy**

Will a vasectomy improve the sexual practice and the overall marriage of the couple by relieving them from the fear of pregnancy? The evidence does not support that view.[28] Dr. William A. Nolen, writing in *McCall's,* noted that men should not have vasectomies in order to solve marital problems. "This is a trap that many couples fall into: They aren't getting along—and they think that a vasectomy will make life wonderful again. It won't. Very few marital problems are solved so neatly. The problems that disrupt most marriages aren't cured by cutting out a bit of tissue."[29]

Furthermore, as male sterilization has become more popular, there have been increasing reports about various side effects. In addition to some nasty, very painful immediate reactions, there is also the problem of long term continued discomfort.[30] A vasectomy does nothing to prevent the continued manufacture of sperm. Normally, excess sperm is discharged through a nocturnal emission, but such a natural process is prevented by a vasectomy. Thus, the sperm, a protein, has to be reabsorbed into the body's tissues; as a result, some men have experienced discomfort ranging from aching testicles to low-grade fevers. In addition, various articles have mentioned problems of psychological health suffered by some men who have had themselves sterilized. Such problems, which began only after the vasectomy, included "complete impotence, persistent premature ejaculation and even one case of vaginal irritation in one wife."[31]

The absorption of the sperm as a foreign protein by the body causes the body to develop antibodies against the sperm. What this will do to the body's natural immunity system is not thoroughly known, but several serious questions have been raised. Doctor H. J. Roberts suspects that a whole series of long term systemic disorders may be caused by vasectomies. His observations of men in their 20's and 30's found a whole series of systemic problems in these men whose "only common denominator was vasectomy."[32] These problems included "unexplained thrombophlebitis, prolonged fever, generalized lymph node enlargement . . . recurrent infection, various skin eruptions, acute multiple sclerosis, liver dysfunction . . ."[33]

Rheumatoid arthritis is added to this list by Dr. John Bernard Henry of Syracuse who told a 1972 medical gathering that he had found suspicious, potentially cell-destroying antibodies in 9 to 12 men who have had vasectomies more than a year previously.[34]

Animal studies with rats, rabbits, and monkeys have shown connections between vasectomy and abnormal conditions in the test animals. The most recent of these was the monkey study in which the vasectomized animals had almost twice as many cholesterol deposits on artery walls.[35] In the human, this is one of the major factors disposing people to heart disease. While causality may not be proved as yet in the human, a definite association between vasectomy and various long-term disorders has been reported.

All of this illustrates the value of an editorial in the *British Medical Journal*. "It is a sound guiding principle of surgery never to disturb the function of a normal structure except as may be necessary for the effective treatment of a related disorder. Consequently, whereas vasectomy may be appropriate in the treatment of established urogenital disease to prevent the spread of infection, its performance in a healthy man for a purpose other than for the protection of his own health is difficult to reconcile with the traditions that normally guide clinical judgement."[36]

In short, nature bats last, and it is not good medical practice to contradict mother nature by performing surgery that has no health benefit but has significant risks.

Reversibility

A related consideration is the permanence of sterilization. Female sterilization (tubal ligation) and male sterilization (vasectomy) are rarely reversible, and because of this, sterilization is truly a drastic step. Thus, it is out of the question for couples who simply want to space their children, and even couples who are satisfied with their present family size are counseled to consider whether they want to destroy their ability to have future children. If one spouse should die and the other should remarry, might not that couple desire another child?

A similar comment can be made about the Pill and the IUD. Sometimes they are not quickly reversible—if at all. The effect of the Pill may be long lasting in some cases; and if the IUD has damaged the uterus, the result may be one miscarriage after another.

On the other hand, with natural family planning there are no such drawbacks. The couple who wish to achieve a pregnancy simply begin having coitus during the fertile phase of the cycle.

Life Itself

The current, popular practice of contraception has raised the question whether the value of family planning is a value greater than life itself. Specifically, the available evidence indicates overwhelmingly that the basic mode of operation of the IUD is to prevent the seven-day-old, newly conceived human being from implanting into the walls of the uterus, thus causing its death.[37] The manufacturers admit this. The Cu-7 patient booklet states that "IUDs seem to interfere in some manner with the implantation of the fertilized egg in the lining of the uterus."[38] Thus the IUD is a method of abortion rather than conception regulation, carrying with it all the moral disvalues that accompany the killing of innocent, weak, and helpless victims.

Somewhat the same thing may be said about the Pill. Drug manufacturers now admit that the Pill may act as an abortifacient (an abortion-causing drug) rather than as a means of preventing ovulation. Researchers have noted that "among women who have been followed over a considerable number of cycles, breakthrough ovulations occur in two to ten percent of cycles,"[39] Since the Pill does not have method surprise pregnancy rates of 2 to 10 percent, the question is raised about how it achieves its effectiveness when it does not suppress ovulation.

It has been known since 1957 that the Pill containing a combination of synthetic estrogen and progesterone has a triple threat mechanism for birth control: 1) suppression of ovulation, 2) thickening of cervical mucus which renders sperm migration more difficult, and 3) changing the endometrium (the lining of the uterus) to make it very hostile to implantation. Regarding the abortifacient potential of the Pill, a late president of Planned Parenthood had this to say: "With combined therapy the endometrium undergoes predecidual transformation very early in the 20 day therapeutic cycle and regresses, ending in a picture of exhausted, inactive glands. The appearance of the endometrium differs so markedly from a normal premenstrual endometrium that one doubts it could support implantation of a fertilized egg."[40] In plain English, the combined Pill shrivels up the lining of the uterus and makes implantation of the new human life almost impossible.

The older higher dosage combined therapy pills probably achieved most of their effectiveness by preventing ovulation, but there are serious questions whether the lower dosage combined pill and the progestin-only minipill prevent ovulation very much or at all.

Some of the pill makers say that the thickened mucus makes sperm migration almost impossible, but experience has shown that a woman must wait for several days of thickened or "dried up" mucus if she wants to avoid pregnancy. In other words, she has to wait long enough for the egg to disintegrate because experience has proved that sperm still migrate despite the absence of the more fluid mucus.

The abortifacient properties of the progestin-only pill are openly admitted. According to the FDA, "The primary mechanism through which [the progestin-only pill] prevents conception is not known, but progestin-only contraceptives are known to alter cervical mucus, exert a progestinal effect on the endometrium, interfering with implantation and in some patients, suppress ovulation."[41] Translated, that means that rarely does it suppress ovulation, and the previous comments about mucus and sperm migration apply. Thus it seems that the primary mechanism of the progestin-only pill is its anti-implantation action on the endometrium.

With regard to users of the IUD, the evidence indicates that if they are having coitus during the fertile phase of the cycle, they and their physicians are in all probability responsible for the death of newly conceived children—possibly each month. We cannot make such a strong statement about all users of the Pill because of the varieties of the Pill and the more confused data about how they work each month. Rather, we can repeat the statement of Dr. Albert Lorincz that it cannot be said for sure that the Pill is not acting as an abortifacient.[42] To put it another way, the evidence indicates that there is a *definite possibility* that the pill is acting as an abortifacient in any woman in any cycle. It is *probable* that this is the most common action of the progestin-only minipill.

When there are other alternatives, whether contraceptive or natural, which carry no such death-causing risks for a newly conceived human being, we fail to understand how anyone who expresses concern about the value of human life can use or prescribe the IUD or the Pill for birth control. Furthermore, if the pill is prescribed as a drug to regulate a menstrual disorder, then it seems to us that the couple should be instructed about the possible abortifacient character of the drug and should be advised not to have coitus during the time that would normally be the fertile phase of the cycle. We are certainly not advocates of the condom or the diaphragm, but at least these are not abortifacient. Thus, they are not directly opposed to the value of life itself, however unesthetic and less effective they may be.

Sterilization: Further Considerations
—Personal Freedom

Normally the topic of freedom would be grouped with the nontangible values, but some recent events have led us to consider it among the tangible values. After all, if you should be sterilized by force, would not that be a very tangible interference with your freedom? If there is a growing acceptance of having one's own self sterilized, then there is also going to be an accompanying decline in the public rejection of sterilization as something wrong or evil. People who have had themselves sterilized are usually not going to admit that they did something wrong; some of them publicly tell the world they did something good. If voluntary sterilization of oneself is no longer regarded as a moral wrong, then it is a small step in the real world (however huge a step it may be according to strict logic) to see it as not wrong but even a good to do to someone else.

Thus, we think it is valid to be concerned that the public acceptance of sterilization may diminish the personal freedom of those who do not want to be sterilized. Certainly, we are aware that the advocates of population control through sterilization tell us that they seek only voluntary sterilization, but it is a difficult for us to believe such talk in the face of evidence from around the world that governments have provided economic incentives for sterilization and have provided very stiff penalties for families larger than the government-approved size. For example, the sterilization programs in India have been a far cry from Gandhi's "birth control through self-control." If a body politic becomes convinced that there is nothing morally wrong with contraceptive sterilization in itself, then we can look forward to arguments such as these: "It is a social good to be sterilized; it is antisocial not to be sterilized; the government has the right and the obligation to enforce social behavior for the common good; therefore the government can impose sterilization." "Just as the government has the right to separate wage-earners from some of their money through taxation, it also has the right to separate married people from some of their fertility through sterilization." Never mind that these arguments proceed from unproved statements; logic hasn't won too many elections. The point is that when a public regards sterilization as morally permissible, it is going to be increasingly less concerned about whether it is voluntary or forced; then the people in a democracy will be softened up to accept arguments that equate forced sterilization and taxation as both distasteful and unpleasant but necessary for the common good. People whose government is less than democratic may not be able to offer any counter-arguments. We have the unhappy precedent that sterilization was one of the first steps taken by the Nazis to exterminate the Jews.

"Of course," many will say, "it can't happen here." The truth of the matter is that it has already begun. In the summer of 1973, the nation was alerted to the fact that certain welfare recipients were being sterilized. The particular incident that made news involved two young black girls who were sterilized with their consent, but the question of their ability to make a *meaningful* consent to a permanent loss of their fertility was challenged. In this case, legal action was taken against the doctor and others, but what will happen in another decade or so if sterilization gains a stronger hold on the public mind?

To avert these dangers we all need to face up to the reality of what contraceptive sterilization is all about. It is a physical mutilation of one's own body, and therefore of one's own self, by the deliberate and permanent destruction of the normal process of fertility.

Contrary to all of this, natural family planning truly respects and builds the value of personal freedom. As we shall describe in the next chapter, it contributes to a true inner freedom, the ability to be free to say "no" as well as "yes" to one's inclinations toward coitus. How great it is to be in control of one's sexual activity rather than to feel driven by uncontrollable urges to engage in coitus or masturbation.

Psychological-Spiritual Aspects

Many find the psychological-spiritual implications of sterilization quite disturbing. Voluntary sterilization says something about the sterility of the whole person. The human person is not just a spirit encased within a body-tool through which it operates. The human being is a body-person, and what we deliberately do to our body we do to our whole self. When a person is born with a defective arm or loses an arm in an accident, we regard it as a physical imperfection and try to help him; but if a person should deliberately cut off his arm, we would judge that he suffered not just a physical imperfection but a sickness of his total person. Likewise, if a person proves to be sterile from birth, we regard it as a physical imperfection; however, when he deliberately sterilizes himself, he does something to the total person. The physical sterilization now reflects the sterility of the total person—spiritual as well as physical. It is a sign of the ultimate biologization of the sex act and a sign of a loss of hope at being able to cope with the stresses engendered by the various factors of family size, sexual urges, and socio-economic conditions. It amounts to a total admission of the inability to control one's use of sex so as to achieve effective natural conception control.

We realize that the preceding statements do not apply to everyone who has been sterilized. Sometimes couples have been led by their doctor to believe that this was the only way, at least for them. In such cases, the physician must bear much more of the responsibility than the couple themselves. In the last analysis, these physicians have dealt with their clients from a veterinary approach. Veterinarians have long been employed to eliminate surgically the fertility of our cats and dogs, but we do not think that such an approach is appropriate or humanizing for human beings. What is humanizing for men and women as made in the image and likeness of God is to understand their natural pattern of fertility and then to govern their sexual activity in accord with their desire to achieve or to avoid pregnancy. This is what natural family planning is all about.

From another point of view, deliberate sterilization offends against the commandment "Thou shalt not kill," for it involves deliberate destruction of the function of a healthy human organ. It has been a long-standing tenet of the Christian tradition that we may not destroy or mutilate healthy bodily organs of the human person. This is a reflection of the Christian recognition that the Christian does not own himself; rather, he belongs to Christ. "You must know that your body is a temple of the Holy Spirit, who is within—the Spirit you have received from God. You are not your own. You have been purchased, and at a price. So glorify God in your body" (1 Corinthians 6:19-20).

References

1. Nicholas J. Eastman. Editorial comments in *Obstetrical and Gynecological Survey,* 10:5 (1955), 661-662, on Gioiosa study (1955). Eastman notes that G. W. Beebe, *Conception and Fertility in the Southern Appalachians,* (Baltimore: Williams and Wilkins Co., 1942, 75) found a pregnancy rate of only 3 per 100 woman-years of exposure in 1,500 months of coincident lactation and amenorrhea compared with 105 per 100 woman-years in some 2,100 months outside of the time in lactation amenorrhea. Furthermore, from Canadian census figures, Eastman calculated that in rural Quebec between 1891 and 1921, when breast-feeding was common and contraception unheard of there, the woman marrying between ages 20 and 24 would average 7.9 live births. Eastman notes how close this is to the figure of 7.8 children for American wives in 1790 (Lotka, *Journal of the American Statistical Association,* 22 (1927) 154.)

2. B. Vincent et al, *Methode Thermique a et Contraception: Approaches medicale et psychosociologique (Paris:* Masson, 1967), 52-73.

3. Josef Roetzer, "The Sympto-Thermal Method: Ten Years of Change," *Linacre Quarterly* 45:4 (November, 1978) 370.

4. Josef Roetzer, "Erveiterte Basaltemperatur-messung und Empfangnisregelung," *Archiv fur Gynakologie,* 206 (1968), 195-214.

5. G. K. Doring, "The Reliability of Temperature Records as a Method of Contraception," (Uber die Zuverlassigkeit der Temperaturmethode Zur Empfangnisverhutung) *Deutsche medizinische Wochenschrift* 92:23 (June 9, 1967), 1055-1061. Abstracted in 1968 *Yearbook of Obstetrics and Gynecology,* p. 354, from which the quotation was taken.

6. Ibid.

7. Frank J. Rice and Claude A. Lanctot, "Results of a Recent Study of the Sympto-Thermal Method of Natural Family Planning," *Linacre Quarterly* 45:4 (November, 1978), 388-391.

8. F. J. Rice, C. A. Lanctot and Consuelo Garcia-Devesa, "The Effectiveness of the Sympto-Thermal Method of Natural Family Planning. An International Study." (Mimeographed reprint of an address given June 23, 1977, at the scientific congress held in conjunction with the First General Assembly of the International Federation for Family Life Promotion in Cali, Colombia.) p. 8. This is an earlier and more detailed paper of the same study mentioned in the above *Linacre Quarterly* reference.

9. Ibid, Tables VII and VIII.

10. Maclyn E. Wade, Phyllis McCarthy, et al., "A Randomized Prospective Study of the Use-Effectiveness of Two Methods of Natural Family Planning," *Am. J. Ob. and Gyn* 141:4 (Oct. 15, 1981) 368-376.

11. The rates used in this text are the mean averages of two figures used in the final report, first entry and formal entry into the study.

12. Robert A. Hatcher and others, *Contraceptive Technology 1976-1977* (New York: Irvington) 1976. For an explanation of his method of calculation, Hatcher refers to T. James Trussell, "Cost Effectiveness of Different Birth Control Methods," *Population Studies,* March, 1974.

13. U. S. Department of Health, Education and Welfare, "Family Planning Methods of Contraception," (DHEW Publication No. HSA 76-16030) 1976.

14. Frederick S. Jaffe, "Commentary: Some Policy and Program Implications of 'Contraceptive Failure in the United States,' " *Family Planning Perspectives* 5:3 (Summer, 1973) 143.

15. Norman B. Ryder, "Contraceptive Failure in the United States," *Family Planning Perspectives* 5:3 (Summer, 1973) 133-142.

16. Morton Mintz, *The Pill: An Alarming Report* (Boston: Beacon Press, 1970).

17. Natalie S. Greenfield, *First Do No Harm* (New York: Sun River Press), 1976.

18. *Federal Register,* 41:236 (Tuesday, December 7, 1976), 53633-53642.

19. Valerie Beral, "Mortality Among Oral Contraceptive Users," *The Lancet* (October 8, 1977), 727-731. Persons wishing to pursue further the medical problems of the Pill would do well to start with the following: Herbert Ratner, ed., *The Medical Hazards of the Birth Control Pill* (Box 508, Oak Park, IL 60603: Child and Family), 1969.

20. *FDA Drug Bulletin,* (May-July, 1978) 19.

21. Jack G. Hallatt, "Ectopic Pregnancy Associated With the Intrauterine Device: A Study of Seventy Cases," *Amer. Journal of Obst. & Gynec.* 125 (1976) 754.

22. H. P. Dunn, "Unexpected Sequelae of Sterilization," *International Review of Natural Family Planning,* 1:4 (Winter, 1977) 318.

23. Ibid, 319.

24. Ibid, 320.

25. Jordan Phillips and others, "Survey of Gynecologic Laparoscopy for 1974," *The Journal of Reproductive Medicine* 15:2 (1975) 50.

26. M. J. Muldoon, "Gynaecological Illness after Sterilization," *British Medical Journal,* January 8, 1972, 84-85.

27. J. R. Neil and others, "Late Complications of Sterilization by Laparoscopy and Tubal Ligation: A Controlled Study," *The Lancet,* October 11, 1975, 699-700.

28. John J. Fried, "The Incision Decision," *Esquire,* June, 1972, 172.

29. William A. Nolen, "Vasectomy: A Cautionary Note," *McCalls,* June, 1972, 136.

30. Fried, op. cit., 118 ff.

31. Ibid., 120.

32. H. J. Roberts, "Voluntary Sterilization in the Male," *British Medical Journal,* August 17, 1968, 434. See also H. J. Roberts, *Is Vasectomy Safe? Medical, Public Health, and Legal Implications* (West Palm Beach, FL 33407: Sunshine Academic Press) 1979.

33. Ibid.

34. "Vasectomy, Ills Linked," *Cincinnati Enquirer,* August 30, 1972.

35. Boyce Rensberger, "Monkey Vasectomies Hint Harm to Artery," *New York Times,* April 1, 1978.

36. Editorial, "Sterilization in Man," *British Medical Journal* 1 (1966) 1554.

37. Thomas W. Hilgers, "The Intrauterine Device: Contraceptive or Abortifacient?" *Marriage and Family Newsletter,* Vol. 5, Nos. 1, 2, 3 (January-March 1974). A slightly shorter version appeared under the same title in *Minnesota Medicine* (June 1974) 493-501.

38. Searle Laboratories, *For the Patient Cu-7* (Chicago, 1977) 3.

39. John Peel and Malcolm Potts, *Textbook of Contraceptive Practice* (New York: Cambridge University Press, 1969) 99.

40. Alan F. Guttmacher, "Prevention of Conception through Contraception and Sterilization," *Gynecology and Obstetrics,* quoted in H. Ratner, *supra,* 33. (See reference 17 above).

41. Food and Drug Administration, "Oral Contraceptive Drug Products," *Federal Register* 41:236 (December 7, 1976) 53634.

42. Albert Lorincz, oral comments in a question-and-answer session at the end of his presentation on the operation of the Pill. Marriage and Family Life Workshop, St. John's University, Collegeville, Minn., June 8, 1972.

43. Hershel Jick, A.M. Walker et al, "Vaginal Spermicides and Congenital Disorders," *JAMA* 245:13 (April 3, 1981) 1329-1332.

44. "U.S. District Court Judge Marvin Shoob said Ortho Pharmaceutical Corp., which makes Ortho-Gynol Contraceptive Jelly, knew its product could cause birth defects and was negligent for not warning its users." *The Cincinnati Enquirer,* January 23, 1985, A-2.

45. *The Cincinnati Enquirer,* November 24, 1983, E-2. The newspaper story reported an article in a current issue of *Family Planning Perspectives,* a Planned Parenthood publication.

Note for page 30, 2nd printing: Spermicidal foams sometimes cause infection or irritation and have been linked to birth defects.[43] In January, 1985 a $5,100,000.00 judgement was awarded to the parents of a birth defects child against a drug firm for the negligent failure to warn of this possible danger.[44] Also, "women who inadvertently become pregnant while using spermicidal contraceptives suffer about twice the rate of miscarriages in the first three months of pregnancy as other women, according to researchers at Temple University and the New Jersey School of Osteopathic Medicine."[45]

2

Why Natural Family Planning?
—Some Intangible Values

Self-Awareness

Many women appreciate the self-awareness they develop in natural family planning. They are able to note physical abnormalities sooner than they would otherwise and thus can seek medical attention at an earlier date. Some women may avoid an unnecessary doctor's visit or surgery. Pregnancy tests can usually be omitted when self-awareness is developed. One woman experienced severe abdominal pain, and upon consultation a doctor scheduled her for surgery. Fortunately, she was able to contact another doctor who suspected ovulation as the cause of her agony. His diagnosis was confirmed by examination and basal temperature readings, and this woman was spared unnecessary surgery and additional hospital expenses.

Some women express a sense of satisfaction from knowing just where they are in their periodic cycle. A former user of contraception told us that whenever her period was three days late, she used to worry about being pregnant. When she started natural family planning, she was very skeptical. Within six months she became very confident. She finds she is no longer fearful when her period begins late. Once her husband teased her about this lateness. To prove that she wasn't pregnant she took her temperature reading which had lowered. She predicted her period would begin by the following day, and it did.

Women can develop a better understanding of their bodily and emotional states through fertility awareness. A married woman writes:

I would like to add a personal vote of thanks as a woman for bringing to me a feeling of true self. That is, now I really seem to grasp the idea of what a cycle consists of—all the changes within me that occur. I've known this, but now all these things I don't take for granted any more. This is a very real and very deep sensation. Once again we thank you for making us aware.

A husband can also become more appreciative of the changes in moods and emotions his wife may undergo during the fertility cycle.

31

Attitudes Toward a Baby

Every known means of birth control results in some babies. Even women who have abortions sometimes deliver babies who refuse to die. The massive use of contraception has tended to absolutize the idea of the "wanted child" to the extent that some have recommended killing the unborn child as a backstop to contraception.

The couple who use natural family planning should be conscious of the fact that they are respecting God's order of creation. With this attitude, if they should experience an unplanned pregnancy they can accept the new life as an unexpected gift from God and grow to love the child for his or her own sake. Unwanted pregnancies are usually a result of carelessness, but unwanted children are a result of lovelessness. If the sex act was an act of loving persons, then the child will be wanted and loved whether he was "planned" or not.

In a more positive vein, it frequently happens that the happy mothering attitudes engendered by proper breast-feeding stimulate a desire to have another child by the time fertility returns. This desire for another pregnancy seems to be a typical consequence of "natural" breast-feeding. It is for this reason that there is an old-time saying among nursing mothers, "Babies are contagious." This should be recognized, discussed, and decided by couples according to their particular responsibilities.

The Christian couple will also want to think about overall family size in a way that differs from that of our culture. Let's face it: our culture bombards us in all sorts of ways with the "ideal" of the two-child family.

For example, how many advertisements show a family with more than two children? On the other hand, the Christian tradition, and that of other world religions as well, calls for generosity in the service of life. For some couples, a two-child family will be a generous response in the light of health, economics and other factors. Other couples may be called to have larger families of five, six, seven or more children.

Almost all of us have been intimidated by the spectre of overpopulation, and we have seen more than ample publicity given to the concept of zero population growth. What is usually not stated in the popular treatment of population statistics is that it takes 2.4 children per ever-married mother simply to maintain the birth rate at the replacement level.[1] For several years, the U.S. birth rate has been below the replacement level. Considering the large number of sterilized couples and one-or-two-child families, it's going to take a significant number of larger families just to get back to a replacement level.

Personal Development

The practice of natural family planning requires the development of personal self-control. This is both an advantage and at the same time the biggest single disadvantage of natural family planning.

More will be said in Chapter 4 about difficulties that may arise in connection with self-control. For the present, let us simply note that it is a necessary part of personal development in every area of life. The person who has gained self-control likewise gains in self-respect; he or she also gains the respect of those who know him or her as one who has self-possession.

Sexual self-control brings about a new freedom, a freedom to refrain from or to engage in sexual relations without feeling compelled to do so because of the sexual urge. The couple who practice natural family planning in effect say to each other, "We, with the help of God, can direct and handle our emotions and instincts. We are persons who are weak but still in control. Our sexual relations are more free because they are freely chosen instead of being the result just of our urges." This doesn't involve denying that these emotions exist or calling them bad or anything of the sort. Rather, it means accepting them and deliberately placing them at the service of authentic married love. The power to do this in marriage is what has been traditionally called the power of marital purity or chastity.

Is Natural Family Planning Natural?

The mere fact that natural family planning calls for self-control and the development of skills and human potential brings up the question, "Is natural family planning natural?" Specifically, questions are raised about two aspects of natural family planning: (1) refraining from sexual relations and (2) the observation of signs and temperatures.

What do we mean by "natural" for man and woman? In the briefest terms, we mean living in accord with God's order of creation. Jews and Christians alike affirm that man and woman were created "in the image and likeness of God" and that we are called to live up to God's plan for us. Christians further affirm that one of the reasons why the Son of God became man was to teach us how to live up to the demands and potential of our human nature. In this view, God's Commandments are not arbitrary rules but are the rules for living up to the demands of our nature. Thus, it is not "just human nature" to lie, steal, murder, and commit various sexual sins. Common as these wrongs may be, they are offenses against the human vocation to be true to one's nature as a person created in the image and likeness of God.

This means that we believe that it is contrary to God's order of creation—and thus contrary to our nature—for married people to have sexual relations with anyone else, or to break up a true marriage and remarry, or for the unmarried to have coitus. Rather obviously, this view is not shared by all. We know that some people think that having sex with anyone at any time is really quite natural to man, and others think that it is unnatural for man to remain faithful to one woman all his life. We could not disagree more strongly, and we would hope that those who share our convictions about sex will also agree that "natural" does not mean doing what seems easiest or most convenient with regard to sex.

When critics question whether natural family planning is "natural," they typically add that a period of refraining from genital contact doesn't fit in with their view of sexual spontaneity. This idea has been voiced so often that it has caused unnecessary difficulties for couples who would like to choose only the natural way of conception regulation. After all, if couples are led to believe that spontaneity is the key to happiness, then they are going to be prejudiced against a form of family planning that requires some restraint at certain times. Thus, because much about sexual self-control is psychological, it is important that the couple take this talk about spontaneity with a grain of salt. What is frequently meant by it is simply letting one's sexual activity be directed by his or her urges. No one in his right mind can deny the reality of these urges, but love is much more than the satisfaction of body urges. If married men and women were to be truly spontaneous according to that concept of spontaneity, we would have a lot more daytime traffic as husband (or wife) got an urge at work and sped home to celebrate it.

Several responses can be made to the question about the naturalness of not having coitus whenever the husband or wife might feel like it. In the Old Testament, the Jews were told to refrain from sexual relations for twelve days beginning with the first day of every menstruation, and everyone recognizes that there may be times in any marriage when the couple may have to refrain from sexual contact for an extended period because of physical health. Some writers have pointed up the psychological benefits to be gained from regular periods of sexual self-restraint within marriage. Thus, in answer to the question about whether it is natural to refrain from sexual relations for some time, we can surely answer that it is by no means contrary to God's order of creation to exercise sexual self-restraint, even within marriage.

Secondly, we should note that "natural" is not the same as "spontaneous." All of us know that is true with regard to sex, for we can all think of social and family needs that make it necessary to control our various sexual inclinations.

We might also note that some former users of contraceptive devices and chemicals have found that their sexual spontaneity was interfered with far more by the use of contraception. One couple put it this way after learning about natural family planning:

We get upset with articles that say natural family planning takes the spontaneity from the marriage act. It is such a wonderful feeling to know that we are not taking the beauty out of the marriage act with an ounce of foam. Our married love has grown and become more spontaneous and beautiful than we ever thought possible.

Lastly, it should be noted that if coital spontaneity is made the guideline to happiness, parents have little to say to their teenagers whose urges and emotional needs may be much stronger than those of the parents.

With a positive approach to natural family planning, a couple can enrich their marriage through periodic self-restraint. The first rule of natural family planning is to keep on loving during times of sexual abstinence. This means finding other ways of showing mutual care and love, somewhat similar to the days of premarriage courtship. With this sort of positive approach, couples can find their marriage enriched through alternating periods of courtship and honeymoon.

A Canadian couple wrote us about their discovery of this courtship phase: "As a married couple, we are particularly enjoying the courtship phases involved in the practicing of this 'art'—they are tempting times with a tension all their own, but they bring back the rich romantic feelings of pre-marital days." Another couple, aware of the concern among married couples that sex may become boring or dull, explained that with the alternating phases "sex never gets old!"

The second question asked whether it was natural to take one's temperature, to observe the other signs of ovulation, and to keep records. What this question really asks is whether it is natural to have to make this kind of effort. Again, what we mean by natural is to be in accord with God's order of creation and not to go against His plans for us. We believe that in this sense study, practice, and hard work are natural to man. We do not think it is unnatural to spend years in study or to put in endless hours developing an athletic or artistic skill. We do not think that people who keep daily charts on their investments in the stock market or people who take their temperatures when they aren't feeling well are acting unnaturally.

Rather, in each of these cases they are developing their human potential as they use their intellectual and physical powers for a good purpose. The same is true of the practices involved in natural family planning. They are actually humanizing since they develop and make use of the powers of observation and judgment in achieving a legitimate human goal. (This is not to say that any use of any human power is humanizing. The man who developed his muscles to assault or seduce another person, the person who used his brain to solve the problem of getting rid of Germany's Jews, and other such "problem solvers" certainly could not be said to be acting in a humanizing way even though they were using their natural powers.)

Personal Moral Authority

The couple who respect God's order of creation and who use only natural family planning methods can make a consistent moral stand when their teenagers begin to wonder about sex. These parents can give not only the "it might hurt someone" answers about sex before marriage; they can also explain how the sex act is meant to be a renewal of the marriage covenant. They can explain how even within marriage the partners have to exercise self-control in order to respect God's order of creation.

On the other hand, what about the couple who tell each other that their marriage will be ruined if they don't have relations for a couple of weeks even though they could still engage in other, nongenital ways of affection? It seems to us that they are on pretty thin ice when they try to tell their teenagers to postpone sexual relations for years. Young people today are quick to sense hypocrisy on the part of the older generation. Once they realize that their parents practiced contraception or were sterilized because they would not put up with any sexual abstinence, how will young people feel about any counsel their parents might give about sexual self-control? Perhaps many such parents sense the hypocrisy of preaching what they themselves refuse to practice and thus no longer say anything to their children about the need for self-control in matters of sex; perhaps that is one cause for the apparent increase in sexual activity by many young and unmarried people today.

Religion

Under the subject of "religion" there are two questions. First, why did the authors include religious values in a book published by an interfaith organization? Secondly, is there a specifically religious reason for choosing the natural-methods-only approach to birth regulation?

As to the inclusion of religious considerations, we have been asked: "Why do you call CCL interfaith when there are religious overtones in its philosophy and in this manual?" By interfaith we do not mean nonreligious; in the same way that Alcoholics Anonymous, certainly a nondenominational organization, recognizes the presence of God, so also do we in the Couple to Couple League recognize Him. We affirm that He is the Creator of man and that He established a certain good order within creation.

To the second question, whether there is a specifically religious reason for advocating natural family planning, we'll address the issue by asking: does God care about birth control?

Undoubtedly, a significant reason why many couples are interested in natural family planning is their religious conviction that contraception, sterilization, and abortion are morally wrong. Thus, in these pages concerned with the intangible or spiritual values that are involved in family planning, it may be worthwhile to examine the reasons why some people have religious or faith convictions about family planning.

When we treat religion and morality in separate chapters, we are not implying that they are unrelated. Rather, we are drawing attention to the fact that religious faith itself provides a reason for calling behavior either moral or immoral particularly for those who believe that their church is guided by God. For example, if someone says he believes that coitus with somebody else's wife is the sin of adultery, he might also give as his *reason* for so believing the fact that his church teaches that way. For him, that is the deciding reason, and he may not be able to quote any scriptural or theological reasons. In effect, he is saying that he believes that God is the ultimate author of his church's teaching and that is reason enough.

The religious issue arises with regard to family planning when some religious groups say that any attempt at family planning is morally unpermissible, others say natural family planning is permissible but not contraception, and others permit contraception, sterilization, and even abortion as means of family planning. An example of the first group is an eastern type religion which is reported to teach that marital coitus is morally permissible only with the intention of trying to conceive a child. The most well-known representative of the second group is the Roman Catholic Church. It is less well known that the teaching of the Eastern Orthodox churches, some parts of Judaism, and some Protestant ministers is also in this group. As to the third group, most Protestant churches and some branches of Judaism either allow contraception or say nothing against it, and some of the same religious bodies have issued statements permitting abortion to alleviate various health or family problems or as a backstop to contraceptive failures.[2]

● **A Biblical Basis**

Within the Bible, is there evidence showing that God cares about birth control? In the Christian tradition, Chapter 38 of Genesis is frequently quoted as providing a basis for the doctrine of noncontraception. Onan, the son of Judah, is obliged by the Hebrew and ancient Near Eastern custom of the Levirate to have intercourse with Tamar, the childless wife of his deceased brother. Onan, however, does not want to give her a child who will then be considered as that of Tamar and the deceased brother. Thus, he has coitus with her but withdraws before ejaculation (coitus interruptus). The text then tells us that God slew Onan because he had done a serious wrong.

Footnote interpretations of the Bible used to say that this showed that contraception was evil in the sight of God; footnotes in some modern versions say that Onan's offense was simply the violation of the Levirate, not the contraceptive means of doing so. We think that the modern interpretations reflect current sexual customs but fail to do justice to the entire Biblical context. First of all, in the same chapter and immediate context Judah admits that he is also guilty of violating the Levirate; and it is clear that Judah's youngest son, Shelah, is likewise guilty of the same offense. Yet neither of them is struck by God. Secondly, the punishment for violating the Levirate is well spelled out in Deuteronomy 25:5-10. The aggrieved woman may bring the offender before the elders, take a sandal off his foot, and spit in his face; then the offending brother shall be called House of the Unshod. Humiliating perhaps, but hardly the equivalent of the death of Onan.

Since the punishment for violating the Levirate is well-defined elsewhere in Scripture and since the father and brother of Onan were likewise guilty of violating the Levirate, an explanation which sees the sudden death of Onan simply and solely as a punishment for violating the Levirate cannot be called faithful to the context. A more adequate explanation must see his punishment corresponding to what he did (and the others did not do). He went through the motions of the act demanded by the Levirate covenant but defrauded it of its meaning; he took its pleasure but contradicted its purpose. Thus, the Genesis text can still be used as a Scriptural basis for the religious doctrine of noncontraception. This interpretation is backed up by the only incident in the New Testament where immediate death is the punishment for sin—the deaths of Ananias and Saphira who go through the motions of a giving act but defraud it of its meaning (Acts 5:1-11).

In the New Testament, it is possible that the Greek "pharmakeia" may refer to the birth control issue. "Pharmakeia" in general was the mixing of various potions for secret purposes, and it is known that potions were mixed in the first century A.D. to prevent or stop a pregnancy. The typical translation as "sorcery" may not reveal all of the specific practices condemned by the New Testament. In all three of the passages in which is appears, it is in a context condemning sexual immorality; two of the three passages also condemn murder (Galatians 5:19-26; Revelation 9:21, 21:8). Thus it is very possible that there are three New Testament passages condemning the use of the products of "pharmakeia" for birth control purposes. Interestingly enough, there were the same questions about those potions as about the modern pharmaceutical product, the Pill: abortifacient or contraceptive?

There is simply no doubt that the entire Biblical notion of human love points to the fact that man is called to subordinate "eros," erotic love to "agape," self-giving love. While not referring specifically to the issue of birth control, St. Paul's most famous discourse on love is still applicable to this discussion. It is noteworthy that he begins and ends on the two aspects of love that are needed for the happy practice of natural family planning. "Love is always patient and kind; ... it is always ready ... to endure whatever comes" (1 Corinthians 13:4, 7). Christian husbands are also told to love their wives as Christ loved the Church and sacrificed himself for her (Ephesians 5:25). All Christians were told by Christ on the night before his death to love one another as he loved them, a statement that has obvious overtones about selfgiving love (John 15:12). St. Paul also tells his listeners that the fruit of the Spirit is "love, joy, peace, patience, kindness, goodness, trustfulness, gentleness and self-control." He reminds them that they cannot really belong to Christ unless they "crucify all self-indulgent passions and desires" (Galatians 5:22,24).

Much more could be said about the overall meaning of the Biblical message concerning love, but the above should suffice for at least one limited purpose. It shows that it is legitimate to state that the religious doctrine of marital noncontraception has a basis in Scripture and that the practice of natural family planning with its necessity of a certain amount of sexual self-control fits well within the Christian Biblical tradition.

For those who want specific proof texts explicitly condemning each and every method of contraception, such references may not satisfy. However, the lack of such explicit references to modern contraception doesn't disturb the person who has a sense of theological realism. Such a person is aware that the Bible could hardly be more explicit in its condemnation of homosexual behavior (e.g. Romans 1:26-32), but those who want to justify homosexual behavior simply dismiss the biblical texts as not relevant to today or interpret St. Paul to mean "promiscuous" sodomy although St. Paul makes no such distinctions. The point is that even if the Bible were filled with explicit condemnations of abortion, sterilization, and contraception, the same techniques used on the sodomy texts would be used on such contraception texts by those who wished to attempt to justify such behavior as compatible with biblical Christianity. Thus it is the belief of the Roman Catholic faith and of many other Christians that Jesus did not leave us only with a book subject to everyone's personal and sometimes contradictory interpretations but also established His church as an authoritative teacher guided by the Holy Spirit. The constant teaching by the Church on a matter of faith and morals is called Tradition.

● **The Christian Tradition**

The "Tradition" approach to the religious question has been raised by an Anglican priest, Robert Capon, in a readable book entitled *Bed and Board*[3]. Father Capon notes that it is very difficult for someone who believes that the Church is guided by the Holy Spirit to say that the Church was wrong about contraception from the first century until 1930. What he refers to is the historic fact that until 1930, all of the churches, Protestant as well as Catholic and Eastern Orthodox, taught that contraception was morally wrong. Or, if every single denomination did not specifically condemn contraception, at least no Christian church taught that contraception was morally permissible. The famed Connecticut laws against the sale of contraceptives were written and passed by Protestants, not Catholics.

The year 1930 is of special interest in the history of birth regulation. As mentioned earlier, in the middle and late 1920's, two medical researchers, the Japanese Dr. Kyusaku Ogino and the Austrian Dr. Hermann Knaus, working independently, discovered that ovulation occurred about two weeks prior to the next menstruation. Recognizing the possibilities of this for birth regulation, each devised a set of rules and made possible the practice of calendar rhythm by 1930. The significance of this breakthrough is seen in the fact that prior to this time it was thought that the only alternatives to a family of indefinite size were complete abstinence or contraception.

In the field of organized religion, 1930 was also a landmark year. In England, the bishops of the Anglican Church voted to allow the practice of contraception for cases of severe hardship. This was by no means a unanimous decision, and Anglican Bishop Gore warned against other moral consequences that would result. The Catholic Church through Pope Pius XI reaffirmed the traditional Christian stance against contraception, and the debate has continued to our day.

The other thing that Father Capon was referring to is the belief of Catholics, Eastern Orthodox, Anglican, and many Protestant groups, that the Church is guided in its teaching by the Holy Spirit according to the promise of Jesus at the Last Supper. Within this belief, when a doctrine is taught consistently within Christianity from the first century until the present, there is a certain presumption that such a teaching has been due to the guidance of the Holy Spirit. Father Capon was in effect asking why we should believe that the Church was wrong in its teaching about contraception for nearly 1,900 years, why we should believe that its historic teaching was not the work of the Holy Spirit. Thus *Humanae Vitae,* the 1968 encyclical of Pope Paul VI did not announce a new doctrine. After a careful review of all the objections that had been raised, the Pope simply reaffirmed the Christian tradition. In effect, he said that the Christian tradition on this matter was so strong and clear that the only interpretation he could put on it was that it was the result of the continued guidance of the Holy Spirit and therefore true.

Pope John Paul II, extremely well informed about conditions in the Roman Catholic Church in America, has strongly reaffirmed this teaching. *And I myself today, with the same conviction of Paul VI, ratify the teaching of this Encyclical, which was put forth by my predecessor 'by virture of the mandate entrusted to us by Christ.'* (Papal address, October 5, 1979, Chicago)

Three comments should be noted about the Roman Catholic tradition on birth regulation. First of all, while it provides a firm and unmistakable negative to abortion, contraception and sterilization, it does allow the use of natural family planning for sufficiently serious reasons. Secondly, the other side of the coin of this doctrine is the positive call to generosity in the service of life according to the various circumstances of the couple. In his October 7, 1979, homily on Capitol Mall in Washington, D.C., Pope John Paul II noted that "decisions about the number of children and the sacrifices to be made for them must not be taken only with a view to adding to comfort and preserving a peaceful existence ... Parents will remind themselves that it is certainly less serious to deny their children certain comforts or material advantages than to deprive them of the presence of brothers and sisters, who could help them to grow in humanity and to realize the beauty of life at all its ages and in all its variety."

Thirdly, the Catholic tradition recognizes the reality of human weakness. It therefore calls its faithful to be spiritually nourished, strengthened and cleansed for the challenge of marital chastity by frequenting the sacraments of the Eucharist and Reconciliation. It also invites its members to gain strength and insight by meditating upon the Scriptures, particularly upon the life, sufferings and teachings of Jesus in the Gospels.

● **Consequences**

A third approach might be said to take up where the second ended. Taking its cue from the words of Jesus, "By their fruits shall you know them," this approach asks what grounds we have for believing that the post-1930 advocates of contraception are giving us something that is the work of the Holy Spirit. It must be remembered that the prime religious or faith question in this matter is about *which* tradition is *really* the work of the Holy Spirit, the tradition of some 1,900 years that forbids contraception or the one of some forty years which either allows it or recommends it as a positive good.

Since the advocates of the contraceptive approach argue that contraception helps to sustain marriage, the critics point to two things. The most obvious is that as the practice of contraception has increased, so also has the divorce rate. Certainly there are other factors involved, but if contraception really helped to sustain and increase the values of marital communion, and if the vast majority of married couples have adopted the contraceptive approach, then the critics of that approach wonder why the unhappiness rate in marriage, as measured by the divorce rate, has increased so much— over 200 percent since 1930.[4] The increased divorce rates make it difficult to believe that contraception is the "marriage builder" it is said to be.

Several other things can also be pointed to as associated with the contraceptive movement. As we shall see in Chapter 3, one well-known writer, Walter Lippmann, in 1929 blamed the use of contraceptives for the growing sexual permissiveness of his day, and the increase of premarital sex and wife-swapping in our day of widespread use of contraceptives certainly tends to support that writer's criticism.

The matter of "who should we believe is giving us the fruit of the Holy Spirit?" has been helped by the growing popularity of abortion. A great many of the Protestant churches that issued statements accepting contraception as a means of family planning have likewise issued statements accepting abortion if contraception fails.[5] Now, the husband half of the couple who have written this book has been mildly taken to task by a well-respected Episcopalian priest for inferring that such pro-abortion statements represented the thinking of the theologians of such churches. In that priest's opinion, many of these statements were heavily loaded with what he called "with-it-ness," and thus the theologians shouldn't be heavily criticized.[6]

If it is the case that the pro-abortion statements of these various Protestant churches are examples more of trying to be "with it" than of serious theological reflection, then perhaps the same needs to be said about their pronouncements on contraception. We think that most people will agree that the moral question of abortion is more obvious than the moral question of contraception. That is, most people would agree that it is easier to see that it is wrong to kill an unborn child than it is to see that it is wrong to practice contraception. Now if in this more obvious area a number of religious spokesmen have erred in saying that abortion is within Christian behavior, then we think it is rather easy to see how they could have erred in a less obvious area. Christians and Jews who understand their religious tradition know that being "with it" is no guarantee of truth. Rather, the Biblical tradition runs directly counter to that idea and raises suspicion about the desire, whether conscious or subconscious, to change doctrine in order to be more "in" with the spirit of the time.

Finally, those who criticize contraception from a religious or faith stance point to the philosophical reflections of the advocates of the contraceptive approach. (Some of these are briefly described in Chapter 3.) When those who say that (1) contraception is religiously permissible *also* say that (2) any other form of voluntary sexual behavior is also religiously permissible, and when they say that the second statement follows logically from the first, the religious critics ask whether anyone has grounds for saying *either* statement reflects the work of the Spirit.

● **An Ecumenical Note**

It has been commonplace among Christians to label the birth control issue as one that divides. Some have tended to pretend that the issue no longer exists and to label as divisive those who say, "Sorry, this long standing tradition on Christian sexuality is true and cannot be ignored."

However, what has not been well publicized is the fact that the Roman Catholic Church is not at all alone in retaining this doctrine. Members of various Christian churches have written us to say, "Our Church teaches against abortion, sterilization and contraception but doesn't provide any help. Thanks so much for enabling us to practice NFP."

● In the public realm, new witness has been given by Protestant theologians and writers. **Pastor Daniel Overduin,** a Lutheran theologian from Australia, has repeatedly hailed the doctrine of *Humanae Vitae* as a vital Christian truth.

●**Ingrid Trobisch,** the charming wife and ministerial partner of Austrian Pastor Walter Trobisch included a chapter about the sympto-thermal method of natural family planning in her book, *The Joy of Being a Woman.*[7] The Trobisches were led to look for NFP by the Africans whom they served, people who instinctively knew there was something unnatural and wrong about the contraceptive approach.

● A German physician and philosopher, **Dr. Siegfried Ernst** has looked at the birth control issue from a unique perspective. He is a Lutheran in a country where there has been probably the least acceptance of *Humanae Vitae* by Catholics; he believes in a divinely guided evolution; and he has lived through the Nazi years. He views the entire "sexual revolution" as counter evolutionary, a regression instead of progress. According to Ernst, "there is a definite contradiction involved in taking both the 'pill' and the host."[8] Speaking of *Humanae Vitae,* Ernst believes that "probably no other papal decision in history has helped so much to cancel the old mistrust against the papacy. When Pope Paul remained steadfast against pressure from the entire world, when he chose the cross instead of an easier way, the credibility of the papacy was restored."[9]

● In the United States a San Pedro pastor and his wife who have developed a national reputation as writers and counselors on Christian marriage (*The Christian Family* entered over a million homes) shared their convictions about birth control in another book, *The Christian Couple.* In Chapter Eight, titled "Contraception: Blight or Blessing," **Pastor Larry and Nordis Christenson** explain how they left the practice of contraception and began the practice of natural family planning through the help of Dr. Konald Prem. Their extensive work in marriage counseling has led them to believe that contraception is a blight upon marriage. Nordis Christenson concludes by saying that they would not return to contraception even if the alternative were twenty children.[10]

Close to home, we had the pleasure of dining one evening with a young Presbyterian minister and his wife. Within the previous 18 months, both of them had given serious consideration to sterilization, but in each something had said "no". Through a prayer group they met a CCL couple who introduced them to the CCL materials. Prayer, reading, and thought followed. By the time we met, they had come to the conviction that only the natural methods of conception regulation are morally acceptable in the sight of God.

We have been criticized by some for calling attention to the religious and moral dimensions of the birth control decision, but our personal experience and the above-mentioned writings lead us to believe that this approach is making a positive contribution to authentic ecumenism.

In summary, the question of religion or religious moral authority in the contraception issue is really the question of which side the authority of God is on. For those who believe that God has revealed Himself in history (the traditional belief of Jews and Christians) and that the Holy Spirit has guided the Church of the New Testament from Pentecost until the present at least in its major teaching, the constant tradition for nineteen centuries against contraception provides a powerful argument.[11] The moral decline and the increased divorce rates that have paralleled the acceptance of contraception, the acceptance of abortion by many of the religious spokesmen who accepted contraception, and the statements of some that they cannot say "no" to any voluntary sexual acts once they have said "yes" to contraception—all of these provide further support for those who cannot agree that the acceptance of contraception by the modern Western world has been the work of the Holy Spirit.

Natural family planning, on the other hand, does not run contrary to the teachings of any major religion although it may not be acceptable to groups that teach that procreation must be sought at each coital embrace. Furthermore, as we have seen, natural family planning frequently involves a significant group of attitudes—respect for one's body and health, respect for each other, respect for the order of creation, respect for life, and the winning of sexual freedom through self-control and the grace of God. All of this is so much in keeping with the Biblical tradition of Jews and Christians that even those who are not disposed to agree that natural family planning is the *only* way might say, from a religious point of view, that it certainly is by far the *best* way of family planning and that it is at least the moral norm.

References

1. U. S. Census Bureau, *Projections of the Population of the U.S. by Age and Sex (interim revisions): 1970-2020* (1970) 3.

2. A rather notable example: Richard S. Unsworth, et al., *Sexuality and the Human Community: A Task Force Study Document* (Philadelphia: General Assembly of the United Presbyterian Church in the U.S.A., August 1970) 26-27.

3. Robert Farrar Capon, *Bed and Board: Plain Talk About Marriage* (New York: Simon and Schuster, 1965) 87.

4. In 1930 there were 1.6 divorces per 1,000 population and in 1977, 5.0 divorces per 1,000 population, an increase of 212 percent. Marriages during the same time increased from 9.2 to 10.1 per 1,000, an increase of only 11 percent. From *Statistical Abstract of the U.S.,* 1978, 59.

5. The task force report cited in Note 2 above was indicative and typical of other statements by various Protestant church bodies.

6. For example, a Methodist pro-abortion statement was issued without the consultation of that church's best known and most respected theologians, including Prof. Paul Ramsey, who is known for his pro-life stance. There is also increasing evidence that other pro-abortion statements purporting to represent a church's official view on abortion in fact have only represented the view of the individual spokesman or committee. Perhaps in time the same thing will be said about the pro-contraceptive statements made a few years back, thus enabling such churches to return more easily to the historic Christian tradition.

7. Ingrid Trobisch, *The Joy of Being a Woman, and What a Man Can Do* (New York: Harper and Row, 1975).

8. Siegfried Ernst, *Man: The Greatest of Miracles* (Collegeville: Liturgical Press, 1976) 143.

9. Ibid., 132

10. Larry and Nordis Christenson, *The Christian Couple* (Minneapolis: Bethany Fellowship, Inc., 1977) 71-89.

11. The force of the argument from Christian Tradition has been put in its most theologically literate form by John Ford and Germaine Grisez who argue that the tradition against contraception fulfills all the requirements of Vatican II for being an infallible doctrine even though *Humanae Vitae* was not promulgated in the solemn manner of defining a matter of faith and morals. John C. Ford, S.J. and Germaine Grisez, "Contraception and the Infallibility of the Ordinary Magisterium," *Theological Studies* 39:2 (June, 1978) 258-312.

3

Questions of Morality

Just as Chapter 2 could only touch on the religious dimension of questions that arise about family planning, so also our comments here can scarcely begin to touch on the moral values in this issue. Certainly, a single chapter is no place to attempt an analysis to which entire books have been dedicated. However, the reader may find it helpful to have something written about the common questions that keep coming up.

Some Common Questions

● **One of the most frequent questions** is usually stated something like this: "If contraception and natural family planning both have the same objective of avoiding pregnancy, how can there be any moral difference between them?" Sometimes, no question is even asked and people bluntly state that it doesn't make any difference which method you use if the end purpose is the same. Such a statement fails to stand up under thoughtful investigation. If somebody wants my car, it makes a great deal of difference what "means" he uses to get it—whether he buys it from me or steals it. If a particular married couple want more money so that they can live in a bigger house, it makes all the difference in the world how they get it—whether they engage in the dope trade (which might get them into that house in a hurry) or whether they try to cut expenses and save (which might never get them into their dream house). In each of these cases, the purpose has been the same but there is a great moral difference in the ways and means of accomplishing it.

Does this also hold true about the various ways and means of family planning? If a person says "no," then he or she is saying that any means of family planning is morally permissible because the end is the same. We think that most readers will reject the killing of the unborn child as a method of family planning, no matter how widely practiced this is in China, Japan, Scandinavia, and in the English-speaking countries as well. At any rate, whoever rejects the killing of the unborn as a morally valid means of family planning accepts the principle that the end does not justify the means and that not all the ways of family planning are morally equal.

● **Another common question** concerns the morality of particular methods of contraception. We have already seen that the IUD is not really a method

45

of contraceptive family planning but rather is an abortifacient means of family planning. The moral judgment that has to be placed on this is the same as for surgical abortion, and it would also hold true for the "morning-after Pill" and the "once-a-month Pill," which flush out the uterus. The use of surgical abortion, the IUD as a mechanical abortifacient, and these abortifacient drugs all have a similar function—the preventing of the *continuation* of pregnancy by the killing of the developing but unborn child. The moral term for such premeditated killing of the innocent is murder.

The right-to-life movement and the reaction against it have made it clear that the pro-abortionists who admit that abortion is killing a young human being still reject calling the act murder. They insist that such a term can only be applied where there is malice involved in the killing. Such a criterion would prevent us from calling Hitler, Eichmann, and Stalin murderers because we cannot prove malice on their part, and thus we think it is a criterion without value. To be guilty of the moral crime of murder, it is sufficient to realize that one is freely killing a helpless and innocent human being, one who has in no way lost his or her personal right of continued existence.

We have already seen that the drugs usually referred to as the Pill operate in somewhat ambiguous and different ways. Some most likely suppress ovulation, others may also act as spermicides, but they all apparently affect the lining of the uterus so as to prevent implantation should conception occur. When conception occurs but implantation is prevented, these drugs have acted as abortifacients rather than contraceptives. We have also noted that there are certain hazards to personal health associated with these drugs. Thus, the moral question about the Pill is actually twofold.

● **Is it morally permissible** to take a drug that may act as an abortifacient and that may also do serious harm to the mother when the desired birth regulation could be effected by less drastic means? Suppose the issue concerned a weight control pill. The same question could be asked: Would it be morally permissible to take a weight control drug that might cause an abortion or seriously injure the woman's health when the desired weight loss could be accomplished by less drastic means? The answer in this case is obvious. It would be immoral because it is wrong to endanger one life unless it is unavoidable in the effort to save another life; it is likewise wrong to endanger one's own life or health except for very serious reasons, especially when less dangerous alternatives are available. What holds true for a weight control pill is equally valid when applied to a birth control drug. This is especially true when there are other means of birth control that carry no risk of being abortifacient and that also entail no risk to the woman's health. Therefore, it is bad medicine and bad medical ethics to prescribe the Pill. This would be clearly recognized by all in the case of the weight control pill, but there are strong forces that work toward diminished moral vision when it comes to birth control.

● **The next question** that usually arises notes that the previous criticisms of various forms of birth control have been based on the moral consideration that these forms have attacked the values of human life and health. But what if a couple used means that were unquestionably "only contraceptive" such as the condom, diaphragm, and the practice of coitus interruptus? This, of course, is the question that has been raised in the religious debate on this issue, and it might be rephrased in this way: Does the practice of contraception within marriage affect the meaning of the marital sex act, the very meaning and the value of the coital embrace, the meaning and the value of marriage itself?

This is the most difficult question to answer because it involves three related but not identical mysteries of life: the mystery of love, the mystery of marriage, and the mystery of sex. We call them mysteries because no matter how much you talk about these aspects of life, no matter how much you read, study, meditate, think, and pray about them, no matter how much you write about them, you know that the thoughts of others and yourself have still not adequately explained these realities. Anyone who attempts to address the morality of any of the modern questions about sex, whether it be premarital relations, group marriages, simultaneous or serial polygamy, homosexuality, contraception, etc., is faced with these related mysteries of life. Still, the human mind that asks these questions also tries to answer them, however incompletely.

The Pro-contraception Arguments

Rather obviously, many people have said that marital contraception does not adversely affect the meaning of marriage, sex, and love. This is not the place for a detailed analysis of the pro-contraceptive arguments, but a few lines may help readers to understand why many people have found their arguments unattractive.

● **The "can do" argument.** This approach says that since man's mind has figured out *how* to practice artificial contraception, therefore he can (morally) do it. Some bring God into the picture by saying that God gave us brains and expects us to use the products of our brainpower. This argument is really amazing, since it would likewise apply to atom bombs, instruments of torture, drug peddling, etc. The ability to do something, no matter how clever, is simply no guarantee that it is morally right to do it.

● **The "man can't do it" argument.** This approach says that man and woman are so weak and the sexual urge so huge that it is impossible for them to refrain from coitus in the face of desire. The Bible has a more optimistic view of man and woman; as already mentioned, the Jewish law forbade coitus for twelve days beginning with menstruation. The words of God that came to St. Paul as he sought the alleviation of some temptation, "My grace is sufficient for you" (2 Corinthians 12:9), also contribute to the

48

inability to accept the pessimistic view of man that is enshrined in this viewpoint.

● **The "lesser of two evils" argument.** This approach grants that contraception is an evil because it directly opposes the order of creation. However, this argument runs, it is a greater evil not to have coitus if the married couple think they need it for their marital happiness. This approach is similar to the previous one and is very closely related to the argument about ends and means; it also tends to incorporate the view that frequent, regular coitus is an absolute necessity for a happy marriage. The evidence on marital unhappiness despite unlimited contraceptive sex plus the very positive experiences of many couples practicing natural family planning leads many to think that this approach is erroneous and based on a very inadequate view of man, woman, love, sex, and marriage. Furthermore, it plays right into the hands of those unmarried couples or individuals who say they need coitus for their happiness.

● **The "argument from proportionalism."** The proponents of this line of thought admit that contraception is a "physical evil" because it takes apart what God has joined together in the order of creation. However, they say that when there is a conflict of values, a physical evil is not a moral evil if there is a proportionate reason for allowing it. In the case at hand, contraception is seen as permissible if in the long run it fosters the values of marital fidelity, human sexuality, and the permanence of the marriage itself.

However, this argument is defeated on the very grounds it seeks for its justification. While an individual couple may say that the practice of contraception has made things easier between them and thus fostered those values, the wider evidence is against it. Increased divorce, increased nonmarital sex, and a general debasing of human sexuality have been the dominant characteristics of an age marked by an almost universal acceptance and use of contraception. (This idea is developed further in the section "Ecology of Morality.") Furthermore, this argument is dangerously similar to the following one.

● **"The end justifies the means."** This approach also accepts that contraception is contrary to the natural order of creation but justifies it on the grounds of marital happiness, solving population problems, etc. It is rather obvious that this ends-means argument can be used to "solve" any kind of problem and has already resulted in such historic landmarks as the killing of six million Jews by the Nazis, the My Lai massacre by William Calley and company, and the current killing of literally millions of unborn children. As a principle for making morally right decisions, it offers no help.

Arguments Against Contraception

Thus, many couples have been faced with the historic Christian view that the practice of contraception is morally wrong and with the additional fact that the typical pro-contraceptive arguments fail to be intellectually satisfying. However, can anything other than the historic tradition, anything in the way of explanation be offered in support of the belief that *natural* family planning is the best not only from the point of view of health, esthetics, cost, etc., but also from the point of view of morality? Again, several approaches should be investigated.

● **"An unnatural separation of powers."** This approach, which has been explored well and in depth by Mary Joyce, notes that the natural law concerning man derives from an essential unity in the human person. Because one reveals himself in his or her actions, this essential unity of the person carries forward into a unity of his actions, at least his conscious ones. It is contrary to the very unity of his nature as a human being to act contrary to this essential unity. For example, in the human action of communication, there is a basic unity between what is in the mind and the expression of it— whether the communication is through the spoken or written word or by a nod of the head. When a person speaks or writes what he judges to be true, then he has respected the unity of his human nature, the order of creation. On the other hand, lying violates this essential unity. "Lying is an internal separation of a communication from its power to express and generate judgments truthfully."[1]

Coital intercourse is another and very special form of communication. Just as one of the powers of intellectual communication is the ability to create a new idea in the listener, so also one of the powers inherent in the human action of coitus is the power to create a new person in the womb of the mother. Contraception violates this unity of the action of its powers. Thus, contraception is "an internal separation of an interpersonal action of coital union from the fully human generative power that is internally structured in this action by the unity of the person's being."[2]

The basic assumption of this approach is that it is not humanly right to violate the unity of the person and his actions. To someone who can see that lying is morally wrong because it violates a meant-to-be unity between the person's judgment and his freely chosen action of expressing it, this argument from the unity of the coital act and its powers can be helpful in understanding why that unity may not be deliberately and internally separated. The proponents of this view note that this does not exclude coitus during the infertile period, for in such acts there is no internal separation of the act from one of its powers. The acts of coitus are accepted in their totality whether they are, in accord with human nature, able to result in conception or not.

This approach is one example of an explanation from the point of view of "natural law." It should be noted that natural law when applied to man and woman does not refer to any sort of physically unbreakable law of nature, such as the "law" of gravity. Rather, it refers to the way in which men and women *should* act to be in harmony with their very *being* and with the design of the Creator. For example, a man is physically able to become roaring drunk, make his way home, and literally terrorize his wife into submitting to coitus with him. In this example, we would think that such a man had acted against the natural law (or order of creation) in three ways: by getting roaring drunk in the first place, by terrorizing his wife, and by forcing her to have coitus when it had absolutely nothing to do with marital love, tenderness, affection, or the desire to conceive a child.

● **"A renewal of the marriage covenant."** This approach can be meaningful to those who see coitus as morally proper only within marriage because it begins by asking, "For this couple, Richard and Mary, what is the moral difference between having coitus before marriage and having coitus only after they have married?" Certainly, between the week before marriage and the week after marriage there has been little change at the level of emotional love or affection. Yet a great many people and the weight of the Jewish-Christian tradition have seen and continue to see coitus prior to marriage as morally unacceptable. The answer provided in this second approach is that coitus becomes morally appropriate only after marriage because it is meant to be a renewal of the marriage covenant, and a couple obviously cannot renew what has not already taken place. In an authentic religious marriage covenant, the couple pledged before God in a true risk of faith their commitment to each other; they promised to exercise caring love for each other until they would be parted by death; they told both God and the world that they were entering upon a sacred unity with each other, that their very lives would be interpenetrated by the other. Thus, the coital act is meant to be a symbol of that unity, that caring love, that risk of faith by which they took each other for better and for worse.

In this approach, there is an emphasis on the risk inherent in pledging such life-long love and faithfulness to each other. Marital love, as contrasted with romantic or erotic love, means the loving acceptance of the other as he or she is now and will become during their life together. If one of the couple is naturally sterile, the faith risk of the marriage covenant does not allow the use of a substitute partner for childbearing purposes, nor does it allow divorce in order to have another marriage fruitful with children. In a similar manner, the faith risk entails the acceptance of that person's fertility as well. To practice contraception would be the equivalent of saying, "I accept you as represented by your body—but not your fertility." Thus, contraception goes contrary to the basic unity of the person and to the meaning of the coital act as a renewal of the love and faith risk of the original marriage covenant.[3]

● **"What God has joined together . . ."** This approach combines elements of each of the first two approaches. It notes first of all that there is rather obviously a natural unity arranged by the Creator in the coital act—the development of marital love and affection and the procreation of children.

It further notes that in this order of creation there is a rhythmic fertility cycle so that at some times the woman is fertile and at others she is not.

This approach then points to the fact that the coital act is rightly called the marriage act. The functions of developing marital love and procreating children are the traditional purposes of marriage, and the *combination* can be sought only through the coital act. Obviously, there are many ways of pursuing the development of marital love and affection, but there is only one way within the natural order of creation for pursuing the procreation of children. In the light of what was said in the preceding section, it might be more appropriate to call coitus the marriage *renewal* or affirmation act.

Since it has this unique place within marriage, the words of Jesus about marriage itself are appropriately applied to marital coitus: "What God has joined together, let no man divide" (Mark 10:9).

Now, rather obviously, the whole purpose of contraception is to divide what God has joined together in the coital act. As such, its function is to separate by positive interference the natural unity of sexual affection and procreation; it must be judged to be dividing what God has put together in a sacred unity and therefore to be contrary to God's design for human sexuality, love, and marriage. Natural family planning, on the other hand, respects what God has joined together and also what God himself has separated.

Anyone who finds this approach helpful may expect the skeptic to ask, "Well, why shouldn't we take apart what God has joined together?" Those who are oriented toward the natural might reply in a way something like this: "We don't know precisely why, but we have ample evidence that the ecological crises have resulted from man's refusing to respect the order within nature. We aren't saying that you can't use trees to build houses or put dams or bridges across rivers, etc., but we are saying that we have learned that it is to man's own interest to respect and to try to foster the natural order of things. The old idea that man can do anything he wanted to nature is truly obsolete."

Those who would answer the question of the skeptic from a religious point of view might answer in a way similar to this: "We honestly don't know all the reasons why we shouldn't divide what God has put together, whether we are talking about marriage itself or the coital marriage act. We can point to all sorts of tragedies that happen when a society starts to think it can take marriages apart at will—broken homes, increasing failure to really love and sacrifice in order to build the marriage, rising divorce rates, unstable homes and children, etc. We can also point to various unfortunate consequences of the practice and mentality of contraception. But in the last analysis, we have to admit that God didn't give us a book of proofs but rather asked for our faithful response to His word. We also believe that whether we are talking about the whole marriage relationship or the coital act, we are talking about very special human realities that are blessed by

God. Because they are uniquely human and interpersonal and because they are sacred realities and far more than just a convenient social form or a biological unity, we have no right to take apart what God has put together."

Needless to say, the description of all of these approaches has been very incomplete. However, the surface has been scratched enough so that an open-minded reader can at least begin to see why many people remain quite unpersuaded by the arguments on behalf of contraception and what sort of moral reasoning is used to support the *natural*-family-planning-only view about birth regulation.

Moral considerations are persuasive only to those who already hold certain values and are frequently rejected by those who hold conflicting values. The couple who have elevated the idea that "sex is only (or mostly) for fun" to the place of their dominant value regarding sexuality may have considerable difficulty in becoming sensitive to the preceding considerations. However, we think that such couples are not the majority. Certainly, marital sex—in all its meanings, not just coitus—can be fun, but indications have appeared in the news media as well as in personal contacts that great numbers of people both young and old are searching for deeper meanings. To ask for such deeper meanings is to inquire ultimately how God meant His creature man to experience sexuality; it is the inquiry into the divine order of creation.

The Ecology of Morality
—The Sexual Logic of Contraception

An inquiry into the order of creation regarding human sexuality, love, and marriage is in some ways similar to the inquiry into the balance of nature that we call ecology. We know that in the physical world one upset in nature leads to others, but what about in the world of human morality? Is there not a reality that we may call the ecology of morality (or an ecological morality)? What happens when one part of an overall sexual ethic is abandoned or rejected? Does that lead to an upset in other parts of the sexual ethic? Specifically, if the practice of contraception is contrary to the order of creation, will its acceptance as permissible lead to the acceptance of other actions that have been traditionally rejected as contrary to God's order of creation? In point of fact, the acceptance and rising use of contraception since the turn of the century (condoms became available in the mid-nineteenth century after the discovery of vulcanizing rubber in 1843) has been followed by rising divorce rates, wife-swapping, increased frequency of nonmarital sex, and, most recently, high increases in the number of abortions.

The question that thinking people simply *must* ask themselves is whether the rise in the use and acceptance of contraception as morally permissible and the rise in these other behaviors has been merely a historical coincidence or whether contraception has been a significant contributory cause to these other areas of sexual behavior.

● This question is by no means new. **Walter Lippmann,** writing in 1929 and reflecting upon the sexual behavior of the 1920's, blamed the rise of sexual promiscuity squarely on the availability, acceptance, and use of contraceptives.[4] Lippmann also criticized the idea of companionate, childless, trial "marriages," which were being proposed as a real advance made possible by the contraceptive separation of coitus and family raising. Such ideas strike us as terribly current, a product of the late 1960s and early 1970s, but they were being publicly promoted in the 1920s as well. In other words, proponents of companionate and temporary marriages were saying that contraception enabled them to promote new and radically changed ideas about human sexuality, love, and marriage.

● Shortly after Lippmann's rather serious book appeared, **Aldous Huxley** published his short novel *Brave New World*[5] which is still being reprinted and read today. Readers of that novel soon realize that the whole society of *Brave New World* is built upon the technology of sex. Contraception has almost completely divided coitus from procreation. Any contraceptive "mistakes" are taken care of at the abortion clinic. Just as logically in this novel, procreation (or rather the reproduction) of children is done by technology: test tube fertilization and development in bottles (artificial wombs) for nine months. Huxley carried the idea of companionate, temporary marriages one step further. Since the reproduction of children was all handled by technology and since the education of these children was in the hands of the state's full-care centers, there was no family and thus no need for parents. Thus, there was no marriage, and everybody was to belong sexually to everyone else. One is hard pressed to say whether Huxley was, at the time he wrote it in 1931, poking fun at the "new sexuality" that had come out of the 1920s or whether he was trying to crystal-ball the future. At any rate, today he looks in many ways, though not completely of course, very much like a "future-teller." It is common knowledge that some people seriously advocate letting the abortion clinic take care of contraceptive failures; others look forward to the day when technological reproduction is as efficient and as well accepted as is technological, contraceptive interference with procreation today.

Thus, we have seen writers of the 1920s and early 1930s spell out what they saw as the sexual logic of contraception. But what about the sexual theorists of today? Do they see any connection between contraception and other modes of sexual behavior? Would it not be a conclusive argument in favor of the idea of an "ecological morality of sex" if proponents of contraception themselves showed the connection between the acceptance of contraception and other forms of sexual or abortive behavior?

●One prolific writer and advocate of contraception notes that "the contraceptive pill technology of the past twenty-five years has forced us to accept procreation and sexual intercourse as two distinct human actions, each governed by its own moral principles."[6] Taking for granted the use of our "sophisticated reproductive contraceptive technology," **Robert Francoeur** then describes some twenty possibilities for various sexual relationships, only one of which is permanent, monogamous marriage—which he thinks only a minority of people in the future will accept. The other nineteen include almost every imaginable combination: trial or two-step marriages, three-party marriages, polygamy for senior citizens, group marriages, temporary contractual marriages, stable unmarried cohabitation and unisex marriages. "Since we can no longer restrict sexual relations to a procreative function, homosexuality can no longer be condemned as immoral or unnatural merely because it is noncreative."[7] We would disagree with the author's conviction that the contraceptive technology has forced us to accept procreation and sexual intercourse as two distinct human actions, but we think that he offers an excellent example of the sexual logic of one who does accept that technological separation.

●**Michael Valente** calls his book *Sex: The Radical View of a Catholic Theologian,* though it is in no way compatible with the official teaching of that church. Joining with those who rejected the official affirmation of the doctrine of noncontraception, and calling himself and other dissenters "revisionists," Valente states that "to accept the revisionist position of the liceity [moral lawfulness] of contraceptive use in marriage is not merely to find an exception to the natural law doctrine, but to destroy it."[8] He also questions the logic of those who would accept marital contraception but prohibit premarital or extramarital coitus.[9] Lest one think that such activity might be forbidden on the basis of Biblical statements, the author assures us that moral statements in the Bible simply reflect the writers' personal ideas about solving problems of living in accord with the dictates of the Judeo-Christian ethic. As isolated statements, they may be wrong and are therefore not binding.[10] Such reasoning, of course, puts Professor Valente out of touch not only with the Catholic tradition but with a great part of Protestant tradition as well.

However, he has now cleared the way to handle various sexual activities, some of which are rather specifically and vigorously opposed in the Bible. Thus,

it seems unreasonable to maintain that there is a difference between allowing a husband and wife to use the condom and allowing them to have anal intercourse, since neither fulfills the natural law doctrine's requirement of insemination in the vagina. Likewise, there is no difference between using the condom and coitus interruptus or any of the other so-called sins prohibited under the doctrine, such as masturbation, homosexuality, and bestiality [intercourse with an animal.][11]

It would be hard to find a more explicit statement of the conviction by an advocate of contraception that the acceptance of marital contraception logically carries with it the acceptance of every imaginable sexual activity, provided such activity would not be condemned on other grounds, i.e., assault (rape), or the development of a bad self-image (promiscuity).

●**Shulamith Firestone** is interested in a revolution between men and women that will include the abolition of the family as we now know it. Her interest in the question of contraception is not from the point of view of a moralist. Rather, Ms. Firestone looks forward to the dissolution of the family and sees technological contraception and reproduction as a necessary means for a revolutionary phaseout of the family. She argues that because of a combination of efficient contraception and nonfamily means of child rearing, it is possible for the first time to attack the family on the grounds that it is neither necessary nor the most efficient means of reproduction.[12] Aldous Huxley may have been either spoofing or ridiculing the sexual tendencies of Western civilization when he wrote *Brave New World*, but Ms. Firestone is perfectly serious in her advocacy of contraception and its societal consequences. In the system that she envisions, a woman's reproductive ability is a tyrant and women are to be freed from it by any and all possible means.[13] Furthermore, in her brave new world of efficient contraception, women and children should have and will have the freedom to do whatever they feel like doing sexually because there simply won't be any reason to refrain from gratification of their various urges.[14] Thus, once again, the cornerstone to both a philosophy and its implementation in eliminating marriage and the family has been technological contraception and its logical counterpart, technological reproduction.

We know that many people do not share the view that there is anything morally objectionable about contraception in marriage, even many people who are interested in natural family planning. We also think that contraception has become so much a part of "the American way of life" that many people have never given it much thought. Various circumstances have combined to make it a professional responsibility for us to read what others are saying and writing about sex, love, and marriage. Their writings have made us aware that there are certainly problems in modern marriage, many challenges to authentic love, and perhaps even increased difficulties in reaching sexual maturity. However, we cannot see that the "new directions" laid out for us by some of these writers lead anyplace except into a blind alley. We must ask our readers: Do you regard the abolition of marriage and the family as a real solution to the problems of the modern family? Do you regard the acceptance of any mutually agreeable sexual activity, even bestiality, as truly ennobling to man—or as consistent with your religion, whatever it may be?

Now, if those who are willing to spell out their theories and follow them to their logical conclusions tell us that to intellectually accept contraception is to logically accept anything and everything in the way of consenting sexual behavior, do we not have an excellent example of interlocking relationships, in other words, an ecology of morality? And when theories of sex end with such morally disastrous conclusions as these after starting with the acceptance of marital contraception, can those be criticized who hold that the starting point must be equally erroneous?

Much to the contrary, natural family planning is associated with a philosophy of sex, love, and marriage that sees the permanent marriage relationship as part of God's order of creation. It accepts the very real differences between man and woman. It does not magnify them but works with them to help the building of a sound and loving marriage relationship.

Certainly, the preceding analysis of the thought of some advocates of contraception has been brief and necessarily incomplete. However, we think that anyone who reads the books from which we have quoted will find that we have not distorted the authors' conclusions. We think it serves a useful purpose in the overall debate about the morality of contraception.

It has been suggested that those who see marital contraception as morally unacceptable do so out of a rather unthinking obedience to various religious authorities. We would hope that the preceding analyses would help to make it clear that at least some people who reject contraception on moral grounds do so because they have reviewed the philosophy, arguments, and conclusions of those who advocate marital contraception and have found them intellectually inadequate. Such people can only conclude that those who accept marital contraception as morally valid either (1) have a different set of standards about the whole ecology of sex, (2) have done so for reasons that are much less than intellectually satisfying, or (3) have done so simply out of a faith in various religious spokesmen who said that they saw nothing wrong with it. With regard to this latter point, many people would want to make a distinction between believing on the basis of a Biblical statement that they should not take apart what God has put together and believing on the basis of statements of various men that it didn't make any difference.

Theologically trained readers may complain that we have built a case by quoting only "far-out" writers rather than the more "moderate" advocates of contraception. Our response is simply that we have quoted those who have made a point of carrying the logic of technological, contraceptive birth control to its conclusions. The contraceptionists who sound more moderate either ignore these conclusions or brush them off with such statements as "We certainly don't intend *that*" or "*Those* things are contrary to the dignity of man." However, what counts is not their intention to stop at contraception but the underlying premises and the logical conclusions. Some of the same people who condemn the conclusions of Valente as being contrary to the dignity of man likewise criticize those who say that contraception is contrary to the dignity of man. They insist that the non-con-traceptionists "prove" their conviction but have offered nothing by the way of proof that they can logically accept contraception and yet condemn such activities as complete oral and anal intercourse, etc. Considering contem-porary sexual behavior, the burden of proof is certainly upon those who would say that the conclusions of Valente and company are not logically implicit in the acceptance of contraception.

Contraception and Abortion

Earlier we asked if it would not be a conclusive argument in favor of the idea of an "ecological morality of sex" if proponents of contraception themselves showed the connection between the acceptance of contraception and other forms of sexual behavior or abortive behaviors. We think that such proponents have done a good job of showing their conclusions about other forms of sexual behavior. But what about that "abortive behavior?" Is there any connection spelled out here? Listen to this:

> I suggest to you that for the individual, the role of abortion will be, as it has been, the second line of defense against harmful pregnancy and the unwanted child. These are contraceptive failures. The societal role will require that we see family planning in a true light; no matter how thin you slice it, ladies and gentlemen, family planning is a euphemism. We don't intend or desire to prevent conception for conception's sake; we want to prevent conception because of what follows conception. Family planning is the prevention of births, and as birth is the end of a sequence which begins with the sexual urge, then family planning is anti-conception, anti-nidation, and the ter-mination of the conceptus if implanted. This is the social role of abor-tion in the future.

The speaker was Professor Irwin Cushner of Johns Hopkins School of Medicine, addressing the Symposium on Implementation of Therapeutic Abortion held in Los Angeles in January 1971. He is quoted in *The Death Peddlers* by Paul Marx, in a chapter titled "How Abortionists Really Think."[15] In the thirty-three pages of this chapter, it is made abundantly clear that the scope of contraceptive family planning has now been widened to include postconception "family planning," that is, abortion at all stages. Thus, in this country the name of the Planned Parenthood Association and that of its late president, Dr. Alan Guttmacher, have become almost syn-onymous with the efforts to gain public acceptance for abortion as just one more means of family planning. People who want to see the planning of the abortionists to get tax money, to deceive women into thinking that they are just "menstruating" when they are really aborting, and to generally in-crease the abortion business should read this little book by Professor Marx. When these indications are coupled to the statement of the Presbyterian

Report[16] that accepted abortion as a backstop to contraception, we find it hard to deny a very real link between the two. We do not know how people can avoid the conclusion that the widespread acceptance of contraception has been responsible for the acceptance of abortion. Thus, there is one more example of the "ecology of sexual morality."

In summary, we have found no indications that the acceptance, use, and philosophy of contraception have led to the raising of public and personal sexual morality since the turn of the century and especially in the fifty-some years since it was first given some religious acceptance. On the contrary, we think that history has shown that Walter Lippmann in 1929 was quite perceptive when he linked the use of contraception with other forms of sexual behavior he regarded as immoral.

If this perception is correct, then there is obviously much more at stake in the natural family planning movement than just helping people to learn about the various signs of fertility and ovulation. History would suggest that when a civilization as a whole abandons a sexual ethic that is truly uplifting and in accord with what is best in man and woman and replaces it with an ethic that cannot really say no to anything mutually pleasurable, then that civilization cannot long endure. Such a thought suggests that the acceptance, use, and philosophy of natural family planning may be a positive and constructive element not only at the level of the individual marriage but also at the larger level of society.

References

1. Mary Joyce, *The Meaning of Contraception* (Staten Island, New York: Alba House, 1970), 26.

2. Ibid., 8.

3. John F. Kippley, "Toward a Unified Theory of Christian Sexuality" *Birth Control and the Marriage Covenant* (Collegeville, Minn.: Liturgical Press) 1976, 97-130.

4. Walter Lippmann, *A Preface to Morals* (New York: The Macmillan Company, 1929).

5. Aldous Huxley, *Brave New World* (New York: Harper & Row, 1969; first published in 1932).

6. Robert T. Francoeur, *Eve's New Rib: Twenty Faces of Sex, Marriage and Family* (New York: Harcourt, Brace, Jovanovich, 1972), 4.

7. Ibid., 223.

8. Michael F. Valente, *Sex: The Radical View of a Catholic Theologian* (New York: Bruce, 1970), 126.

9. Ibid.

10. Ibid., 147.

11. Ibid., 126.

12. Shulamith Firestone, *The Dialectic of Sex: The Case for Feminist Revolution* (New York: William Morrow and Company, Inc. 1970), 250.

13. Ibid., 233.

14. Ibid., 236.

15. Paul Marx, *The Death Peddlers* (Collegeville, Minn.: St. John's University Press, 1971), 122.

16. Previously referred to in Chapter 2, reference 1. See also Chapter 2, reference 4.

4

Marriage Building with Natural Family Planning

I urge the advocates of artificial methods to consider the consequences. Any large use of the methods is likely to result in the dissolution of the marriage bond and in free love.

— *Mahatma Gandhi, 1925*

In this chapter there is some good news and some bad news, and we'll take the bad news first.

Was Mahatma Gandhi, the great Indian leader, a prophet when he spoke the above words in 1925? We do not know the results in India, but in the United States, the increasing use of contraceptives has been accompanied by a steadily increasing divorce rate. In 1910 there was one divorce for every eleven marriages;[1] by 1925 the philosophy of contraception and Havelock Ellis's ideas about companionate marriage were being well circulated and the divorce rate had risen to one in seven marriages. In 1965, a few years after the Pill helped to foster the "new morality," the ratio was approximately one divorce for every four marriages. More and more people began experimenting with all sorts of new sexual "freedoms," and by 1970 one in three marriages was ending in divorce. By 1977 the happiness promised by unlimited sex through the pill or sterilization still had not materialized, and the divorce rate was at a tragic all time high — one divorce for every two marriages. The propagandists for contraception have traditionally argued that freedom to have sex at any time without fear of pregnancy will make people happy and build better marriages. To continue such an argument is to ignore current history which has proved Gandhi correct.

Contraception is not the only factor that has contributed to the breakup of marriage and the family, nor does contraception always bring divorce. However, the practice and philosophy of contraception must be recognized as a major cause of marital unhappiness and divorce.

Why? We believe that there are at least three reasons. First of all, the philosophy behind contraception preaches an unreal, overly orgiastic idea of marriage and sex. The erotic element of marriage is good, but overemphasis on it is leading many people to enter marriage with the utterly

59

unrealistic notion that enough sex will solve all their problems. Current divorce rates prove the size of that error.

Secondly, the unreality of the overly orgiastic concept of marriage leads couples to ignore the proper development of married love. Those of us who are happily married recognize that the words of St. Paul about love apply fantastically well to marital love. "Love is patient . . . kind . . . ready to endure whatever comes" (I Corinthians 13: 4-7).

Thirdly, couples who are influenced by their culture to try to solve problems by taking apart through contraception what God has joined together in sexual intercourse may also be more inclined to try to solve marriage problems by taking apart the union that God established in their marriage.

On the other hand, natural family planning requires couples to broaden and deepen their understanding of marital love, and the habit of respect for what God has put together in the sex act helps them through other periods of marital stress. One informal survey showed a divorce rate of less than 1% among couples practicing natural family planning,[2] and such marriage building good news is the subject of the rest of this chapter.

Marriage Building

When the Couple to Couple League was first started, it was not its intention to get involved in the rather huge challenge of trying to help married couples improve their marriages. Practically a whole industry of psychiatrists, psychologists, clergy, marriage counselors, and organizations was already working at this task. Thus, CCL had and continues to have as its main objective the more limited purpose of helping couples to learn how to practice natural family planning. However, right from the beginning it was realized that a couple who wanted to practice natural family planning successfully had to have certain attitudes. The old idea of the wife being there in bed as the immediate relief valve for any and all sexual urges of her husband had to be replaced by something more meaningful without denying that the relief of sexual tension can be a valid reason for marital coitus.

As a result, two things happened. First of all, leader couples at CCL meetings have talked briefly about the necessity of marital teamwork, mutual decision making, open communication, and the importance of expressing marital love and affection in nongenital ways. The second thing that happened is that various couples have told Couple to Couple League leader couples such things as "CCL has saved our marriage," "Our marriage has become richer as a result of CCL," etc. Of course, CCL has not really saved any marriages; the couples themselves, with the help of God, have healed or saved their own marriages by changing their marital attitudes and behavior and pursuing other values that are all part of the "logic" involved in natural family planning.

Mutual Decision Making

Natural family planning is built upon mutual fertility awareness and decision making. During each menstrual cycle, the couple become aware of the changes in the wife's fertility pattern. We don't attempt to lay down any hard-and-fast rules about how *both* husband and wife are involved in this, but the following guidelines have been derived from the successful practice of various couples.

1. The process of fertility awareness should not be left up to the wife alone. There are several things that will normally be done by the wife, such as taking mucus observations, but there are other things that can and should be done by the husband.

2. The husband should be involved in some of the daily practice of fertility awareness. Obviously, if he is traveling or has to leave the house hours before his wife gets up, modifications will have to be made; however, under normal conditions he should participate. For example, among many couples who use the sympto-thermal method, it is the practice for the husband to give his wife the thermometer in the morning and to record the temperatures.

3. Decision making should be mutual. The husband should be actively engaged in the interpretation of the signs of fertility. Some couples think that the decision to resume coitus should be *only* the husband's, thus forcing him to become involved in the art of interpretation. These people want to do everything possible to avoid the situation where the husband leaves everything up to the wife and places her under a certain psychological pressure to announce "safe day" as quickly as possible. If the only possible way to overcome such an attitude is to leave the decision making entirely to the husband, then we would have to go along with it reluctantly. Such a couple would have a problem that has nothing to do with natural family planning but was merely brought to the surface by the occasion of having to work together. Once on the surface, it can be dealt with constructively. It would be something entirely different if the couple agreed that the husband should make the final and important decisions because of his role as "head of the family." However, we think that normally it should be a matter of mutual interpretation and decision making.

All of this should not give the impression that there is some huge and difficult decision to make every month. Normally speaking, the rules of natural family planning make the wife's fertility stage rather self-evident, but even an easily made decision is still a decision. When the interpretation of the signs of fertility is difficult for an inexperienced couple, they may decide to seek help from others who are more experienced. Providing such counsel is another service of the Couple to Couple League and other natural family planning groups.

Recurring Thought about Meaning

Another way in which the commitment to natural family planning contributes to marriage building is that it provides the couple with a regularly recurring opportunity to think about the meaning of their marriage, sex, and their spiritual values. This is nothing new in human sexuality. As mentioned earlier, for over three thousand years the Orthodox Jew has been required by his Law to refrain from sexual relations at certain times. Through the observance of the Law, the believer was thus asked to think about God, the ultimate lawgiver, and to reaffirm his spiritual values.

Many Christians believe in a reality called "the communion of saints" in the creed. One aspect of this belief might be called the spiritual unity of mankind. The prayers, good deeds, and sacrifices of one person can help someone else through the universal mediation of Christ. Why is this mentioned here? Many people who are interested in natural family planning are also concerned about the degenerating sexual morality that characterizes a significant part of our society. The mere fact that a couple make a commitment to natural family planning does not mean that they are never going to experience any difficulties of self-control during the time when they have decided not to have coitus. For one who believes in this spiritual unity of mankind, such difficulties can be spiritualized; they can be transformed into a positive work for the uplifting of the sexual habits of the world in general or of other particular persons in the world, their children, for example. The Christian couple can go even further and unite any of their difficulties with the sacrifice of Christ in a living prayer for divine guidance and the grace to be good parents. Such a positive approach can bring the couple closer together at the spiritual level and be a most effective marriage builder.

A Remedy for Satiety

When the popular television show "All in the Family" dealt with wife-swapping (October 28, 1972), the topic of sexual satiety was touched upon indirectly. The wife-swapping couple explained that they had taken up this way of life because the zip had gone out of their own married life. That was about as close as anyone could get on television to saying, "We became tired of each other as sex partners, we've had so much of each other, we're bored." We have seen no studies that have analyzed the wife-swapping scene, but we find it hard to imagine that couples who had solid and satisfying marriages would be very interested in such activity. We would be willing to guess that the couple in the television show gave a fairly good reason why some couples take that route in an effort to do something about a crumbling relationship. Interestingly enough, wife-swapping was infrequently practiced before the Pill gave people an added feeling of security.

Is it merely coincidental that the growth of wife-swapping and the use of the Pill occurred at the same time? Could it be that the practice of contraception has increased the quantity but lowered the quality of marital coitus? It would seem that the quantitative approach to sex easily results in "having it more but enjoying it less."

Periodic abstinence is good for the marriage relationship because it helps avoid the feeling of sexual satiation, the feeling of having too much quantity, and a corresponding lack of joy and meaning. Such voluntary and mutual refraining from intercourse is part of the normal pattern of natural family planning and as such can contribute to building the marriage. Once the couple resume intercourse it is a common experience for them to have a heightened appreciation of it. This has led to the saying among some couples who practice natural family planning, "Every cycle has a period of courtship followed by a honeymoon."

Nongenital Ways of Marital Affection

As indicated above, when a husband and wife are in a period of refraining from coitus, they do not simply forget or ignore each other. Rather, it can be compared with the period of courtship that preceded the marriage and honeymoon. There are very significant differences between a chaste and loving premarital courtship and the regular "courtship" phase of natural family planning, for the married couple may morally engage in nongenital behavior that would be highly inappropriate for the unmarried. However, the comparison we would want to make still has validity. During the period before marriage, the couple with a commitment to premarital purity looked for and found nongenital and nonpassionate ways of expressing their love and affection. The fact that they did not have intercourse provided no deterrent to their love; on the contrary, the other little niceties of courtship helped to develop their relationship. Tenderness and gentleness instead of passion, conversation rather than coitus helped to broaden and deepen their friendship.

In a similar fashion, when a married couple choose to refrain from intercourse for a period of time—whatever the reason—they should remember some of the pleasantries of courtship. Conversation without coitus is once again especially appropriate. Her making him a special dinner or his taking her out to dinner provide traditional ways of courtship for the married as well as the unmarried. His performance of some of the household jobs that she has wanted done or his taking out the garbage without complaint can be most helpful in the process of marital courtship. So also can be her verbal thanks for such little things and her compliments for his help with the children. Some couples find that a bit of cuddling is very helpful; the wife feels more loved for her own sake when her husband puts his arm around her and sprinkles their conversation with a few kisses without coitus than when it is known that all such activity is simply a preliminary to coital gratification. There is no universal recipe for the periodic courtship-without-coitus phase of marriage; an excellent exercise in marital communication would be a discussion of what each might do for the other in such periods. The important thing is that they still show each other that they care and are friends. In this way, they can actively work against one of the worst enemies of the marital relationship—taking each other for granted.

Increased Respect

If the feeling of being taken for granted is a prime cause of marital discontent, the feeling of being used must run a close second. For reasons that are probably obvious to most readers, this is particularly true of women. When the frequency and the conditions of intercourse lead a woman to feel that she is being used pretty much just as a means of sexual relief for her husband, her respect for him is hardly increased, no matter how sympathetic she is to his sexual urges. On the other hand, when couples give up their practice of contraception and turn to natural family planning, it is a fairly common experience for the wife to develop greater respect for her husband.

Encountering Difficulties

Even with firm moral convictions that natural family planning is the only way to go, even with convictions that the natural way is not only best for the individual couple but even for our civilization, couples will still experience occasional difficulties. Natural family planning involves some voluntary sexual self-restraint, and that can be difficult. Some experienced couples may refrain from genital contact for less than a week; others go for two or three weeks or longer without genital relations. The approach taken to any difficulties will have much to do with the couple's happiness and success.

We certainly don't have a ready-made formula that we can hand to every couple that guarantees they will have no problems. However, common sense plus the experience of couples practicing natural family planning suggest some thoughts and guidelines that may be helpful not just in developing a positive approach to difficulties but also in developing a deeper, more mature marriage relationship. Indeed, it is a frequent comment from couples we meet in CCL that natural family planning demands a certain amount of maturity to begin with but results in an even more mature, stable, and happy marital relationship. Repeatedly, we have been told by others that the efforts involved in natural family planning have been repaid tenfold in marriage enrichment.

Accept Difficulties as an Enriching Part of Life

The famous Jewish psychiatrist Victor Frankl reflected deeply upon his experiences as a prisoner in the Nazi concentration camps during World War II. His book *Man's Search for Meaning* is the type that you can hardly put down, and many read it in one sitting. (A common experience is that it quickly makes the rounds in a neighborhood because it is something people want to share.) He notes that

suffering is an ineradicable part of life, even as fate and death. Without suffering and death human life cannot be complete. The way in which a man accepts his fate and all the suffering it entails, the way in which he takes up his cross, gives him ample opportunity—even under the most difficult circumstances—to add a deeper meaning to his life . . . . Everywhere man is confronted with fate, with the chance of achieving something through his own suffering.[3]

Of course, whatever difficulties one may encounter in natural family planning are different from the sufferings Frankl and his associates endured in prison, not just because the natural family planning difficulties are much, much less severe but also because these lesser problems are freely accepted as part of the price of pursuing and upholding certain values.

Another indication that the willing acceptance of difficulties can be a real source of meaning and life-enrichment is the statement of Jesus: "Whoever tries to gain his own life will lose it; whoever loses his life for my sake will gain it" (Matthew 10:39). That doesn't apply just to ultimate martyrdom; it also applies to the little martyrdoms of everyday life in which we "die" to some expression of self-will and find ourselves correspondingly enriched, especially if we have done it for the sake of Christ. Many of the "Jesus people" witness to the fact that by giving up their free-love sexual activity for Christ, they have indeed become more free and more loving as total persons.

Count Your Blessings

One of the most unfortunate things that can occur in any person's life is the state of feeling sorry for oneself. It is quite imaginable that occasionally men and women, whether married or single, may start to feel sorry for themselves because they think they are not having as much sexual pleasure and fun as other people. (And that "as much" can mean either quantity or quality.) For the single, such thoughts, if allowed to develop, can dispose them to engage in fornication; for the married, we would imagine that such attitudes weaken their defenses to the temptation to engage in various forms of adultery.

It is hard to imagine that some men and women practicing natural family planning have not also been tempted to feel sorry for themselves during times of genital continence. Such people may choose to reject such temptations by reflecting on their blessings. Or, to look at the other side of the coin, they can realize how much worse it could be. In any marriage, one of the couple could have an injury, an infection, or some other problem that would mean having no coital relations for a long time—months, or even for life. And how much better to go to bed at night with a faithful and loving spouse than to go to bed alone, wondering where your spouse is.

More positively, married couples should be glad they are not endangering each other's health or taking the life of a newly conceived child through the current popular forms of birth control. They can be proud of the fact that they have learned to understand this aspect of human nature; millions of people wouldn't know where to start. We think it is a fundamental rule of life: Count your blessings.

Take One Day at a Time

Another attitude that is helpful in dealing with any sexual frustration that may arise is "Let each day take care of itself." We are married for life, but we only have to live one day at a time. In the Lord's Prayer, we pray only for this day's bread.

Keep Communication Open

Throughout the whole range of the experience of marriage, open communication is a necessity. Many little problems can be solved or greatly reduced simply by talking about them, sometimes just by admitting they are there. If, for example, the husband should be feeling a few urges, knows he must exercise self-restraint, but is having a bit of difficulty, the situation may be greatly relieved by his telling his wife the situation. It will probably be much more helpful if they are both willing to joke about it: "Honey, I'm feeling oversexed . . ." A couple who can laugh together at any of the difficulties of sexual restraint are on the road to sexual maturity and are miles ahead of the couple who begin to feel sorry for themselves.

Use Common Sense and Mutual Support

An attitude of mutual care and support is important. Part of this is by way of communication but also included are some little things. For example, if a husband has told his wife, "When you wear that shorty nightgown, all I can think of is making love to you all the way," then it is simply a matter of common sense for her not to tease his imagination in that way when they have already chosen to refrain from coitus at that time.

In a similar vein, common sense dictates that they should avoid TV shows, movies, magazines, and books that have a definitely erotic effect. Many people have a sexual drive that receives ample stimulation just from being alive and in the presence of one's spouse. Why complicate matters by patronizing those whose sales effort is directed toward further sexual stimulation?

Furthermore, it is common experience that alcoholic beverages can reduce inhibitions, make one feel sexier, and generally create problems with self-restraint. Again, it is simply a matter of common sense not to make things harder for oneself by drinking to the point where these things occur. For some, that may mean complete abstinence from alcohol; for others, it may mean stopping after one drink. People who take two or more drinks are quite probably creating unnecessary difficulties for themselves and their spouses.

In a similar vein, Dr. Pierre E. Slightam has suggested that a healthy diet makes it easier to practice natural family planning. "Many women would have more regularly spaced, natural periods and menstrual cycles if they would eat better."[4] Dr. Slightam counsels his patients to avoid as far as possible the "factory foods" from which the nutritional value has been taken, e.g., white flour and sugar, to avoid or limit the intake of caffeine, and to eat natural foods. He believes that a one-a-day type vitamin supplement may be helpful to make up for the deficiencies in today's processed foods. This applies to men as well as women, because an improper diet results in poor body balance and may provide increased difficulties with one's nervous system and self-control.

Don't Blame the NFP Decision for Basic Marital Problems

This warning is addressed primarily to those who feel that the decision not to practice contraception was more or less imposed on them from the outside. Thus, it becomes a convenient scapegoat for all sorts of problems, especially by those who would see more coital relations as the answer to their marital needs.

Dr. Max Levin, a Jewish neurologist and clinical professor at the New York Medical College, some time ago addressed an audience that was acquainted with the outlook of some Catholics on this matter:

In cases where rhythm is a problem, the husband regards sex not as something he can give his wife but as something to give *himself* as a compensation for his various grievances. In cases I have seen where periodic continence was presented as an intolerable burden, there has not been a single case where I didn't find something seriously wrong with the marriage. There was no love, no spirit of devotion. One or both partners were immature, egocentric, selfish. They were wrapped up in themselves, not each other. It was not the frustration of the rhythm method that was disturbing them. Even if the Church were to change the rules and raise all bars, they would still be miserable living together. What they need is not permission to use other contraceptive methods. They need therapy.[5]

Make the Decision Your Own

When a policy of marital noncontraception is also the official teaching of major religious bodies—Roman Catholicism, the Eastern Orthodox churches, Orthodox Judaism—then it is quite possible that certain believers will accept the teaching in faith but in a most grudging way. Their attitude may be that this is something imposed upon them by some old-fogey ecclesiastics, and consequently the practice of periodic marital continence may seem like quite a burden indeed. Now, however meritorious it may be for such people to accept what they feel is a burden out of a spirit of loyalty and faith, their own religious leaders would greatly prefer that they internalize this decision, that they make the decision on the basis of a moral conviction that the practice of contraception fails to uphold the divine order of creation and the sacredness of human sexuality.

Such couples might do well to remember that other couples are making the same decision for reasons that have nothing to do with religious faith; we would hope that both types of couples will find in these discussions various facts and reasons that will clarify and support their decision.

Expand Your Ideas About Making Love

You have probably noticed that we have regularly used the technical terms "coitus" or "genital relations" as substitutes for the less technical terms "sexual intercourse" and "sexual relations" and have generally avoided the term "making love." Our reason for doing this has been very deliberate. Our culture has tended to identify "sex" with "genitals," "sexual intercourse" with "genital intercourse," and "making love" with "genital intercourse." In reality, any sort of human interchange between any man and any woman can be termed an intercourse that is sexual in a broad sense of the term. However, because of the common limitation of the term "sexual intercourse" to coitus, we have followed the general usage in this manual.

When it comes to the term "making love," who can say that any particular act of coitus is one of "making" love? The term is used frequently for coitus outside of marriage, where the appropriate moral terms are "fornication," "adultery," and even "prostitution." Even within marriage, many honest couples will admit that there is no direct and necessary relationship between coitus and the "making" or "expression" of love. Sometimes, their marital coitus is very expressive of love and is truly constructive, or a "making" of marital love. At other times, their marital coitus is hardly more than a sexual relief mechanism. This is not to level some sort of condemnation of the idea of coitus for sexual relief, but it is to say that honesty requires that we admit that "making love" is frequently just a euphemism that is more useful in describing what coitus is meant to be at its best instead of what it actually is. Thus, we think that our talk about sex would be better off if we eliminated any sort of identity between "making love" and "coitus." On the other hand, we should use the term "making love" in a much wider context. There are all sorts of "love making" or "love building" activities that have nothing to do with coitus.

Just a few days before writing these lines a friend who knew we were working on the manual gave us a couple of short articles on marriage. One of them carried the following thoughts by an anonymous contributor.

"Each couple will need to find or rediscover for themselves the ways to say, 'I love you and I want you to be happy.' It is an art that is not acquired without effort. It may include:

HIS remembering the good-bye kiss or the hello kiss.

HIS bringing her something occasionally (even a bag of peanuts) to let her know that he thought of her during the day.

HIS sharing the goals and problems of his work with her.

HIS doing at least the masculine jobs around the house.

HIS helping in the physical care and particularly the discipline of the children.

HER preparing his favorite meal even though it is by no means her favorite.

HER sprucing up before he is due home at night.

HER overcoming shyness to give a spontaneous and unexpected physical show of affection.

HER learning enough about it to appreciate his sports or political interests.

The project may be as subtle and as long-range as HER sensitizing him to the emotional element of love and HIS educating her in sensuality and the physical response.

Cultivating a sense of proportion and sense of humor . . . in all areas, but, particularly, concerning the sexual life. Laughter can relieve tensions. *Love is not necessarily increased by solemnity.*"

We would go even further and try to examine the "love-making" aspects of what typically takes place when a couple engage in the coital embrace. Typically, they begin with romantic talk and kissing, then engage in necking and petting, and all of this may have been done fully or partially clothed. Then, they engage in the coital act; soon the husband alone or husband and wife together experience orgasm, and rather shortly thereafter it is typically all over. Now, of all these elements, can we say definitely that some are more constructive of "love-making" than others? In other words, can we say for sure that in this typical series of marital activities the actual coitus and orgasm are any more constructive of the love relationship than what is typically called the foreplay? Or could a good case be made for the statement that the foreplay, the talk, and the kissing and petting are at least equally constructive of the marital love relationship?

We have heard from several sources that some Europeans, Orientals, and Americans think that the practice of coitus reservatus is the height of the art of love-making. (Coitus reservatus means engaging in physical coitus but controlling oneself so that neither party has orgasm.) Now, sperm may be present in the slight nonorgasmic lubricatory discharge that comes from the penis of the sexually stimulated man, and thus genital contact and certainly the practice of coitus reservatus are excluded on practical grounds during the fertile period. Furthermore, such a practice carries with it a certain risk of accidental orgasm, especially among those who are accustomed to orgasmic coitus. But still, one wonders whether these people may not have a grain of truth in their de-emphasis on orgasm and their positive emphasis on some of the other aspects of erotic marital love.

At any rate, marital continence is not the same thing as living as brother and sister; it is not the continence of those who have dedicated themselves to a single, celibate state. The periodic marital continence of natural family planning does exclude coitus and genital contact, but it does not exclude the sexual intimacy of kissing, necking, and petting. Certainly, it takes self-control to firmly hug and kiss one's spouse and not think immediately or exclusively in terms of carrying through to orgasm, but this type of self-control is part of what is meant by the development of sexual maturity.

Now, some couples may decide to engage in no more than a kiss goodbye, hello, and a quick good-night. They may find that to engage in any further intimacy puts too much strain on one or both parties. Other couples may find that they can engage in these marital pleasantries without feeling any sort of overpowering drive toward coitus; they may find that such activity helps reduce sexual tension. Most of these latter couples will have arrived at this state only little by little. We only wish to point out that sexual self-control within natural family planning does not necessarily mean avoiding all husband-and-wife contact that is sexually arousing. It also includes being able to experience moderate sexual stimulation and still being able to control oneself from going further. We would think that one of the best times to begin to develop this sort of self-control would be during the *infertile* times so that if passion should take over, the complete act of coitus and orgasm would not result in pregnancy.

From what we have said thus far, we think it is obvious that masturbation—solitary or mutual—oral sex or anal sex are not included as morally acceptable "expanded ideas of marital love" during the fertile time. We are not condemning oral-genital contact as part of the foreplay that leads to completed intercourse, but orgasmic oral sex is contrary to the Christian tradition of sexual morality which holds that deliberate ejaculation must take place only within the vagina. Orgasmic oral sex is called oral sodomy.

Natural family planning calls for sexual continence during the fertile time. A combination of fertility awareness with oral sodomy during the fertile time simply is not natural family planning but rather is just another means of non-natural birth control using masturbatory types of acts. We regret having to mention this unpleasant subject and do so only in response to published recommendations for such behavior.

Couples who manage to expand their ideas about making love will also be less concerned or anxious in looking forward to the resumption of coital relations when they find the indications of infertility. If coitus is simply one of many ways in which they have learned to express their marital love and affection, then the first day of the infertile phase will not take on undue importance. Perhaps they won't feel like engaging in coitus that night anyway.

Quite obviously, this process of expanding one's view of the practice of love-making deemphasizes the quantitative approach that has been so much a part of our culture especially since Dr. Kinsey reported on his study of coital customs of married Americans—so many times per week for this age group and so many times for that group. In effect, the approach inherent in natural family planning says, "Dare to be different. Put more emphasis on the quality of your marital love as a whole than on the quantity of coital acts. Learn to be lovers." Another writer put it this way some years ago:

If a husband and wife have not learned in a few years how to give themselves to each other totally in the intimacy of an understood look, they had better get busy learning how to love each other. They are simply lousy lovers. And I don't care if they hustle off to bed every night of the week for the so-called marital embrace. If that is the only love-making they do, they are at best only half-alive.[6]

Expand the Meaning of the Marital Embrace

Just as it is necessary to expand the meaning of love-making to include many noncoital activities, so also is it necessary to expand the meaning of the coital act. If it is seen only in terms of biological urges, it is being viewed too narrowly. We believe that it may be helpful to make use of some of the ideas touched upon earlier in order to have a more adequate understanding of the meaning of the coital embrace.

Marriage is both a state and a process of being. We have all heard talk about "the married state," which refers to the status of the couple before God and the world. For some reason, we have heard less talk about "the marriage process," which refers to how this man and woman are continuing to develop their marital status with each other. Perhaps one reason for this is that it is a relatively easy and one-time step to enter the married state, but the marriage process is never completed. To put it another way, when two people commit themselves in marriage, they promise to give of themselves in a caring love for each other for the rest of their lives. They give themselves without reservation to each other for better or for worse. However, most married people will acknowledge that it is easier to make this commitment than it is to engage in the day-to-day process of carrying it out and renewing it.

In this perspective, the coital embrace is seen as a unique expression of married love; it is seen as embodying and renewing in a symbolic way their original marriage commitment of *total* giving to each other. In this way, the meaning of the coital embrace takes on the very meaning of marriage itself; this is certainly a view of coitus that is considerably more expansive than the idea that coitus is chiefly the expression of biological urges.

In such an expanded view of the meaning of the coital embrace there is no room for contraception. The coital renewal of the marriage covenant calls to mind the couple's vow of giving *without* reservation to each other, but contraceptive coitus is very simply the expression of the sexual encounter *with* serious reservation. As such, it fails to fulfill the rich and real meaning of the marital embrace.

Be Positive About the Difference

Because couples who practice natural family planning are apparently a minority with respect to those who use mechanical and chemical contraceptives and abortifacients, they are frequently not only soft-spoken about their conviction but even apologetic. However, there are increasing reasons to be more positive. We have already reviewed such values as esthetics, health, cost, and life of the newly conceived baby, and we have spent time on religious and moral values that are involved in the choice of methods for birth regulation.

We have heard from various couples who made a thoughtful decision to use only natural family planning and who yet found themselves at a loss for words to answer the question, "Well, what difference does it make which way you choose? After all, we all have the same purpose in mind." We have already tried to provide a response to that at the level of moral principles in Chapter 3 but a related example may be helpful.

Periodically, we read about a "marriage contract" in which the couple agree to a five-year term of legal marriage with an option to renew; sometimes the "contract" is for no time period but lists the various conditions under which they will remain married or will call it quits. The aim is quite simple: to eliminate the risks of an unhappy marriage.

Most people contemplating Christian marriage likewise hope to avoid an unhappy marriage. If they have any idea of what marriage is, they realize it is a risk, so they try to cut down the risks. They try to find a mate who is truly compatible; they try to have some financial basis for living. Many will postpone the wedding until some milestone has been achieved, such as graduation, military discharge, or employment. But still, within the Christian principle, when that couple finally marries, they take each other for better or for worse. If the sky falls in on their plans a week after marriage, they are still married. They have accepted each other, committed themselves to each other in a risk of faith and love. The unconditional character of their commitment is the core of what makes their union a marriage.

Both the "five-year option" pair and the carefully selective couple hoped to avoid an unhappy marriage, and both took steps to reduce the risks. However, in the first case, they destroyed the very meaning of marriage, while in the second case they accepted it for all that it is.

Contraception is like the "five-year option." It so absolutizes the elimination of risk that it contradicts the meaning of the sexual act as a renewal of the marriage covenant for better or for worse. On the other hand, the couple who practice natural family planning may engage in the sexual embrace only when the possibility of conception has been naturally reduced or eliminated. When they engage in the marital embrace, they—unlike our second couple—accept it for all that it is, thereby keeping it as a symbol of unconditional giving of each to the other. The difference is significant.

Develop Authentic Notions About Freedom

A proper approach to freedom is helpful in natural family planning, and a false idea of freedom can bring chaos to a marriage. Some people don't want to marry because they feel it will restrict their sexual freedom, and others pursue freedom and happiness in extramarital affairs. Such unfortunate people are more slave than free.

If the coital embrace is viewed almost solely in terms of being the result of various biological or romantic urges, then it tends to be seen as "inevitable" or "absolutely necessary." Such a limited view about the meaning of the marital embrace leads to erroneous and narrow conclusions about our freedom to say "yes" or "no."

Most of us have found that freedom isn't really free. To be free to run a mile without stopping, we have to put forth a great deal of training effort. The same is true of sexual freedom. To be sexually free means to have enough sexual self-possession so that we are masters over our urges and can place sex at the service of authentic love. To attain that degree of freedom requires the help of God, and no one should feel ashamed at admitting his or her need for divine help in this area of life.

The Christian will recall the frequently quoted words of Jesus, "And the truth will make you free." Less frequently quoted is the preceding sentence, "If you continue in my word, you are truly my disciples and you will know the truth" (John 8:31-32). Thus, in the Christian perspective, authentic freedom comes from discipleship, and no one has ever said that authentic

Christian discipleship was easy. Furthermore, the statement of Jesus that "without me you can do nothing" makes it a responsibility for those who wish to be his disciples to acknowledge their need for his help and to pray for the gift and development of authentic sexual freedom.

* * *

Current awareness teaches us that many people do not see everything the way we have written in this manual; many have never thought about some of the things we have touched upon. Though we have written many words on a number of related topics, this has not been the place to develop in any adequate way a complete rationale of natural family planning or a critique of the contraceptive and the abortifacient approaches. Despite these limitations, we are led to believe from our correspondence that the preceding considerations may prove helpful to people who have already made the decision for natural family planning and to those who are still in the process of making up their minds.

Furthermore, we think that a great many couples of good-will have made a decision for contraception based on a seriously limited consideration of all the values involved; we would hope that many such couples will reevaluate that decision and choose to follow only the natural way in the future, and perhaps this book may offer them some food for thought. At any rate, we would hope that even our critics would agree that a well-rounded, consistent, and intellectually satisfying case can be made for the statement that natural family planning is the best approach to birth regulation because it is the only one that is at the same time—

—highly effective

—without medical hazards

—morally and religiously acceptable

—humanly challenging and appropriate

—and a marriage enriching process in which husbands and wives are considered as creatures of God, called and empowered to respond to the divine order of creation.

References

1. The marriage and divorce statistics from 1910 to 1977 are from the *Statistical Abstract of the United States,* 1978, 59.

2. Nona Aguilar, *No-Pill, No-Risk Birth Control* (New York: Rawson, Wade, Publishers, Inc., 1980. In press.)

3. Victor Frankl, *Man's Search for Meaning* (New York: Washington Square Press, Inc. 1963). 106-107.

4. Pierre E. Slightam, *Coverline* (New Haven: Natural Family Planning Association) vol. 2, no. 16. Spring 1973.

5. Max Levin, "Sexual Fulfillment with Rhythm." *Marriage* (June, 1966), 32.

6. Frank M. Wessling. "Is It Immature Loving?" *America* (May 2, 1964), 595.

Part Two

Fertility Awareness

The "How To" of

Natural Family Planning

The Sympto-Thermal Method

The method of Natural Family Planning emphasized in this book is called the Sympto-Thermal Method (STM). It is a universal system that incorporates all the common indicators of fertility and infertility in crosschecking ways.

We strongly recommend learning the full Sympto-Thermal Method as contrasted with learning just a single symptom approach whether that be mucus-only or temperature-only, etc. By learning how all the symptoms work together for you as a married couple, you can then make your own decision about whether to continue with the full Sympto-Thermal Method, or to use two symptoms, or to adopt a single symptom approach. You can make such a decision based on your own experience, and you have the freedom to return to the full STM at any time.

We believe that by instructing you in the full Sympto-Thermal Method of Natural Family Planning, we are providing you with the most effective means of NFP known today. We also teach you about "ecological breastfeeding," another highly effective but temporary natural means of spacing but one which we wouldn't call "systematic" in the manner of the STM.

In this manual, we also provide you with rules of thumb for using the single symptom approaches: mucus-only (the so-called "Ovulation Method") and temperature-only. We believe that by doing so we are expanding your freedom to choose among several different systems of Natural Family Planning even though we personally prefer the crosschecking approach that is at the heart of the Sympto-Thermal Method.

5

The Basic Physiology of Human Reproduction

The Man's Part

The man's part in human reproduction is relatively simple compared with that of the woman. The testicles, which are contained in a sac called the scrotum, manufacture sperm on a regular basis. The prostate gland produces a fluid that combines with the sperm and is called semen. When the man is sexually excited, his penis stiffens so that it can be inserted into his wife's vagina. When he is sufficiently stimulated, an ejaculation occurs which expels the semen into his wife's vagina.

Millions of sperm may be deposited in any act of sexual intercourse. It takes only one of those sperm to join with his wife's egg (ovum) to create a new life. Under the microscope each sperm looks like a tadpole with a headlike body and a "tail." The tail thrashes around and enables the sperm to swim upward in the woman's reproductive channels to meet the egg. If an egg is present, the woman is fertile and one of the sperm may penetrate it. If the sperm and the egg unite, a new human life begins. This process is called conception or fertilization.

If an egg is not available, conception cannot occur even if sperm are present. Instead, they will simply disintegrate within a short time. The length of sperm life after ejaculation in the vagina varies according to conditions in the woman's reproductive channels, especially the vagina. Ordinarily, sperm life after ejaculation is short. If there is no cervical mucus in the vaginal tract, sperm life is anywhere from 1/2 hour to 24 hours, depending on the acidity of the vaginal tract. In the presence of cervical mucus, sperm life is usually 72 hours (3 full days) at most. While sperm life of 6 days or longer cannot absolutely be ruled out, pregnancies caused by such sperm life are extremely rare.

A man reaches biological sexual maturity during his teens, sometimes even earlier. The growth of hair in the armpits, on the face, and in the area around and above his penis indicates this new biological power. However, in contrast with his biological sex, the young man's inner sexual maturity is by no means automatic, nor will he always progress in maturity. In his behavioral life, he may be more immature at age twenty-four, even sinfully immature in a sexual exploitation of others, than at age fourteen. In short, the young man typically has a struggle of many years to place his biological power at the service of authentic love.

It should be noted that once the normal biological sexual power has developed within a young man, he is capable of fathering a child at any time. In contrast, a woman is fertile only a few days each month.

The Woman's Part

The woman's part is considerably more complex than the man's. A normal man possesses a relatively simple reproductive system and continuous fertility; a woman has a much more elaborate reproductive system that gives her a rhythmic cycle of fertility and infertility. She undergoes certain hormonal changes each month that may affect her both physically and emotionally. An understanding of these changes is necessary for successful natural family planning.

There are six body parts or organs that will be mentioned regularly in discussing the woman's role in becoming pregnant. This chapter describes the bodily changes and signs related to fertility for which these organs are responsible.

● The Ovaries

Ovary is the name given to each of the organs that act as the storehouses of all the eggs (ova) the woman will ever have (see fig. 5.1). A woman has two ovaries, one on each side of the uterus. Within the ovary each ovum has its own container called a **follicle.** Once a young woman has reached a certain level of biological sexual maturity, one of these follicles ripens and ejects an ovum approximately every month except during pregnancy and for a variable time after childbirth. (This latter time may be considerable during ecological breast-feeding, as will be explained in Chapter 10.)

The process by which an ovum is released from its follicle is called **ovulation.** After ovulation the ovum lives from 15 to 24 hours. The range of life makes it apparent that ovum survival is not the same for all women. During this time, the ovum may join with a sperm to begin a new human life. If it does not join with a sperm, the ovum begins to disintegrate and is no longer capable of fertilization.

After ovulation, the follicle that released the egg has a new role to play and gets a new name. It is now called the **corpus luteum,** and its function is to send out a chemical signal, a hormone called progesterone. This hormone is secreted after ovulation for about 10 to 14 days and has several effects related to fertility: it keeps the lining of the uterus intact; it prevents another ovulation from occurring; and it causes the basal body temperature to rise, the cervical mucus to thicken or disappear, and the cervix to close. When the corpus luteum ceases to produce progesterone, the lining of the uterus breaks down and is sloughed off during **menstruation.** The time between ovulation and menstruation is called the **luteal phase,** and it is usually about two weeks long with a normal range of 10 to 16 days.

● The Fallopian Tubes

Next to each ovary is the Fallopian tube that connects to the uterus. When an ovum is released from the ovary, it enters the tube and begins to travel toward the uterus. Conception/fertilization takes place in one of the Fallopian tubes when a sperm cell has come up the tube and united with the ovum.

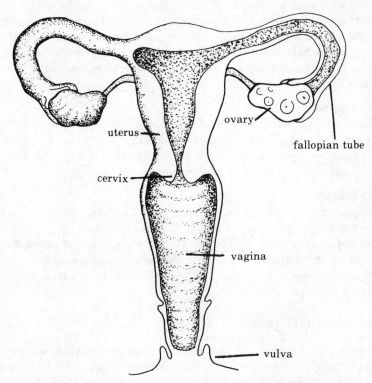

ovary

uterus—

fallopian tube

cervix—

vagina

vulva

Figure 5.1 A Woman's Reproductive Organs

● The Uterus

Within this organ, sometimes called the womb, the baby develops. The uterus is normally about the size of a small pear, but it stretches many times that size to accommodate the growth of the baby. Each month a lining called the **endometrium** builds up inside the uterus. The purpose of this lining is to provide a place for the newly conceived life to implant itself and to give it nourishment. If conception takes place, then the lining remains during the entire pregnancy.

If conception has not taken place, about two weeks after ovulation this lining begins to disintegrate and passes out of the woman's body. This process of sloughing is sometimes called the monthly "bleeding," although the woman is not really bleeding in the same sense as from a cut. More technically, this process is called menstruation. It is also called menses because it usually occurs once a month, and the Latin word for month is "mensis."

● **The Cervix**

The cervix is a channel about an inch in length that joins the body of the uterus to the vagina. The lower end of the cervix has an opening called the **os** (the Latin word for mouth). The cervix and the os can be felt by a finger inserted into the vagina. The os undergoes certain physical changes around the time of ovulation. During childbirth, the cervix opens wide to allow passage of the baby from the uterus into the vagina. Lining the cervix are glands or crypts that secrete mucus under the stimulus of the hormone estrogen.

● **The Vagina**

The vagina is the female sexual organ that receives the male penis. As mentioned before, sperm deposited in the vagina enter the cervix, if it is open, then progress upward through the uterus and into the Fallopian tubes, where conception may take place.

● **The Breasts**

The mammary glands or breasts are likewise part of the woman's overall reproductive physiology even though they are not directly involved in the process of uniting sperm and ovum. During the process of breast-feeding, the sucking stimulation at the breast, through a complicated hormonal interaction, suppresses ovulation and hence fertility for a variable length of time (see Chapter 10).

The Menstrual Cycle

Once a girl reaches a certain stage of biological sexual maturity, she begins to have a regular cycle of ovulation and menstruation. In some girls, this begins as early as age ten, and most are experiencing it by age fourteen. This process normally continues well into a woman's forties and sometimes into her early fifties. However, in the later years she is much less fertile for a number of reasons. Toward the end of her years of fertility, a woman enters stages called premenopause and menopause, the latter frequently called the change of life. During this time ovulation and menstruation may become irregular, and eventually they cease completely. The actual cessation of all menstruation is called menopause. Popular usage tends to group premenopause and menopause under the latter term.

On the average, most women menstruate about every 28 days. This is an average figure and should not be applied to any individual case. Some women regularly have shorter cycles of 25 or 26 days or less; others may have cycles up to 40 days or more. Almost all women vary somewhat from their own average. For example, Mrs. A may have an average cycle length of 28 days. A cycle range of 5 days is well within normal variation. Therefore, it would not be unusual for Mrs. A to have some cycles of 26 and others of 30 days. This degree of variation is not considered irregular or abnormal. Some women, however, may have cycles ranging from 25 to 50 or more days, and these rare cases are considered irregular and abnormal.

Regardless of the length of the cycle, there are usually only 5 to 7 fertile days in each cycle, that is, only 5 to 7 days on which coitus can result in pregnancy. The seven day figure allows for a maximum sperm life of 5 days plus the day of ovulation and the next day. Determining these days is part of the art of natural family planning.

For an individual woman, the interval between ovulation and the following menstruation—the luteal phase—is usually quite regular (see fig. 5.2). Mrs. A may have a luteal phase of 12 days while Mrs. B has a luteal phase of 15 days, but neither luteal phase will ordinarily vary more than one or two days on either side of its average length. An exception is frequently found in the first few ovulatory cycles after pregnancy when the interval between ovulation and the next menstruation may be relatively short.

When there is significant cycle variation, it occurs between menstruation and ovulation as indicated in figures 5.2 and 5.3.

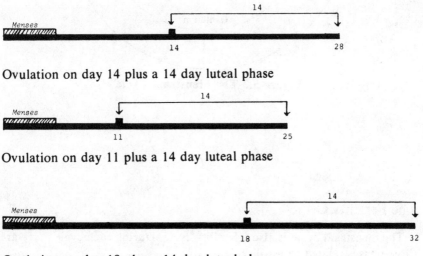

Ovulation on day 14 plus a 14 day luteal phase

Ovulation on day 11 plus a 14 day luteal phase

Ovulation on day 18 plus a 14 day luteal phase

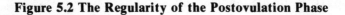

Figure 5.2 The Regularity of the Postovulation Phase

All of the causes of cycle irregularity are not known. However, it is known that stress can delay ovulation and that sickness is one such stress (illustrated in the CCL Practical Applications Workbook). Efforts to induce greater cycle regularity are discussed in Appendix I.

The diagram in fig. 5.3 shows a typical menstrual cycle. If a woman is not pregnant or lactating abundantly, she has recurring cycles. After one menstrual period, the lining (endometrium) of the uterus begins to build up. Then she ovulates. If she doesn't conceive, the endometrium is discarded and menstruation occurs. That is what creates the menstrual bleeding, and the cycle is under way again.

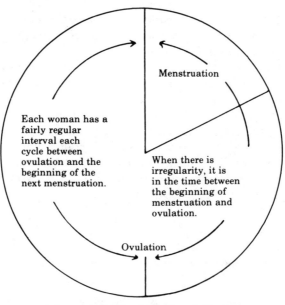

Menstruation

Each woman has a fairly regular interval each cycle between ovulation and the beginning of the next menstruation.

When there is irregularity, it is in the time between the beginning of menstruation and ovulation.

Ovulation

Figure 5.3 The Menstrual Cycle

The Fertility Cycle

The menstrual cycle is also a fertility cycle. During each cycle there are three phases related to fertility:

Phase I: pre-ovulation infertility;

Phase II: the fertile time;

Phase III: postovulation infertility.

● Phase I

Pre-ovulation infertility begins with the first day of menstruation. It would be an extremely rare situation for conception to occur during the first few days of heavy menstrual flow, but once the flow begins to decrease, conception is a possibility.

Phase I infertility is sometimes referred to as the relatively infertile phase to distinguish it from postovulation infertility, sometimes called the absolutely infertile phase. This is because Phase I infertility will be followed by the fertile time, Phase II. There is a slight possibility that a couple may think they are still in Phase I infertility and actually be in the early part of Phase II. Part of the art of natural family planning is for each couple to learn enough about the wife's fertility cycle pattern to be able to make intelligent decisions about the end of Phase I. Several guidelines are provided in Chapter 8.

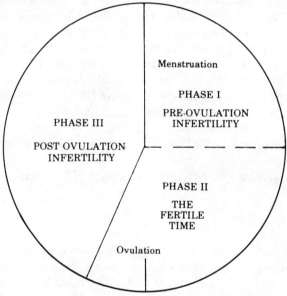

Figure 5.4 The Fertility Cycle

● Phase II

The fertile phase consists of a relatively few days in each cycle. If sperm life is three to five days and ovum fertilization is possible on two days, then there are only five to seven days in that cycle on which coitus or genital contact can result in pregnancy. However, in natural family planning, days of safety are normally added at both ends of the most fertile days to take into account an early ovulation or a second ovulation within twenty-four hours of the first.

One very positive sign that the fertile phase has begun is the appearance of pre-ovulation cervical mucus, but for a few women the fertile phase may begin before the first observable sign of cervical mucus. That is, enough mucus may be present for fertility before the woman actually is able to observe it. A sure sign that the fertile phase has ended is a basal temperature thermal shift that has been sustained through the third morning reading. (These terms will be explained in Chapter 7).

Within the fertile phase, some days are more fertile than others. For those who have experienced some difficulty in achieving pregnancy, part of the art of natural family planning is determining the *most* fertile days, and guidelines are provided in Chapter 8.

●Phase III

Postovulation infertility begins a few days after ovulation. Shortly after ovulation has occurred, the postovulatory hormone progesterone suppresses further ovulations, and there is no firm evidence of a second ovulation occurring a considerable time after the first one. Thus the time of postovulation infertility has frequently been called the absolutely infertile phase to distinguish its greater infertility from that of Phase I infertility. However, the term *absolutely infertile* should not be interpreted to mean that all couples having coitus only in Phase III will never have a surprise pregnancy. Depending upon the system used, Phase III can have a pregnancy-avoiding effectiveness at the 99% level, but no system of natural family planning can promise 100% effectiveness in avoiding pregnancy—or in achieving it.

Various guidelines for determining the start of Phase III are provided in Chapter 8.

The Hormonal Cycle

The underlying cause of the changes in the menstrual and fertility cycles is a hormonal cycle. A hormone is a chemical substance secreted by one of the body's endocrine glands that affects some other bodily function.

Let us start with the time of menstruation. Shortly after the menstrual period starts, the pituitary gland (located near the base of the brain) secretes a hormone called follicle-stimulating-hormone, FSH (see fig. 5.5). FSH stimulates the development of an ovarian follicle and the ovum it contains. The stimulated follicle then secretes another hormone called estrogen. The estrogen has three effects relevant to fertility.

1. The inner lining of the uterus (the endometrium) builds up.
2. The glands or crypts lining the cervix secrete a mucus discharge.
3. The cervix opens slightly, raises slightly, and becomes softer.

The increasing level of estrogen usually causes the mucus discharge to become more abundant and like raw egg white—clear and stretchy. The cervix becomes more elevated and higher as the estrogen level increases.

About a day prior to ovulation, the estrogen level reaches a peak and the pituitary gland secretes another hormone called luteinizing hormone—LH. The surge in LH stimulates the follicle to release the ovum in the process called ovulation.

After ovulation the estrogen level falls sharply but then regains slightly and continues at a level lower than its high pre-ovulation levels until menstruation.

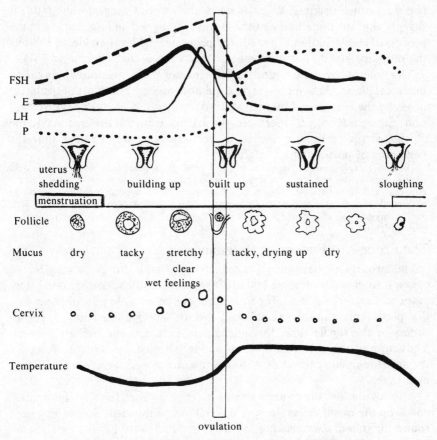

Figure 5.5 The Hormonal Cycle and Its Effects

Figure 5.5 illustrates the relationships between the hormones, the menstrual cycle, the ovarian follicle-corpus luteum, and the symptoms of fertility and infertility—mucus, cervix and temperature changes.

The follicle that released the ovum assumes a different appearance and function after ovulation. It is called the corpus luteum (yellow body), and it secretes a second ovarian hormone—progesterone. The increased level of progesterone has five effects relevant to fertility.

1. The lining of the uterus is maintained at a thick level with a rich blood supply.
2. Further ovulation is suppressed.
3. The basal body temperature rises.
4. The mucus thickens and forms a plug in the cervical canal.
5. The cervix closes, becomes lower, and becomes firm again.

The corpus luteum continues to secrete progesterone for approximately two weeks more or less. When it stops, the level of progesterone falls off sharply, and the thick lining of the uterus is sloughed and discharged in the process of menstruation. The reduced progesterone level no longer inhibits the pituitary gland, and it once again starts the cycle by secreting FSH.

The time of the cycle under the influence of the corpus luteum is called the luteal phase; the sympto-thermal method measures the start of the luteal phase by the first day of thermal shift (described in Chapter 6). The elevation of the basal body temperature, the disappearance of the mucus, and the closing of the cervix are used in a cross-checking way to determine the beginning of postovulation infertility.

The above explanation is simplified but still valid. A more complex explanation would have to include the hypothalamic-pituitary relationship, threshold levels of pre-ovulatory estrogen, and the relationship between the ovaries. While appropriate for a course in physiology, such detail would be excessive and is quite unnecessary in a manual of this sort. See "A Physician's Reference to Natural Family Planning," a CCL pamphlet publication, for greater detail.

The Process of Becoming Pregnant

The process of becoming pregnant begins with coitus (sexual intercourse). At ejaculation some 100 to 500 million motile sperm are deposited in the vagina (see fig. 5.6). If coitus occurs at an infertile time of the cycle, the sperm remain in the vaginal tract and die within a few hours. If coitus occurs in the fertile time, the mucus acts as a nutrient and a transport medium, and the sperm rapidly (at about 1/8 inch per minute) swim up through the open cervical os, through the uterus and then into the Fallopian tubes.

After ovulation, the ovum starts its journey through the Fallopian tube, and soon the ovum meets the sperm. Well over a thousand sperm may surround the ovum, each seeking to pierce its outer wall. Finally, one sperm penetrates the wall of the ovum which immediately undergoes a change to prevent any others from doing so. The sperm proceeds to unite with the nucleus of the ovum in the process called fertilization or conception and a new human life has been created. Each person begins life in his or her mother's Fallopian tube, and that's where all hereditary characteristics are determined.

The human person has a primary instinct for survival, and he begins to exercise this instinct soon after conception as he manufactures and secretes a hormone called HCG, human chorionic gonadotropin. HCG tells the corpus luteum to keep on secreting progesterone. Thus instead of ceasing

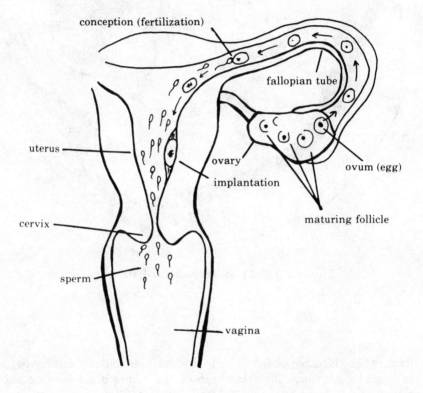

conception (fertilization)

fallopian tube

uterus

ovary

implantation

ovum (egg)

maturing follicle

cervix

sperm

vagina

Figure 5.6 The Process of Becoming Pregnant

its production of progesterone about two weeks after ovulation (which would cause menstruation), the corpus luteum continues to function for several months until the production of progesterone is taken over by the placenta. In this way the lining of the uterus is maintained.

Approximately a week after fertilization/conception, the new life implants in the rich and thick lining of the uterus. After two more weeks, the

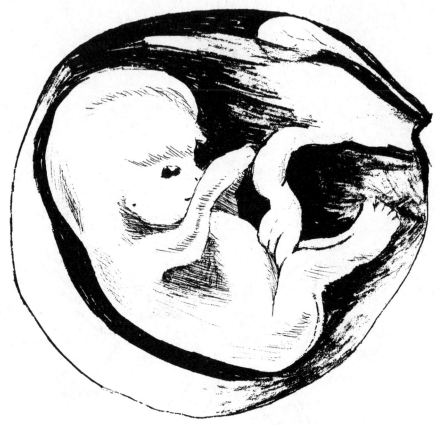

Figure 5.7 Baby at Six and one-half Weeks

nascent baby is taking on familiar physical features, and its heart has begun to beat. By six weeks after fertilization, the baby's brain waves can be measured; and by eight weeks after fertilization, the baby has all the organs it will have at birth.

6
Charting

Good charting makes interpretation both easier and more accurate. Therefore, we emphasize the value of complete and accurate records. The chart in fig. 6.1 is used by the Couple to Couple League and was designed to include the information we think is important. Once a person becomes familiar with it, it is simple to understand and to use properly.

● Daily Observation Chart No._____

When you first start using this particular form of chart, place a "1" in this space, and add one for each succeeding cycle. This may seem arbitrary, but such uniform notation will be helpful when charts are presented to counselors for help in interpretation.

CCL Daily Observation Chart No. _____ **Month** _____ **Year** _____

Name_____ **Age**_____

Address _____ **Phone (** ____ **)**_____

City _____ **State**_____ **Zip**_____

● Month and Year

Write in the time covered by this particular cycle. Frequently a menstrual cycle will overlap two months; then be sure to write in both months, for example, November-December. Write in the year, which may seem so obvious at the time as to be unnecessary, but if someone else is looking at it later, it will be quite necessary. Again, if this cycle overlaps December and January, be sure to write in both years, e.g., "*Month* December-January; *Year* 1979-1980."

● Name, Address, etc.

All this information is important when charts are submitted to the Couple to Couple League teachers or other counselors.

Attention is called to the value of recording your telephone number on any chart submitted to the Couple to Couple League or other counselors. CCL teaching couples are instructed to review the charts handed in at

90

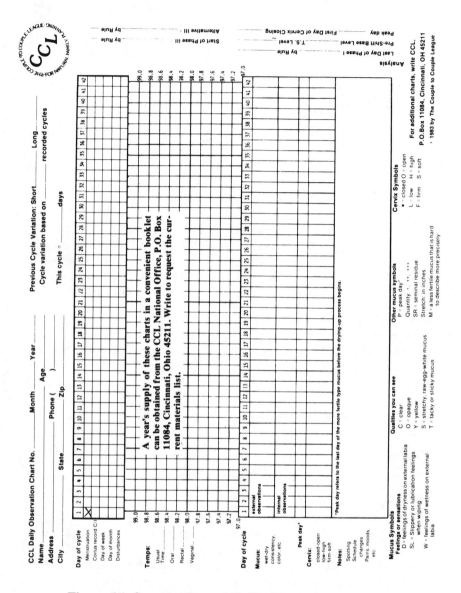

Figure 6.1 Sympto-thermal Daily Observation Chart

meetings and to call the couple if the charting seems to indicate some lack of understanding. For example, one couple told us they understood the method perfectly and were using it to postpone pregnancy; yet their chart showed coitus during the fertile period. A quick telephone check revealed that they had turned the system backwards and were abstaining during the infertile time and having coitus during the fertile period. (By some chance, the woman did not become pregnant in that cycle). When people have coitus is their own business, but if they have come to the Couple to Couple League to learn when coitus will not result in pregnancy, then we would like them to understand the method correctly. Thus, CCL teachers have a policy of reviewing the charts of couples attending our meetings.

If your instruction is solely through this manual, you may send us your charts for review. If you do so, please note if you will accept a collect phone call, or send a self-addressed stamped envelope. It will also be important for you to provide the coitus record, and you should indicate your judgments about the dividing lines between Phases I, II, and III.

● Previous Cycle Variation

This refers to the range of previously recorded cycle lengths. For example, if you have records showing that your shortest cycle was 28 days and your longest cycle was 34 days, you would record "28-34" in this space. If another cycle is either shorter or longer than the previous variation, then you change the "cycle variation" figures accordingly.

Previous Cycle Variation: Short_____ Long_____

Cycle variation based on _____ recorded cycles

This cycle = _____days

● Cycle Variation Based on _____ Recorded Cycles

In this space, you record the number of cycles that are included in the "Previous Cycle Variation." Do you have only three recorded cycles on which to base this range? Then write down "3" in this space. Do you have records of two years of cycles? Then write down the appropriate number of cycles, which will probably be between 24 and 27.

If you have been keeping records on some chart or form other than this one, use those records in determining the previous cycle variation and the number of cycles on which that variation is based. Thus on Daily Observation Chart No. "1", there could be a Previous Cycle Variation of "28-34" based on "17" recorded cycles, etc.

● This cycle:_____Days

This space is for recording the length of the cycle on this chart. A cycle begins with the first day of menstruation and ends on the last day before the next menstruation. The figure placed here should tie in with the recording on the Menstruation line below.

● Day of Cycle

Day 1 is the first day of menstruation. The chart provides for 42 cycle days; for longer cycles, another chart should be used and the numbers changed. Always start a new chart with the beginning of a new menstruation.

Day of cycle	1	2	3	4	5	6	7	8	9	10	11	12	13	14	15	16	17
Menstruation	X																
Coitus record C/I																	
Day of week																	
Day of month																	
Disturbances																	

● Menstruation

An **X** or a / is placed in the square for each day of menstruation. The first **X** has been prerecorded on the chart; write an **X** for the rest of the days of the heavy flow and a / for the days of light flow. In addition, record an **X** on this chart for the first day of the next menstrual period. For example, if the next period begins on what would have been day 32 of this cycle, record an **X** on day 32. This indicates that the present cycle has been 31 days long.

Then record a 31 for This Cycle: _____ days as in this example:

This cycle = ___31___ days

23	24	25	26	27	28	29	30	31	32	33	34	35	36	37	38	39	40	41	42
									X										

● Coitus Record C/I

On your own charts, indicate every instance of coitus. This is so that if a surprise pregnancy should occur, a counselor can help you to understand why.

On the other hand, some couples may not like putting such information on a chart to be handed to a teaching couple. However, for a teaching couple to know whether a learning couple understands the sympto-thermal method, it is necessary that they know what the learning couple regard as the limits of the fertile period. Thus, such charts should include two things:

1. A definite indication of the intellectual judgment about where the fertile period began and ended. Draw a line between Phases I and II and another between Phases II and III.

2. An indication of at least the last 2 occasions of coitus (if any) in Phase I and the first coitus during Phase III. Also record any coitus in Phase II.

The C/I after Coitus record refers to "Complete" or "Incomplete" recording. If the chart has a record of every coitus during that cycle, then the "C" should be circled. If the Coitus record line on a chart has omitted any recordings of coitus, then it is incomplete, and the "I" should be circled.

●Day of Month
●Day of Week

These lines are to be filled in beginning with the first day of menstruation. If menstruation begins before midnight of a given day, then that day is placed in the same column as Cycle Day 1. If menstruation begins after midnight, then the date of the new day is placed in the column for Cycle Day 1.

● Disturbances

This line is for marking any sort of disturbance that might affect the basal temperature recordings. This is more fully explained in connection with temperature recording in the next chapter.

● The Temperature Graph

The heavy dark line on the left is day 1, and the other heavy vertical lines occur at weekly intervals—days 7, 14, 21, 28, 35 and 42.

The horizontal lines indicate the temperature levels; each line represents a difference of 2/10 of one degree Fahrenheit from the next line.

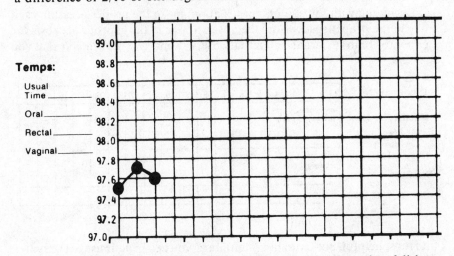

Make your recordings on the vertical lines. For readings that fall between the 2/10 lines, make your recording halfway between the lines. For example, in the illustration above, the reading for day 1 is 97.5°, for day 2 it is 97.7°, and for day 3 it is 97.6°. If a reading is exactly between 97.5° and 97.6°, pick the lower number; in this example, it would be 97.5°.

● Temperature

Write down the usual time at which the basal temperature is taken, and check off the method of taking it—oral, rectal or vaginal. Remember that rectal and vaginal temperatures may give more consistent readings than those taken orally and that the vagina is usually more germ-free than the mouth. This last point is made to alleviate any qualms about being unsanitary if the vaginal method is used.

The most important thing about temperature recordings is consistency. Take the temperature at the same waking time each day. If you change the method of taking your temperature, do it at the beginning of a cycle, because rectal and vaginal temperatures will be a little higher than oral temperatures. If you should change during a cycle, be sure to note the changed method.

● Day of Cycle

The Day of Cycle line below the temperature graph is identical to the one above it; it is provided simply for easy reference.

Day of cycle	1	2	3	4	5	6	7	8	9	10	11	12	13	14	15	16	17

● Mucus Notations

Beginning with the end of menstruation, make the proper notation each day in the proper space. Note the observations in the appropriate rows for either (or both) external or internal observations. Use the symbols that you

Day of cycle	1	2	3	4	5	6	7	8	9	10	11	12	13	14	15	16	17	18
Mucus: external observations																		
wet-dry consistency, color, etc. internal observations																		
Peak day*																		

find most helpful, but try to be as definite as you can in your use of the symbols. For example, use **T** for tacky or sticky mucus; use **S** for stretchy, raw-egg white mucus. Use **SL** for definite feelings of slipperiness when you wipe yourself. Use **W** for sensations or feelings of wetness or lubrication you notice at the outer lips, the external labia. (Note well: you will always notice wetness in the vagina if you make the internal observation for mucus; the W refers **only** to the **external** feelings.) Use **C** for clear or cloudy mucus. Use **SR** for seminal residue. Use **M** as the symbol of last resort: you notice something which is definitely not the more fertile type of mucus, but it's hard to be any more specific.

The T and M stand for the less fertile types of mucus; the C, S, SL and W symbols are for the more fertile types.

● **Peak Day**

Place a "P" in the space for the day of peak mucus and then number the following spaces 1, 2, 3 and 4 for the first four days of drying up. Remember that you cannot determine the peak of mucus until the next day when the mucus symptom has changed. Where there is more than one day of the peak type of clear, stretchy, wet mucus, regard only the last day as the peak day.

● **Cervix Notations**

Some women find one form of cervix notation more helpful than another; some will want to use only one feature for notation; others may want to use more. The most important thing is to be consistent in your method of recording. For the open-closed notation, use circles of varying sizes ranging from a dot to one that is as wide as the daily observation space. Use the

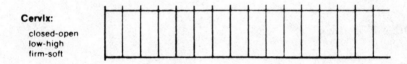

Cervix:

closed-open
low-high
firm-soft

initials "F" and "S" to note firm or soft, and the initials "L" and "H" to note low and high. Better yet, use the open-closed dots and circles to illustrate the rising and lowering pattern (see fig. 6.2). Remember that the cervix opens up, softens, and rises to prepare for ovulation and then follows a reverse pattern after ovulation.

The blank space for notes should be used for writing down explanations for any "disturbances" marked above as well as for jotting down anything else that may be helpful in understanding or learning the fertility pattern.

Notes:

Spotting
Schedule
  changes
Pains, moods,
  etc.

*Peak day refers to the last day of the more fertile type mucus before

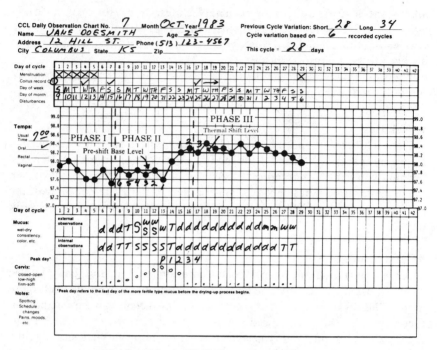

Figure 6.2 A Well Completed Chart

● **Other Notations**

●● **Phase division lines.** In the above example, Phase I ended on day 7. Note that the phase division line comes between the temperature lines for days 7 and 8. Phase III began on day 17 (in the evening). Note that the phase division line is drawn between the temperature lines for days 16 and 17. Phase II consists of the days between the 2 lines.

●● **Pre-shift Base Level.** During the learning stage and whenever a chart is to be submitted for counseling purposes, it is recommended that the couple draw a line showing their judgment of the pre-shift base level. This is set primarily by the normal highs of the six temperatures immediately before the rise in temperature begins. In the above example, it is set at 97.8.

●● **Thermal Shift Level.** As above, during the learning stage and whenever a chart is to be submitted for counseling purposes, it is recommended that the couple draw a line showing the level of the thermal shift. This will normally be 4/10 of a degree above the pre-shift base level. In the above example, it is set at 98.2.

7

The Signs of Ovulation

In this chapter the major observable signs that accompany ovulation are described and related to a typical example of the sympto-thermal method. The signs of ovulation are described in the order in which they occur within the menstrual cycle. This necessarily involves reference to or repetition of certain things mentioned in the preceding chapters.

Sign 1. Cervical Mucus

General Description

Under the influence of increasing levels of estrogen, certain cells in the cervix secrete a mucus discharge which passes through the vaginal tract and is discharged at the vaginal opening. (see Glossary of Terms near end of book for any unfamiliar words.) The following points are important for understanding the cervical mucus symptom of fertility.

● **Biological purpose.** The cervical mucus is present prior to ovulation as nature's way of assisting conception. It provides a favorable environment in which sperm can live. Under ideal conditions, it is possible for sperm to live beyond the ordinary life of 72 hours. In the absence of mucus, or with adverse mucus conditions, sperm may live only a few hours. However, couples practicing natural family planning should not plan on a shortened sperm life.

The presence of cervical mucus provides a natural medium in which the sperm can swim up the vaginal tract, through the cervical canal and into the uterus on the way to the Fallopian tubes.

● **Quantity.** The quantity of the mucus discharge varies greatly. Some women report such a heavy flow that they have to wear a sanitary napkin, while others report that they cannot notice any mucus at all. However, it appears that the vast majority of women can identify the mucus symptom of fertility.

The typical mucus flow starts with a rather small amount and then increases in quantity as ovulation approaches. About one or two days before ovulation, the quantity frequently begins to decrease, and it usually disappears by a few days after ovulation. While the *quality* of the mucus is *more* important, the quantity is still important, and certainly a large quantity of mucus cannot be ignored as a sign of continuing fertility.

● **Quality.** The cervical mucus discharge usually begins as a rather tacky substance that is also rather unclear or opaque. If obtained on the finger-tips, it breaks as soon as any effort is made to stretch it. It might be compared to nasal mucus in the last stages of a cold. This tacky mucus is *less* fertile than what follows, but it can still be conducive to fertility.

As ovulation approaches, the mucus usually becomes stretchy and clear (or somewhat cloudy) in appearance, much like raw egg white. It may stretch one to six inches. It becomes slippery and will cling to one's fingers. Of great importance, this mucus causes feelings of lubrication, slipperiness, or wetness on the outer lips (labia) of the vulva. This is the more fertile type of mucus that indicates the time of greatest fertility, and it may last from one to several days.[1]

As long as the mucus has *any* of the characteristics of being clear, stretchy, slippery and/or providing feelings of lubrication or wetness, it is to be considered the more fertile type mucus. This mucus is usually more clear than at other times, but it may be cloudy, tinged with blood, or brown or yellow as well.

Around the day of ovulation, the mucus begins to change in quality. It loses the characteristics of the more fertile type mucus. Instead, it becomes non-stretchy and tacky, thicker, more opaque, and then it usually disappears. In this manual, the **drying up process** refers to the days of distinctly changed, less fertile, tacky mucus that come after the days of the more fertile type mucus and before the completely dry days.

Some women notice a mucus discharge every day. However, most and perhaps all of these women can learn to distinguish the difference in their own types of mucus upon close observation and with experience.

After ovulation, there may be mucus of varying quality. For example, sometimes a secondary postovulatory rise in estrogen will bring on a day of mucus, even the more fertile type, after several days of dryness. Again, it is common to have one to three days of mucus, even the more fertile type, prior to menstruation. These occurrences need not concern the woman if the basal temperatures and the initial post-peak drying up days have assured her of being in Phase III and if the temperatures have remained in an overall thermal shift pattern (to be explained in the temperature section).

● **Peak day.** The peak mucus day is very simply the **last day of the more fertile type mucus** before the drying up process starts. When the more fertile type mucus lasts for several days, the **last** day is the peak day. This usually does *not* coincide with a peak in the quantity of the mucus; the day of the greatest amount of mucus typically occurs one or two days before the peak in quality.

Sometimes one symptom of fertility lasts longer than others. For example, there may be very distinct feelings of wetness on the labia after the mucus no longer stretches. This might be caused by the mucus becoming extremely watery, much like the watery nasal mucus of a really drippy head cold. Such watery cervical mucus is still helpful for sperm migration, and days of continued feeling of wetness must be regarded as "wet" days of high fertility. If it's "wet" for part of the day and "tacky" for another part, the whole day is interpreted as "wet."

Sometimes a symptom takes more than one day to change from "most fertile" to "less fertile." For example, at a time of very high fertility, the mucus might stretch five inches. The next day it might stretch only one inch, and the next day only 1/8 of an inch. Consider any mucus stretching more than 1/2 of an inch as a "more fertile" type. Thus in this case the day on which it still stretched one inch would be the last day of more fertile type mucus, i.e., the peak mucus day. See fig. 7.1 for an illustration of a somewhat typical pattern of stretchiness, keeping in mind that the pattern for any given woman may not be at all the same. **NOTE:** The feelings of wetness are even more important than the stretchiness even though less dramatic.

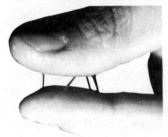

Tacky	Less Stretchy	Very Stretchy

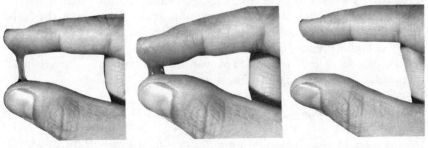

Less Stretchy	Tacky, Drying up	Nothing

Figure 7.1 Changes in Mucus Stretchiness

Observing the Mucus Symptom

You can observe the mucus symptom in several ways. Some are called "external observations" because they are used to detect cervical mucus at the vulva or outer lips; the "internal observation" checks for mucus at its source, the cervical os.

●**The external observations.** There are two types of external observations: 1) sensations or feelings of either wetness or dryness on the outer lips of the vagina (the external labia); 2) visual observations of mucus obtained on tissue paper by wiping the outer lips. Perhaps a step by step explanation will help you to understand what you are looking for and how to observe it.

●●**Using tissue paper.**

1. Use white, unscented toilet paper, folded instead of crumpled.

2. After urination, wipe yourself and concentrate on the feelings produced.

Did it feel positively dry? That indicates no mucus and you'll record that as D on your chart.

Did it feel slippery? Did the tissue glide through as if well lubricated? Those sensations indicate that mucus is present, and you'll record the observation as SL on your chart.

Did it feel neither dry nor slippery? Be sure to check the tissue paper visually for any mucus.

3. Look at the tissue paper. Do you see any mucus? If not, then a wiping sensation of neither dry nor slippery nor lubricated can be interpreted as an externally dry observation. Do you see a bit of dampness or shininess on the tissue paper? Some teach that *in the absence of any sensation of lubrication,* the observation of damp or shiny can still be interpreted as a dry observation.[2] However, we think that more research may be needed and that the situation is best clarified by the internal observation. If no mucus is found at the cervical os and there are no sensations of lubrication or wetness, then a bit of dampness or shininess on the tissue paper may be regarded as some sort of vaginal secretion rather than cervical mucus.

4. Use the touch test if you have what appears to be mucus on the tissue paper. If you can raise it off the tissue anywhere up to a half inch, it's called tacky or sticky mucus and you record it with a T on your chart; more than a half inch is called stretchy. You can do this same test by getting it between your thumb and forefinger as in figure 7.1.

●●**Vaginal sensations**

While the wiping observation is an important way to detect mucus externally, you may also notice feelings of lubrication or wetness at the entrance to the vagina at other times. These are also important, and you'll want to record them as "wet" or "slippery."

Becoming aware of vaginal sensations can be compared to other forms of awareness. One who brushes her teeth after eating or has an apple or carrot develops a feeling for clean teeth and can notice the distinctly different sensation of "dirty" teeth after having eaten sweets and before cleaning. Or, a person easily becomes aware of the feeling of dry, clean skin as opposed to sweaty, sticky skin. Again, the easiest way to distinguish between water and oil is simply by "feeling."

To develop this sort of awareness, you will probably have to think about it constantly for the first few cycles. Then it will gradually become more or less "second nature." At first you may think you have no mucus, but you can most likely develop this awareness with initial effort, detailed charting of your mucus observation, and persistence. Then with experience you may suddenly notice the feelings of wetness while shopping, gardening or doing other ordinary day to day activities. You would record such feelings with a W on your chart.

To have accurate sensations of vaginal wetness, wear cotton underpanties. The synthetic fiber underpanties (e.g. nylon and polyester) are basically non-absorbent and can produce vaginal feelings of wetness completely unrelated to the cervical mucus secretions. In warm weather such nonabsorbency can also contribute to the persistence of vaginal yeast infections. Tight slacks, shorts and jeans can also cause problems with mucus observations.

●●**When and how often?** Start the external observations right after menstruation. However, if you have a history of short cycles — 25 days or less — start the tissue paper awareness as soon as your heavy flow is over. Always start at least by day 6 even if you still have some spotting.

Make the external wiping observation after each urination and bowel movement during Phases I and II. (Women experiencing a scanty mucus flow will sometimes notice a mucus discharge only after a bowel movement.) Strictly speaking, you can omit these observations during Phase III **if** you are using the sympto-thermal method with its temperature crosscheck. However, if you are **not** using the temperature crosscheck, you must make the mucus observations with the same diligence every day of the cycle. The reason will become more clear when you study the double-mucus-patch syndrome.

Another suggestion for mucus observation in the case of a very scanty discharge came from a woman who found that a tampon was helpful. Inserted for several hours, it allows the mucus to accumulate on it for an easier observation. This observation has not been researched, and is not recommended as a general practice. However, it may be helpful in an occasional case and is therefore passed on for whatever it may be worth.

●**The internal observation.** The purpose of the internal mucus observation is to obtain the mucus at its source, the cervix. The distinct advantage of this method of observation is that a woman may notice the mucus directly from the cervix a day or two before she notices it by either external observation method.[3]

To make this observation, a woman inserts her index and middle fingers into the vagina to the cervix (see figs. 7.4 and 7.5). She opens her fingers, places one on either side of the cervix and then closes them as she comes to the lower tip. Keeping her fingers together, she withdraws them. Separating them, she examines for the absence or presence of any mucus between her fingers. If mucus is present, she examines it for stretchiness and other characteristics. This examination is sometimes called "milking the cervix." It should be done **gently** because the purpose is to obtain the mucus that is at the cervical os already, not to squeeze anything from the cervix. Another advantage of this observation is that it is not affected by the discharge of vaginal infections.

Note that a woman will always notice "wetness" in the vaginal tract. Such wetness is there all the time and should not be confused with the feelings of wetness on the external labia which indicate the presence of mucus. That is, "the feeling of wetness" as a symptom of fertility refers **only** to such a sention at the external labia.

Ordinary soap and water clean fingers hygiene is sufficient and should be used before making the internal examination for mucus.

●●**When and How often?** Remember that the big advantage of the internal observation is that you may find the mucus at the cervical os a day or more before you would notice it at the outer lips. Therefore, you'll make this observation more often in Phase I than at other times of the cycles.

Start the internal exam as soon as your menstrual flow has stopped or by day 6 at the latest, even if some spotting should continue. During Phase I, make it two or three times a day — either at midday and bedtime or in the late morning, late afternoon and before bed. More than three times a day may actually obscure the mucus by giving it insufficient time to accumulate. During Phase II, twice a day should be sufficient. During Phase III it is not necessary to make the internal exam if you are using the temperature crosscheck.

●**Observation details.** If you make both the external tissue observation and the internal observation at the same time, make the external observation first.

Because you may experience some confusion in the learning process, regardless of the method used, it is important to write down in some detail whatever you notice during the day. After a short time, the amount of detail can be greatly reduced.

To repeat, whatever your method of mucus observation, make it **periodically throughout the day** and record it at night. Experienced women note that the mucus discharge is not constant throughout the day. Trying to notice the mucus only once a day during Phase I is simply not sufficient.

As the mucus patern starts, you may notice mucus only on part of the day. Such a day is still a mucus day and shows that Phase II has started. As the more fertile mucus pattern is ending, you may notice more fertile types and less fertile types of mucus on the same day. Such a day is considered a "more fertile day" and not as part of the drying up process.

1	2	3	4	5	6	7	8	9	10	11	12	13	14	15	16	17	18	19	20	21	22
external observations			d	dd	d	d	dw		S W	S	S	S	d	d	d	d	d	d	d		
internal observations			d		M	S	S	S	S	S	S	S	d	d							
												P	1	2	3	4					

Figure 7.2 Mucus Charting

● **Mucus charting.** In the above real life example, menstruation lasted for five days. No mucus was noticed either internally or externally on days 6 and 7. On day 8, some mucus was noticed at the cervical os, and this was recorded in the lower row for internal observations. External feelings of dryness continued until day 11. The internal exam indicated the start of the mucus flow 3 days before mucus was noticed externally. Such an earlier warning may be a bit out of the ordinary, but the above pattern is an actual case (including the absence of an internal observation on day 7). When "D" is recorded for the internal observation, it means "no mucus found."

In fig. 7.2 the last day of the more fertile type mucus was the same for both internal and external observations. If there had been a difference, a conservative interpretation is indicated and the last day of more fertile mucus from either type exam is interpreted as the peak day.

Practical Use in Fertility Awareness

The mucus sign can be used most of the time to determine the transition from Phase I to the fertile phase and then the transition from the fertile phase into Phase III.

● **The pre-ovulation mucus sign of fertility.** Typically, but not always, you will have several dry days after menstruation before the mucus discharge starts. Then you will probably notice some tacky or sticky mucus when the mucus flow first starts. **The first apppearance of mucus, even the less fertile type, marks a positive start of Phase II.** Therefore, couples wishing to avoid pregnancy should not have sexual intercourse or genital contact from the time when mucus appears until the beginning of Phase III. It should be remembered that the mucus provides an environment that keeps sperm alive. Cases have been reported where sexual intercourse six days prior to the estimated time of ovulation has resulted in pregnancy. That would be quite unusual, but it points up the fact that under certain mucus conditions sperm can be long-lived.

To repeat, although the days of the clear and stretchy mucus are more fertile, the first day of the less fertile mucus marks the beginning of the overall fertile time, and these days of merely tacky mucus are highly fertile for some couples.

Ovulation frequently occurs on the first day of the drying up process. However, as measured by hormonal analysis, ovulation sometimes comes as early as three days before peak day and sometimes as late as three days after peak day.[4,5]

The days of highest fertility are the days of the more fertile type mucus and the first day of drying up.

● **Determining the peak day.** For the purpose of determining the beginning of Phase III, it is the drying up or disappearance of the mucus that is significant. The day before the drying-up process begins is the **last** day of cervical mucus that is 1) like raw egg white in its consistency **or** 2) that produces the feeling of vaginal lubrication or wetness. This day is called the **peak day** even when there are several days of practically identical mucus signs. Thus **the peak mucus symptom day is known only by hindsight.** For example, Mrs. A. noticed clear stretchy mucus on Tuesday and Wednesday. On Thursday it wasn't stretchy, but she still noticed distinct feelings of wetness or lubrication at the vulva. Then on Friday and Saturday, she noticed that it was tacky and opaque, and she no longer had the feeling of vaginal wetness. Thus, she would then label Thursday as the peak day — because it was the last day of a more fertile type of mucus as indicated by the continued wetness on that day.

● **Postovulation infertility.** In the crosschecking sympto-thermal method, the following rule of thumb has been developed to indicate the start of Phase III: "Beginning of Phase III = Evening of the 4th day past the peak day *crosschecked by 3 days of sufficient thermal shift after the peak mucus day.*" The meaning of the italicized phrase will become clear as the basal temperature sign of ovulation is explained later in this chapter and when the various signs are combined for interpretation in chapter 8.

If the mucus symptom is used by itself as an indicator of the start of Phase III, at least one extra day should be added to make up for the lack of the temperature crosscheck. In our opinion a mucus-only guideline would be as follows: "Start of Phase III = Evening of the 5th day past the peak day." This is not the same guideline used by the Billings method as will be clarified at the end of this chapter.

●**The double mucus patch syndrome.** Bodily stress such as sickness or psychological stress and probably other causes can postpone ovulation despite an apparent readiness to ovulate according to the mucus and cervix symptoms. Take a look at the real life mucus pattern in figure 7.3.

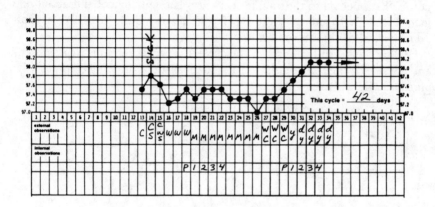

Figure 7.3 Double Mucus Patch

What happened here? The woman was sick on day 14, and that may have delayed ovulation. At any rate, there was a true peak day on cycle day 18 followed by this woman's typical drying up pattern — never all the way dry, as can be seen by the second drying up pattern after the second peak day, cycle day 29. In the sympto-thermal method, this provided no particular problem: the temperature stayed low after the first peak, alerting the couple that they had no positive sign of being past ovulation. When the temperature pattern began rising on day 29, the second peak day, the couple were given a positive crosscheck of being in post-ovulation infertility by day 32.

The frequency of the double patch syndrome has not been documented, but our experience indicates it is neither quite common nor extremely rare. It's a "sometimes" type of thing. However, it provides an excellent reason for using the sympto-thermal temperature crosscheck if you have a serious reason to postpone or avoid pregnancy. (Incidentally, this is the type of thing that created problems for calendar rhythm which didn't have either the temperature or the mucus information.) See chart 9 in the CCL *Practical Applications Workbook* for the complete chart and explanation.

Please note: this is **not** a case of double ovulation: Only one ovulation occurred, and it happened in all probability between days 28 and 30 inclusive.

Sign 2. Changes in the Cervix

General Description

The second sign of ovulation takes place in the cervix, the part of the uterus that opens into the vagina. It is firm and cylindrical and about one inch thick. The opening of the cervix, the os or mouth, feels like a small donut or hollow in the center.

During the infertile phases of the cycle, the cervix remains firm, closed, and is easy to reach. As ovulation approaches, the following changes take place (see fig. 7.4).

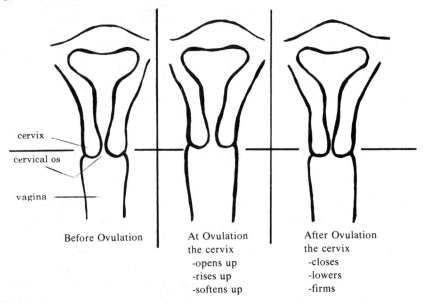

cervix

cervical os

vagina

Before Ovulation	At Ovulation	After Ovulation
	the cervix	the cervix
	-opens up	-closes
	-rises up	-lowers
	-softens up	-firms

Figure 7.4 Changes in the Cervix

1. The os opens enough to accept a fingertip.
2. The portion of the cervix protruding into the vagina becomes softer, attaining a rubberiness and softness similar to the walls of the vagina.
3. The cervix rises and becomes more difficult to reach.
4. There is an abundance of mucus.
5. The mucus makes the cervix feel more slippery.

These signs appear gradually in the cycle; it takes several months to recognize the changes and become experienced in their interpretation.

After ovulation, the cervix soon changes back to the way it was before ovulation.

1. The os closes, frequently more tightly than before its pre-ovulation opening.

2. The whole cervix becomes firmer; the tip becomes like the tip of the nose.

3. The cervix moves lower, is easier to reach, and is sometimes lower than before its pre-ovulation rise.

4. The mucus changes in quality or consistency and is difficult to obtain.

5. The absence of mucus makes the cervix feel drier when compared to the time of peak mucus.

● **Biological purpose.** The opening of the cervical os prior to ovulation aids sperm migration, and the same may be true of the elevation of the cervix. No function of the softness is known. The tight closing after ovulation combines with the thickening of the mucus in the cervical canal to prevent the migration of sperm and other organisms into the uterus.

Observing the Cervix Symptom

The changes in the cervix can be observed by the woman herself through examination by touch. Perhaps the easiest way to make this examination is for the woman to sit on an open toilet. She then inserts her middle finger or index finger or both into the vagina to touch the cervix (see figure 7.5).

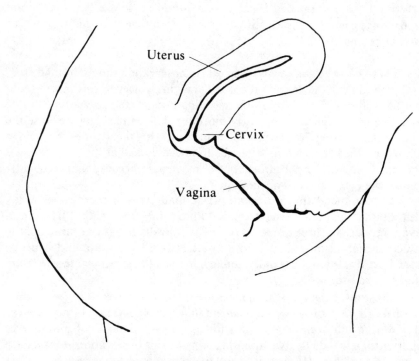

Figure 7.5 Side View of Vagina, Cervix and Uterus

If she finds difficulty in reaching the cervix at all times in the cycle, she can press down and a bit forward on her abdomen with her other hand. Since this pushing may make the cervix lower and easier to reach, it should be done either all the time or not at all lest a woman confuse these "pushing" differences in the ease of reaching the cervix with those caused by the natural rising and lowering of the cervix during the cycle.

Another way of making this observation is in a standing position with one foot on a stool or low chair.

Some women find the lower end of the cervix sensitive to touch during the fertile time, but most women do not. A woman will typically feel the cervix as cylindrical and about one inch thick, and she will be able to circle it with her examining finger. She will notice that the lower end has an indentation, much like the stem end of a small pear after the stem has been removed.

● **The first finding.** Many women have difficulty in finding the cervix at first. Two suggestions may be helpful. First of all, some women find that the cervix is lowest in Phase III, so this may be the best time to make the first efforts at finding it. Secondly, some women have been assisted by their husbands in finding it the first time. Once he finds it, he can describe its feel and location so that she can find it. Since this may be erotic for some, Phase III would again be the best time for such initial assistance. The main point is that once a woman has identified it for the first time, she usually proceeds well after that.

● **When to observe and record.** The cervix observation should be made several times during the day and recorded at night. However, this exam should not be made the first thing in the morning because the cervix tends to be almost always higher in the early morning. This is probably because the muscles supporting the uterus contract a bit during the night as the woman sleeps and then stretch a bit after she has been up and around. Nor should this exam be made right after a bowel movement because that frequently causes the cervical os to open a bit.

We recommend that observations be made two or three times a day during Phase I and towards the end of Phase II. DON'T make this internal exam more than three times a day or you may disturb the accuracy of the mucus observations. If you do it twice a day, try a noon and bedtime schedule. For three times daily, make it in the late morning, late afternoon and before bed.

Because all of the cervical changes are relative — lower or higher, closed or open, firm or soft — we recommend that this observation be made every day during the cycle beginning with day 6 — or sooner if menses was shorter than five days. By continuing to make this observation at least once a day during Phase III, a woman will literally keep in touch with her cervix during a very stable time, thus giving her a good base for comparing the changes at either end of Phase II.

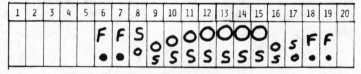

Figure 7.6 Cervix Charting

● **Cervix charting.** In the above example the letters F and S were used to designate firm and soft. The dot represented "closed," and then it was drawn as an open circle to show relative opening and closing again. Its location on the chart was used to designate the rising and lowering of the cervix. In this case, the first day of closing was day 16, a finding that can be used in conjunction with the other sympto-thermal signs even though some softness continued.

● **Value of experience.** Experience with the cervix symptom of fertility is a real asset to the nursing mother and the woman approaching menopause; some women find that during these times the cervix provides a more interpretable indication of pre-ovulation infertility than the mucus symptom.

Thus because of its long range value we encourage women not to become discouraged if they find difficulty in interpreting this symptom at first. It will take many women two to six cycles of daily observations to develop experience and confidence.[6]

Practical Use in Fertility Awareness

● **Pre-ovulation.** In the first part of the cycle, while the cervix remains low, firm and closed and there are no indications of mucus even from "milking" the cervix, there are good indications of still being in Phase I. With increased estrogen activity and the beginning of the fertile time, the cervix starts to rise, open and become softer.

● **Post-ovulation.** Once the cervix has begun to close, lower and become firmer, at least four days of closing etc. should be crosschecked by at least three days of overall thermal shift. There are no scientific studies relating only the cervix changes with the temperatures, and thus the following rule of thumb is not based on experience but upon the fact that the cervix reacts to the same hormones as the cervical mucus. The sympto-thermal rule of thumb can be stated thus: "Beginning of Phase III = Evening of the 4th day of closing crosschecked by at least 3 days of overall thermal shift."

"Day of closing" represents all three of the changes. If a woman notices that the cervix is wide open at noon but has distinctly closed by nighttime, that is the first day of closing.

Because of lack of experience with the cervix changes alone as an indicator of postovulation infertility, cervix-only usage is not recommended.

If conditions made it impossible to obtain a thermometer, at least 4 days of cervix closing should be crosschecked by at least 4 days of mucus drying up. If no help was given by the mucus sign or the temperature, the practical start of Phase III should be delayed until the evening of the 5th day of closing.

Sign 3. Ovulation Pain

General Description

Somewhere around the time of ovulation a pain in the area of one or both of the ovaries is felt by many women. This pain is technically called "mittelschmerz" meaning pain in the middle. Sometimes it lasts a few hours; at other times it may last for one or two days. For some the pain is negligible, but some women have been known to experience great discomfort, even to the point of doubling over with pain.

● **Biological explanation.** The cause of this pain is debated, and we cannot provide an explanation on which there is universal agreement. One explanation says it is caused by a pre-ovulation congestion in the Fallopian tubes, a filling up with mucus to facilitate sperm migration. Another explanation holds that it is due to a vigorous pulsing of the Fallopian tubes at and just after ovulation, a peristaltic motion to move the ovum toward the uterus. A third explanation points to the process of ovulation during which the follicle containing the ovum ruptures. Frequently a small surface blood vessel is broken by the rupture and a slight bleeding occurs. The lining of the body cavity is very sensitive to internal bleeding, and its reaction results in pain.

Practical Use in Fertility Awareness

Because of the ambiguities stated above, we cannot say if "ovulation pain" comes before, during or after ovulation. However, it is still useful as a secondary crosscheck to be used in conjunction with the other symptoms. Furthermore, the woman who notices this pain in conjunction with the other signs of fertility has a pretty good idea it is "mittelschmerz" and not a symptom of some other problem.

Couple to Couple League policy is to recommend that a couple not rely on the ovulation pain as a primary means of detecting ovulation. For one thing, it might be confused with minor intestinal pains or cramps, and if it occurred during sleep, it might not be felt at all. The signs of the mucus, cervix and basal temperature are far more reliable.

Sign 4. Temperature Rise

General Description

As soon as the ovarian follicle has ejected its ovum, it begins a new function. It becomes the corpus luteum and begins to release progesterone. This hormone causes a woman's basal body temperature to rise slightly, usually at least 4/10 of one degree Fahrenheit — for example, from 97.7° to 98.1°.

A person's basal body temperature is the temperature of the body at rest, uninfluenced by food or drink or activity. It rises and falls in a cyclic pattern throughout the day and night, with the lowest point being at some time in the very early hours of the morning. Normally, it continues to rise after a person's regular wake-up time and rises about 1/10 of 1°F. every half hour until it reaches the normal high base which is around 98.6°. Both the rate of rise of 1/10 of a degree per half hour and the 98.6° temperature are averages and may not hold true in any individual case. This daily rising and falling of the body temperature affects everybody and is called a circadian rhythm.

Ovulation is followed by a sustained rise in temperature called the **thermal shift**. The **thermal shift level** will usually be 4/10 to 6/10 of 1°F. higher than the **pre-shift base level**. The pre-shift base level is established by the normal high temperatures on the six days immediately preceding the beginning of the rising temperature pattern. When the basal temperature has been elevated at least 4/10 of 1°F. above the pre-shift base for at least three consecutive days, a full thermal shift has been established.

Note: In previous printings we used the term "pre-ovulation base level" (POB) instead of "pre-shift base level." Experience has shown that "pre-shift base level" is better for educational purposes. You may find the older term in the CCL *Practical Applications Workbook* and even on some pages in this book.

Observing the Temperature Sign

●**The basal temperature thermometer.** Although it is not absolutely necessary, it is customary to use a basal temperature thermometer from a reliable manufacturer. This type of thermometer records only within the range of 96° to 100°F. and is very accurate. It is also more readable than the typical sickroom thermometer (See fig. 7.7).

Figure 7.7 A Basal Temperature Thermometer

●**When to take it.** The basal temperature should be taken for five to seven minutes **at the same waking time** each morning. The reason for sameness in temperature-taking time is the circadian rhythm mentioned in the general description. If the basal temperature is rising at the rate of 1/10 of

1° F. per half hour at a normal waking time — say 6:30 a.m. — then taking it two hours later at 8:30 a.m. could result in a temperature recorded 4/10 of 1° higher than it was at 6:30. This could interfere with proper interpretation. It is especially important to take the temperatures accurately during Phase II but not so important when well into Phase III.

When it is practically impossible to take the temperature at the same waking time, exceptions can be made. We have seen good records from women who took their temperatures at a consistent time just before going to bed in the evening. One woman who worked evenings took her temperature regularly between 1:30 and 2:00 a.m., her normal bedtime, and obtained an easily interpreted record.[7] Consistency is very important in all of this.

● **How to take it.** How should a woman take her temperature — orally, rectally, or vaginally? Rectal and vaginal temperatures tend to be more accurate than oral temperatures because oral temperature readings can be affected by insufficient mouth moisture, having one's mouth open, etc. Some people who teach natural family planning recommend using only the rectal or vaginal method. However, the experience of those associated with the Couple to Couple League is that most women can obtain satisfactory temperature recordings by taking the temperature orally. If temperatures taken orally tend to be irregular, then a woman should use one of the other methods. The basal temperatures of the vagina and rectum will record a little higher than those of the mouth. Therefore, a woman should not change her method of temperature-taking during any given cycle. Those who take their temperature rectally or vaginally do not need to insert the thermometer very deeply, and they must be careful not to break it while it is thus inserted. With oral temperatures, the thermometer is always placed under the tongue.

Does a woman have to remain in bed while taking her temperature? Rather obviously, this question applies only to those taking their temperature orally. The experience of the Couple to Couple League is that many women can get accurate oral temperatures even if they do not remain in bed. Therefore, a woman can spend her five minutes of temperature-taking in bed, or she can get up with the thermometer in her mouth and perform light morning duties such as going to the bathroom and getting dressed. Such light activity will usually not affect the temperature pattern, but it is advisable to have a uniform practice of either staying in bed or getting up. She may test this practice simply by recording her temperature at the end of five minutes in bed, shaking the mercury down, rising as mentioned above, and checking the temperature again after five minutes of such light activity. After a few mornings of this, she can see for herself whether her temperature has been raised by this light activity or has remained the same.

Some special notes:

1. A woman who takes her temperature orally should never have a drink of any kind or a cigarette before taking the temperature. On the other hand, common sense indicates that a glass of water at 4:30 a.m. isn't going to affect an oral temperature reading at 6:30 a.m.

2. A woman who gets up while she is taking her temperature should be careful; women have broken thermometers while brushing their hair.

3. A woman should not fall asleep while taking her temperature.

4. A woman suspecting she has a fever over 100°F. should use a regular clinical thermometer. If the mercury in a basal thermometer rises too high in the presence of a fever, it may separate and be impossible to shake down properly.

5. If the thermometer has become very cold during the night, it may actually cause a slight chill spot in the mouth, thus yielding a false low reading. A woman gets around this simply by warming it up on one side of her mouth for a few minutes and then switching it, without shaking it down, to the other side for the five minute reading.

● *Night risings.* Does getting up during the night affect the morning basal temperature? Usually this question has reference to taking care of a child during the night, and the amount of actual activity is negligible. This will not significantly affect the morning basal temperature. Even when the woman is up for quite some time during the night, her morning basal temperature will usually be quite normal if she has been able to get a good hour's sleep before taking her temperature. If the temperature should be unexpectedly elevated after a night of interruptions, a notation of the disturbance should be made on the chart.

● **Recording the temperatures.** When and how should the temperature be recorded, and who should do it? Once the temperature has been taken for five minutes, either the woman or her husband may record it. The authors of this manual recommend giving the recording job to the husband as his part of their team approach. It is a good practice, but not absolutely necessary, to record it immediately on the temperature graph (see fig. 7.8). If that isn't practical, a notation can be made in a notebook, etc. If no notation is made, then be sure to keep the thermometer away from any heat until a recording is made. The mercury won't go down unless it is shaken down, but it might go up if subjected to heat. Thus the thermometer should be stored in a top dresser drawer, for example, but never on a radiator, in front of a hot air vent, on a table where the sun can reach it — or in the reach of children.

After the temperature has been recorded, the reading and recording should be rechecked, and then the thermometer should be shaken down so that it is ready for the next day. Two notes of caution:

1. Do not shake down the thermometer in the bathroom or kitchen.

There are too many hard things around to hit it on and break it. The best practice is to shake it down over your mattress. Thus, if it should slip, it would likely hit some soft blankets instead of a hard floor or sink. Hold on to the thermometer firmly, even on the upstroke.

2. A thermometer is a delicate instrument, the basal thermometer more so. If you wash it, do so *only with cold water.* It is not necessary to wash it when the temperature is taken orally or vaginally as the bacteria from these areas die after a few hour's contact with air.

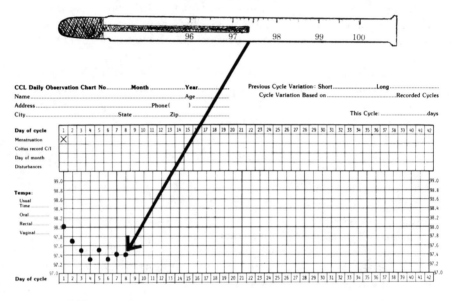

Figure 7.8 Basal Temperature Thermometer and Graph

●*A personal note to husbands from the husband half of the author-couple.* I like the information given me by the basal temperatures so I don't mind the temperature taking. Here's how we do it. At night I shake down the thermometer over the bed, replace it in the rubber holder in its original box, and then slide the open box between the mattress and the box spring. When the clock radio wakes us up, I reach under the mattress, hand the thermometer to my wife who then takes her oral temp, and we listen to a five minute news program. When that's over, I take back the thermometer, replace it in the rubber holder, and place it under my pillow till I get up. When the lights are on, I record the temp, double check it, and store the thermometer in its open box in the top dresser drawer.

On weekends in Phase II, I set the alarm for our usual wakeup time, get the temp taken and then just leave the thermometer in its box under my pillow till rising. On weekends in early Phase I and in Phase III, we don't set the alarm and simply take the temp when we wake up.

All of this seems so simple to me and such a little price to pay for such important information that I have a hard time understanding why some people think daily temp-taking is a big chore. I hope you will find it equally easy and informative.

Interpreting the Basal Temperature Pattern

The important thing about the basal temperature sign is that after ovulation the temperatures will remain elevated. The rise has to be sustained at this higher level to be reliable as a sign that ovulation took place. What is looked for is the shift from a lower level to a higher level.

By way of review, the lower level is called the **pre-shift base level** (PSB) and is simply the *level from which the rise is measured*. The higher level is called the **thermal shift level** (TSL), and the rising process is called the **thermal shift.**

In the interpretation of the thermal shift, three kinds of shifts are recognized in the sympto-thermal method.

A **full thermal shift** consists of at least three valid, **consecutive** temperatures that are **all** at least a full 4/10 of 1°F. above the PSB level.

A **strong thermal shift** consists of at least three valid, **consecutive** temperatures that follow this pattern:

1. each one is at least **2/10** of 1°F. above the pre-shift base level;

2. the **last** one is at or above the normal TSL of 4/10 of 1°F. above the pre-shift base level.

An **overall thermal shift** consists of at least three valid temperatures that follow this pattern:

1. each one is at least 1/10 of 1°F. above the pre-shift base level;

2. they are in an overall elevated or rising pattern;

3. at least one of them has reached the normal TSL of 4/10 of 1°F. above the pre-shift base level.

●**Setting the PSB and TSL.** The PSB (pre-shift base level) is set in conjunction with the TSL (thermal shift level). Both are set when there is a series of three or more temperatures that are all consecutively above the previous six temperatures. The six temperatures immediately before the first elevated temperature are then called the **pre-shift six.**

Two questions are asked as the temperature pattern develops:

1. Are there three temperatures above the previous six?

2. Are those elevated temperatures **enough** above the pre-shift six to satisfy the requirements for a particular rule of thumb? That is, have at least some of them, if not all, reached a level 4/10 of 1°F. above the PSB?

This may appear complicated at first, but it is easy to do in practice. Here is an example adapted from one of the co-author's charts as this was being written.

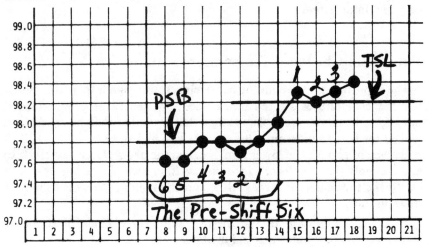

Figure 7.9 Setting the PSB and TSL

By the time we reached day 16, it was very easy to see that we had three temperatures (days 14-16) in a strong thermal shift pattern above the pre-shift six temperatures on days 8 through 13. Note how we counted backwards from the first day of an overall rising pattern, day 14.

The PSB is set by the normal highs of the pre-shift six, namely 97.8 in this case. By a **normal high** we mean the higher temperatures among the pre-shift six that have not been disturbed by sickness, late temperature taking, etc. In fig. 7.9, the normal highs are on days 10, 11 and 13.

We drew a line at 97.8 to indicate the PSB level. Then we added 4/10 of a degree to arrive at the calculated thermal shift level of 98.2. That is, even if all of the higher temperatures had been at 98.3 or 98.4, we still would have drawn the line at 98.2 simply to mark off the ordinary amount of thermal shift, 4/10 of 1° above the PSB.

In figure 7.9 the temperatures on days 15, 16 and 17 constitute a **full** thermal shift. They are all consecutively 4/10 of 1°F. above the PSB.

The temperatures on days 14, 15 and 16 constitute a **strong** thermal shift. Note that the temperature on day 14 was 2/10 above the PSB. Thus it could be counted as part of a *strong* thermal shift but *not* as part of the stricter *full* thermal shift. The significance of this difference will be seen in Chapter 8 where the crosschecking rules of thumb are explained.

●**Shaving irregular highs.** The occasional difficulty in establishing the PSB is illustrated in this example:

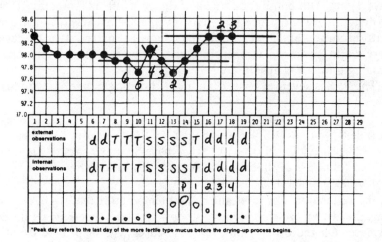

Figure 7.10 A Shaved Pre-Shift Base Level

By day 18 in fig. 7.10 it is apparent that there has been a definite shift from a lower level to a higher level, but it doesn't fit within the standard guidelines that call for the TSL to be 4/10 of 1°F. above a PSB determined by the normal highs of the pre-shift six. The temperature on day 11 was a "normal high", not disturbed by late temperature taking, sickness, etc. Using the standard rules, we should have set the PSB at 98.1 based on the temperatures on days 11 and 15, and the standard requirements of the 4/10 of 1° shift would never have been fulfilled.

Thus the following rules have been developed. In these the **basic principle** is that when the interpretation of an **otherwise obvious shift** in temperature levels is held up by **one or two** temperatures among the pre-shift six, these higher, out-of-line temperatures may be "shaved" slightly in order to get a standard application of the basic rules.

●●**Rules for shaving irregular highs.**

1. Don't shave unless it's the only way to get one of the standard rules to fit.

2. Shave only when there is an obvious thermal shift above the rest of the pre-shift six temperatures.

3. Shave **only one or two** irregular high temperatures down to the **next highest level** among the rest of the pre-shift six. In fig. 7.10, the temperature on day 11 was shaved down to the level of the next highest temperatures in the pre-shift six, and the shaved PSB was thus established at 97.9°. The temperature on day 15 is seen as the first day of an overall rising pattern, especially since it occurs on a day past the peak day of the mucus symptom.

4. If there are **three** temperatures that are causing the problem, they cannot all be shaved to the level of the other three. Instead, the PSB may be set by **averaging.** This entails adding all of the pre-shift six temperatures and then dividing by six, a process open to arithmetic mistakes. It can also lead to cutting corners and disregarding the other signs of fertility in the face of a very slight sustained temperature rise. Thus we do not recommend averaging unless it is absolutely necessary.

5. The PSB is never set lower than the arithmetic average of the pre-shift six.

6. Shaving can be used with sympto-thermal rules A, B, and C but not with Rule R; you can also shave with the four and five day temperature-only rules. When shaving with Rule A, if you have only two days of drying up, you need four days of thermal shift with the last three temperatures at the full thermal shift level.

In the vast majority of cases, the highest temperature reading or readings among the last six pre-shift temperatures are the ones that truly set the pre-shift base. On the other hand, in some cases it is helpful to do some "shaving" or "averaging" in conjunction with the other signs of ovulation.

●**False rises.** Pre-shift temperatures may occur that are above the general level of the rest of the temperatures, and a decision must be made whether to determine the pre-shift base level by the higher temperature, to exclude it, or to shave it as mentioned previously. The following guidelines should be used to arrive at such a decision.

1. High temperature readings that are obviously due to a fever or some lesser illness such as a bad cold or a sore throat should be disregarded.

2. The alcohol from a couple of drinks the night before can influence the next morning's basal temperature.

3. Arising later than usual typically yields a higher temperature. A change in daylight saving time has the effect for about 2 or 3 days of rising an hour earlier (slightly lower temperatures) in the spring and rising an hour later (slightly higher temperatures) in the fall.

4. An unaccustomed chill or heat may affect the basal temperature. For example, one woman had an apparent three-day thermal shift, but she was sure that ovulation had not occurred due to the absence of the pre-ovulation mucus sign. This mother, who always slept with her baby, remembered that on each of those three mornings her five-year-old had crawled into her bed several hours prior to the temperature-taking time. She reasoned the second child's close presence must have given additional warmth to her body.

Erratic temperatures due to explainable causes are sometimes called "false rises," and they can be disregarded in setting the PSB. In such cases, the conservative policy is to go back for one or two more undisturbed temperatures in order to have six for setting the PSB. In doing so, it is frequently necessary to shave the temperatures farthest away from the start of

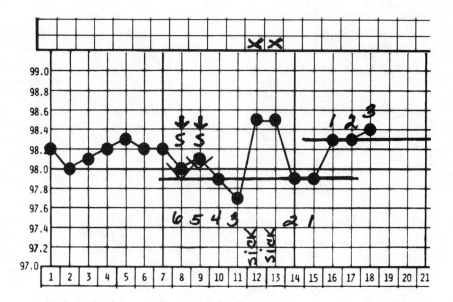

Figure 7.11 Disregarding Disturbed Temperatures

the shift as in fig. 7.11 because it is a typical experience for the pre-shift six to be a bit lower than the previous temperatures, possibly because of a slight temperature depressing effect of the higher levels of estrogen in the half-dozen days before ovulation.

● **Unexplained rises.** In some cycles, one or two temperature readings may occur that cannot be explained by the above types of causes. The following factors are used to evaluate such readings.

1. Does the questioned temperature reading make any difference, or have the thermal shift temperatures risen to at least 4/10 of a degree even above it?

2. If the pre-shift base is set without the questionable temperature, is a thermal shift from that level crosschecked by the mucus and/or cervix signs of ovulation? If so, the questionable temperature may be shaved.

3. When in the pre-shift phase of the cycle did the questionable temperature elevation occur? If it was seven or more days before the thermal shift, it can be ignored.

4. How many "questionable" temperatures are there? One and sometimes two temperatures may be unexplained "false rises" that can be shaved. Three or more are pattern setting, not erratic, and would have to be considered in establishing the pre-shift base, either as setting the pre-shift base by their highs or at least to be used in calculating an average.

● **Thermal shifts of less than the normal amount.** A few women regularly show a thermal shift pattern that is less than the normal shift of at least 4/10 of 1°F. Well instructed couples can learn to interpret such rises *in conjunction with the other signs of ovulation* and successfully use the sympto-thermal method. A cross drawn on the chart in such a way that the horizontal line is *above* six temperatures to the left of the vertical line and *below* three (preferably four) temperatures to the right of the vertical line can help in determining the thermal shift in conjunction with the other signs of ovulation.

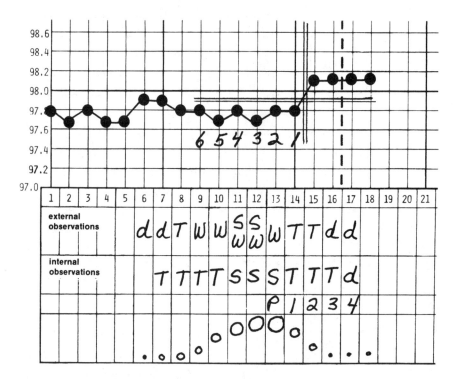

Figure 7.12 Thermal Shift of 3/10 of 1° F.

In fig. 7.12 a thermal shift of 3/10 of 1°F. is accepted as a crosscheck on the mucus drying up pattern. Normally, a CCL teacher would want to see at least two or three consecutive cycles before accepting anything less than the standard thermal shift of 4/10 of 1°F. CCL teachers would always want at least three well charted previous cycles before accepting a thermal shift of only 2/10 of 1°F. because that would be such a very rare occurrence. Overall, CCL teachers find that with the correct application of the shaving principle it is quite rare to have to settle for a thermal shift of less than 4/10 of 1°F.

Practical Use in Fertility Awareness

The best proven test of the start of Phase III is a clear thermal shift of at least three days accompanied by the disappearance of the mucus signs that had previously indicated fertility. Sexual relations may be resumed on the evening of the third day of such sustained basal temperature elevations with confidence of being in Phase III. An additional margin of safety can be gained by waiting until the fourth day of sustained temperature rise. Such a practice can also provide psychological reassurance, but it is not necessary as a general rule for natural family planning. Thus, the following rules of thumb have been developed.

● **Sympto-thermal method.** The mucus and cervix signs can be of great help in the interpretation of the temperature pattern. These other signs of ovulation can make it evident that the rise in temperatures is due to the postovulation progesterone and not some other cause. Thus, in the sympto-thermal method the thermal shift is determined by a temperature rise that has been preceded by the appearance of the mucus sign and is accompanied by the drying up and/or disappearance of the mucus. Therefore, the general rule of thumb emphasizing the temperatures is as follows: "Beginning of Phase III = evening of the 3rd day of a thermal shift accompanied by the disappearance of the mucus and/or cervix signs of fertility for 2 to 4 days."

This description has been left vague with regard to the required number of days of drying up because that is provided in chapter 8.

● **Temperature-only.** For years many couples used basal temperatures alone to determine the beginning of Phase III, and most of them used a rule of thumb calling for a 3 day full thermal shift. However, in the absence of a crosscheck from the mucus and/or cervix signs, a 4 day thermal shift pattern should be required. In this pattern, the last 3 temperatures must all be at the full thermal shift level, but the first can be a day of partial rise. Thus in fig. 7.9, the 4 temperatures on days 14-17 would fulfill the requirements of the 4 day temperature-only interpretation to yield the evening of day 17 as the start of Phase III.

Other Signs

Some women will experience other signs that will indicate the period of greatest fertility. Dr. Konald A. Prem notes that these signs include "increased libido, abdominal bloating, ovulation pain (mittelschmerz), vulvar swelling and slight bloody staining. These usually occur simultaneously with mucorrhea just prior to the temperature rise."[8]

The woman who has these or any other particular signs should note them on her charts. If they occur regularly, they may prove to be very helpful in determining the approximate time of ovulation.

Putting It All Together

The purpose of this chapter has been to describe each of the main symptoms involved in fertility awareness with some reference to their use in the crosschecking sympto-thermal method. The real putting it all together occurs in Chapter 8.

The Debate About the Mucus Sign

Because the mucus sign can indicate the beginning of fertility, the time of greatest fertility, and the beginning of postovulation infertility, it has been suggested by some that natural family planning use this sign alone without reference to cervix and basal temperature signs that are also indicators of fertility and infertility. This mucus-only approach has been stressed by the Australian physician Dr. John Billings who prefers to call it the "ovulation method." However, since all methods of natural family planning are ways of determining the approximate time of ovulation, other people call it the "Billings approach" or the "mucus-only-method." We will use the latter term.

The Couple to Couple League recognizes the distinct contributions to the science and art of natural family planning that are made by the mucus sign during regular cycles. Furthermore, it is invaluable during the time following childbirth and during the period of premenopause, and it is of great help for most situations of severe irregularity. Nevertheless, the League is not prepared to recommend the mucus-only-method as the best or only method of natural family planning. First of all, it is the philosophy of the Couple to Couple League to instruct couples in all the methods of natural family planning and to recommend the use of a combined system. However, a couple may choose to use one sign only, and that is their own choice to make. Secondly, information from several sources indicates that the mucus-only systems have a much higher user surprise pregnancy rate. Thirdly, there are some cases in which we do not believe that a mucus-only system is particularly helpful. Some of these will become evident as we explain the system.

Rules for the Mucus-Only System

1. During menstruation and any vaginal bleeding, do not have coitus or genital contact. The reasons for this are twofold. First, the menstrual flow obscures the mucus sign. Secondly, sometimes a bloody discharge or spotting occurs at or about the time of ovulation, and since the mucus-only system does not provide the positive assurance of ovulation that is provided by the basal temperature, this method has to caution against coitus during any bloody discharge or spotting. That is, in the mucus-only-

method, a woman does not know if a bloody discharge is a light menstruation or spotting due to ovulation.

2. Immediately after menstruation, begin making the mucus observation periodically throughout the day, preferably after each urination. (This should also be done under the combined system.)

3. The dry days after menstruation are available for coitus as days of Phase I relative infertility.

4. During the time between menstruation and the appearance of mucus, do not have coitus on successive days. The reason for this is that the residue from intercourse on one evening may be still present the next day and obscure the mucus observation. Again, a woman might observe the mucus but *think* it was just the seminal discharge, thus thinking she was still quite infertile when her fertile phase may have actually begun.

5. Do not have coitus in the morning in Phase I because a dry day is known only by the sum total of the observations during the day.

6. Once the mucus appears, even the less fertile type, refrain from coitus and genital contact until the evening of the fourth dry day past the peak mucus day. Note: Dr. John Billings in 1978 stated that Phase III starts at 12:01 a.m. on the fourth dry day past the peak. However, as mentioned previously, research has indicated that ovulation has been noticed as late as peak day plus 3. Thus CCL recommends that couples using only the mucus symptom without any temperature or cervix crosschecks should delay the practical start of Phase III until at least the evening of peak day plus 4 and preferably until the evening of peak day plus 5.

7. Continue regular observations and recording of the mucus symptom throughout the cycle.

8. If the more fertile type mucus should appear again during the cycle, treat it just as the first mucus period: refrain from coitus until at least the fourth dry day past the last day of the fertile-type mucus.

9. In all of this, we repeat that the woman should remember that the mucus sign is frequently observed just by noticing the lubricative feeling of vaginal wetness. Secondly, the quality or consistency of the mucus is much more important than the quantity. (See also Chapter 8 for further comment about the detection of mucus.)

Some Questions and Answers

● *Does the mucus-only system provide positive proof that ovulation has actually occurred?*

No. Only the elevated basal temperatures provide positive proof that ovulation has occurred. Rather, the mucus indicates a time of overall fertility. It is a possible though an infrequent occurrence to observe the mucus sign without a subsequent ovulation even when a woman is having regular cycles. The cycle may be anovulatory (without ovulation), or a second phase of mucus may indicate ovulation later in the cycle. Therefore, it is important that users of the mucus-only approach continue to be aware of any development of a second patch of mucus and to regard it as pre-ovulatory and fertile. This obviously necessitates daily observations, a good idea whether following the mucus-only or the combined system. Basal temperature observers would be alerted about such an anovulatory first phase of mucus by the absence of the required thermal shift.

● *Can every woman use the mucus-only system?*

The experience of women associated with the Couple to Couple League indicates that as high as 15 to 20 percent of women have difficulty in observing the mucus. Some say they cannot find any at all.[9] This may be due to a complete absence of mucus (and possibly an infertility problem) or the presence of a relatively small amount, or it may be due to inexperience. On the other hand, some women indicate that they notice mucus continuously. Even though most of these women learn to distinguish the special qualities of the mucus that comes before ovulation, we believe that a definite cutoff day in the relatively infertile period is still helpful and sometimes necessary.

● *If a woman observes mucus continuously, can she use the mucus-only system?*

This is one of the real problems associated with the mucus-only system. Many, perhaps most, women learn to distinguish the more fertile mucus from the ordinary mucus they experience continuously. However, they will usually need to relate the mucus sign to the basal temperatures in order to become familiar with the changes in mucus consistency. Furthermore, during some cycles, even the relatively experienced woman who has a continuous mucus discharge may become confused and have difficulty determining the first appearance of the pre-ovulation mucus or the post-ovulation changes in quality.

In cases where a woman has difficulty in determining the beginning of the more fertile type mucus because of a continuous mucus discharge, the mucus-only system would call for continence not only during the menstruation period but also until the fourth day past the peak day, assuming the woman could distinguish the peak day. In such cases, the combined system using a 21-day rule for determining the end of Phase I, the basal temperatures, and perhaps also the cervix and the mucus sign is clearly superior to the mucus-only-method.

● *Does the mucus-only system actually provide more days available for intercourse than other methods of natural family planning?*

It all depends upon the comparison and the cycle length; almost all the variation comes in the pre-ovulation phases. For short and average length cycles, the sympto-thermal method with the 21-day rule (or a cutoff based on clinical experience) provides more days for intercourse since it allows coitus in the menstruation period, and this is not allowed under the mucus-only system. On the other hand, where there is a cycle variation of 28 to 40 days or more, the Phase I allowed with the 21-day rule remains constant even in the longer cycles, while the mucus-only system provides a longer Phase I. The maximum number of days in Phase I is allowed by a version of the sympto-thermal method which uses the mucus and/or cervix symptoms as positive indicators of the start of Phase II.

● *Does the peak mucus symptom always come a full day before ovulation?*

No. According to research done with twenty-two women and reported by Dr. Billings, ovulation, as determined by hormonal tests, occurred about twenty-two hours after the peak mucus symptoms *on the average.* However, in one case ovulation occurred two days before the peak symptom; but, more seriously, in others it occurred as late as three days after the peak symptom.[10] Having coitus in the morning of "Peak day + 4" could be quite close to a first ovulation with a definite possibility of pregnancy. On the other hand, the basal body temperatures do not become well elevated until after ovulation, thus providing positive assurance that ovulation has occurred. In the sympto-thermal method of fertility awareness, the basal temperatures provide a check on the mucus sign, and the mucus sign helps to interpret the temperatures.

● *Is the mucus-only method as effective as the sympto-thermal method?*

Not according to the available evidence. A comparative study in Los Angeles sponsored by HEW showed that at the level of user effectiveness, the unplanned pregnancy rate was 146% higher with the ovulation method than with the sympto-thermal method, although both showed excellent results at the level of pure method surprise pregnancies.[11]

For these and other reasons, the Couple to Couple League leadership continues to think that natural family planning normally should include basal temperature records and reference to past cycle history for the greatest effectiveness.

Each symptom of fertility has its advantages and limitations, and the limitations of the mucus symptom by itself should not be interpreted as a criticism of its true value in the sympto-thermal method. In typical cycles, its presence and subsequent drying up provide an excellent check on basal temperatures. This is particularly useful when the temperature rise is somewhat ambiguous. The third or fourth dry day past the Peak day will normally coincide with the third day of thermal shift.

Among the vast majority of women who are able to observe accurately the pre-ovulation mucus, it takes on a special significance in three cases because it provides a sign of impending ovulation: (1) the lactating mother if she ovulates before her first postpartum menstruation (see Chapter 10 on breastfeeding), (2) the woman who has serious irregularity during her childbearing years, and (3) the woman who has the irregularity frequently associated with the premenopausal period.

126

Because the available evidence indicates that when compared to the "ovulation method," the sympto-thermal method is easier to learn, easier to use and more effective in general use, the Couple to Couple League will continue to recommend an approach that combines observations of mucus, the cervix, and basal temperatures. However, we know from experience that some women who start out on a combined system decide to rely primarily on one or another sign, sometimes mucus alone or in combination with the cervix, sometimes primarily the cervix sign, and sometimes primarily or exclusively the basal temperatures. This is not at all opposed to the Couple to Couple League's teaching philosophy which is to instruct couples about all the natural signs and then let them choose the combination that they find the most helpful.

References

1. E. L. Billings, J. J. Billings, J. B. Brown, and H. G. Burger, "Symptoms and Hormonal Changes Accompanying Ovulation," *Lancet,* February 5, 1972, 283.

2. Thomas W. Hilgers et al, *The Picture Dictionary of the Ovulation Method and Other Assorted Teaching Aids* (Omaha: Creighton Univ. NPPE and R Center, 1982), 7.

3. J.F. Kippley, "The Cervix Symptom of Fertility: A Comparative Study," *The CCL News* 7:2 (November-December 1980) 2 f. Also in *International Review of Natural Family Planning,* VI:3 (Fall, 1982) 272-277.

4. W.M. Moore, "Ovulation Symptoms and Avoidance of Conception," *Lancet,* March 11, 1972, 588. Dr. Moore notes that there is no solid evidence of a second ovulation occurring several days after the first one.

5. T.W. Hilgers et al, "NFP 1. The Peak Symptom and Estimated Time of Ovulation," *OB & GYN,* 52:5 (November, 1978), 575-582. Using slightly different ways of estimating the day of ovulation, Dr. Moore found ovulation occurring from 2 days before peak day til 3 days after peak day, and Dr. Hilgers found ovualtion occurring from 3 days before peak day till 3 days after peak day, inclusively.

6. Edward F. Keefe, "Self-Observation of the Cervix to Distinguish Days of Possible Fertility," *Bulletin of the Sloane Hospital for Woman,* VIII:4 (December, 1962) 129-136. Dr. Keefe suggests that a woman who examines her cervix through three cycles should be able to recognize the changing signs.

7. See also R. Vollman, *The Menstrual Cycle* (Philadelphia: W.B. Saunders Co., 1977), figure 38, p. 78.

8. Konald A. Prem, "Temperature Method in the Practice of Rhythm," *Child and Family,* Fall, 1968, 313.

9. Dr. Josef Roetzer has reported 4.8% of 311 fertile women having no perceptible mucus secretion and another 1.9% having only the less fertile type. "The Sympto-Thermal Method: Ten Years of Change," *Linacre Quarterly* 45:4 (November, 1978), 369.

10. Billings, op. cit., 283.

11. Maclyn E. Wade and others, op. cit.

8
Putting It Together
—Rules and Interpretations

Most of us learn best by example. This chapter provides examples that illustrate different types of cycles and some of the variations in signs and symptoms of fertility that are seen on some charts. The interpretation of charts really means "the interpretation of the recorded signs of fertility."

Section A: Rules for Interpretation

In interpreting these signs or symptoms, certain rules or guidelines are followed. These are based on the following scientific facts which have already been mentioned.

1. Cervical mucus appears several days prior to ovulation. It reaches a peak of clearness, stretchiness, and wetness about a day before ovulation.

2. Changes in the cervix itself take place both before and after ovulation.

3. After ovulation, the corpus luteum secretes progesterone, which does five things of interest to natural family planning.

   a. It maintains the endometrium.

   b. It suppresses further ovulation.

   c. It causes the basal body temperature to rise.

   d. It increases the viscosity of cervical mucus (i.e., makes it less fluid).

   e. It causes the cervix to lower, close, and become firm.

4. After ovulation, a second ovulation may occur; however, it will occur only within 24 hours of the first ovulation (due to the action of the progesterone as mentioned above).

5. The ovum is capable of being fertilized for about 24 hours after ovulation. NFP rules must allow for the lifespan of the ovum from a possible second ovulation.

6. Sperm are capable of fertilizing the ovum for about three days (72 hours) after sexual relations under normal conditions of fertility, although there is both shorter and longer life under certain conditions. (For further explanation of these matters, see Chapters 5 and 7.)

The first set of rules deals with determining the limits of Phase I. Second, there is a brief reminder about Phase II. Third, there are rules for determining the start of Phase III.

I. Rules for the end of Phase 1, the time of pre-ovulation infertility

There are basically three ways to determine the end of Phase I. One is based on data gained from **clinical experience**; the second is based on **personal previous cycle** history; and the third depends upon the **absence of any mucus.**

Of these three ways, the first two are more conservative while the last one may call for less abstinence but may also be less accurate.

In all of these, the first day of menstruation is almost always counted as day 1 of the fertility cycle. However, there are two rather rare exceptions. 1. If the basal temperatures should drop from the thermal shift pattern to or below the pre-shift base level just before menstruation starts, it may reflect a sharply reduced progesterone level. In such a case, the more conservative practice is to count the first day of temperatures at or below the PSB level as day 1 of the new cycle. 2. The other exception is in connection with "irregular shedding" and is explained with Figure 8.6.

Phase I ends on the night of the cycle day indicated by the rule you use.

1. End of Phase I by Clinical Experience

This set of guidelines and rules comes from the wide experience gained about the relative infertility of the first six days of the menstrual cycle.

● **Complete continence.** Total continence in Phase I is one option and obviously has the lowest surprise pregnancy rate. Starting continence on the first day of menstruation yields a Phase I surprise pregnancy rate of zero. Treating the days of heavy flow as still in Phase III and starting continence on the first day of light flow would yield a surprise pregnancy rate close to zero.

● **Days 3 and 4 guidelines.** One member of the CCL Medical Advisory Board has reported from over 40 years of experience one pregnancy attributable to coitus on cycle day 3. CCL Central has observed only 2 recorded pregnancies resulting from coitus on cycle day 4. Although there are no scientifically controlled studies that can be quoted for an effectiveness rate, the extensive experience of the members of the CCL Medical Advisory Board suggests that coitus through cycle day 4 yields a surprise pregnancy rate no greater than that for surgical sterilization.

●**Day 5 rule.** CCL Central has observed only three pregnancies resulting from coitus on cycle day 5. Again, no scientifically controlled study can be quoted, but the experience of the CCL Medical Advisory Board indicates that cycle day 5 is an extremely infertile day. Based on this experience and the study of Dr. Roetzer, we estimate that coitus on day 5 has a surprise pregnancy rate of no more than 1/2 of 1% (1 per 200 women years) provided that 1) the woman has not had previous cycles of 22 days or less, and 2) there is still no detectable mucus on day 5.

●**Day 6 rule.** In the study reported by Dr. Josef Roetzer in 1978, couples used day 6 as the end of Phase I.[1] The overall user pregnancy rate from this study was 0.8 per 100 women years; the pregnancy rate of the first six days of the cycle was 0.2 per 100 women years based on one pregnancy in 8,532 cycles. The very rare day 6 pregnancies that have been observed have almost always been associated with a history of very short cycles — less than 26 days.

Based on the experience of Dr. Roetzer, Dr. Prem, and others, we estimate that for the general population the day 6 pregnancy rate is less than 1 per 100 women years provided there is no observable mucus. However, experience also indicates that the few women who have become pregnant from coitus during the first six days almost always have had a history of short cycles. Therefore, for the highest effectiveness, use the following rules:

If you have had short cycles of **23 to 25 days** during the last two years, use a day 5 cutoff.

If you have had very short cycles of **22 days or less** during the last two years, use a day 3 cutoff.

Cycles with 9 days (or less) of rising or elevated temperatures can be ignored for the above calculations.

Most couples can use a day 6 rule even when first learning the sympto-thermal method.

●**Beyond day 6 rule.** Fertility returns with increasing frequency starting with cycle day 7. Thus, beyond day 6 couples must have enough experience to apply the 21 day rule or the last dry day rule.

2. End of Phase I by Previous Cycle History

This rule is based upon the shortest cycle within the last 24 cycles and is called the 21 day rule of thumb. Simply subtract 21 from the shortest previous cycle to obtain the last day of Phase I.

● **The 21 day rule of thumb** is as follows:
"Shortest previous cycle minus 21 yields the last day of Phase I, provided that mucus is not present on or before that day."

Shortest Cycle	Minus 21 =	Last day of Phase I
32	-21	11
30	-21	9
28	-21	7
26	-21	5

It should be noted that the 21 day rule is **subordinate to the presence of early mucus** which provides a positive indication of the start of Phase II, the fertile time. Therefore, if the 21 day rule indicated day 8 as the end of Phase I but mucus was present on that day, the couple should regard themselves as already in Phase II on day 8.

● *What is the basis for the 21 day rule?* One basis for the 21 day rule is that ovulation may occur from 10 to 16 days before the next menstruation, and sperm under some conditions may live up to five days. The rule is conservative and uses the 16 and 5 day figures. By using these figures it also tends to make allowance for an ovulation that might occur one or two days earlier than in any previously recorded cycle. A practical basis for this guideline is that too many surprise pregnancies occurred when a 19 day guideline was used, so the rule of thumb was extended to 21 and has been working very well. The Los Angeles study found zero unplanned pregnancies with the 21 day rule. [Ref. 10, p. 29, Wade et al.]

● *How do you know the shortest previous cycle?* Here is seen the importance of accurate record keeping. A couple must have accurate cycle length records before the 21 day rule can be meaningful. The more records they have, the better. How many months' records are necessary? Dr. John Marshall has studied this extensively. On the basis of 4,593 cycles he concluded that at least six cycles should be known to make a fairly accurate prediction about future cycle lengths. In his study he found that with six months' records of cycle lengths, 82 percent of the next three cycles fell within the same range; if there were twelve months' records, 90 percent of the next three cycles fell within the already recorded range. However, on the basis of three months' records, only 64 percent of the next three cycles were within the range.[2]

Thus CCL recommends that a couple should have **at least six** or more cycles of experience before applying the 21 day rule of thumb.

The cycle experience of the recent past is more important than cycle history of years ago. Once you have several years of experience we suggest using only the last 24 to 30 cycles as a basis for the 21 day rule. Short cycles obviously caused by an unusually short luteal phase can be disregarded for purposes of this calculation. (This is illustrated in the *CCL Practical Applications Workbook,* third edition, chart 12).

The 21 day rule is not applicable when a woman has a luteal phase of more than 16 days. Thus, if a woman has more than 16 days of rising and elevated temperatures, the couple should add one day to the 21 day rule for every extra day (beyond 16) of elevated temperatures to formulate their own rule of thumb. In all cases, the wife should be very observant for the appearance of mucus.

The 21 day rule of thumb may be modified for short cycles in accord with the rules for cycle days 4, 5 and 6 given previously on pages 128-129.

Based on wide clinical experience and the Los Angeles study, we estimate that the correct application of the 21 day rule will yield a surprise pregnancy rate of not over 1% (1 per 100 woman years.)

3. End of Phase I by Last Dry Day (Absence of Mucus)

Without the presence of cervical mucus, sperm life is very short and is measured in terms of a few hours rather than days. The appearance of mucus provides a positive sign of the start of Phase II, the fertile time. Thus, before the beginning of the mucus symptom, "dry days" may be used for coitus with a high probability of natural infertility. Such a practice can extend Phase I beyond the limits of the previous rules, especially in longer cycles, thus requiring less continence than may be required by the other rules of thumb.

The effectiveness of this rule depends upon the woman's ability to detect mucus when it begins. Therefore the following practices are recommended for the highest effectiveness in detecting the start of mucus.

● **Internal observation.** The woman making the internal observation of mucus at the cervical os ("milking the cervix") may detect the start of mucus one to three days before she would notice it at the external labia. It must be noted, however, that "feelings of wetness" as a sign of fertility refer only to the sensations at the external labia; a woman will always notice ordinary wetness in the vaginal tract.

No matter how the mucus observation is made, it must be made **periodically throughout the day.** The external observation should be made after each urination. The internal observation should be made two or three times during the day during Phase I.

● **Evenings only.** A dry day is known only by the sum of the observations made during the day. However, the mucus may begin to flow during the night but still be undetected upon waking especially if relying only upon external observations. Thus there is greater probability of having an adequate mucus warning of fertility by having coitus only in the evening during Phase I.

● **Not on consecutive days.** Do not have coitus on consecutive days in Phase I. This guideline serves to reduce the possibility of confusing seminal residue and mucus. Coitus on Monday night will generally result in feelings of wetness from seminal residue on Tuesday. If the woman thinks it is only seminal residue, she should chart SR. However, it might be a combination of both SR and mucus. Thus, the couple should wait till the next day. If the next day is dry all day, then it can be presumed that the preceding day's discharge was just SR and that the couple are still in Phase I.

   If, on the other hand, all of the seminal residue drained during the night and the woman felt dry all the next day, this rule would not have to be followed.

● **When mucus starts, abstain,** if you are postponing pregnancy. Consider yourselves in Phase II as soon as mucus starts even if it is the less fertile type. The last dry day is the last possible day of Phase I.

● **Gain experience first.** Do not rely upon the "last dry day" guideline until the woman has had **at least six cycles** of experience and has developed both ability and confidence in the detection of the mucus sign.

   What is the effectiveness of the last dry day rule to signal the start of Phase II? More good research is needed. Some mucus-only-method advocates say it's at the 99% level of pure method effectiveness, but other studies lead us to think that in actual practice the unplanned pregnancy rate may be a bit higher, perhaps at the level of 3 to 7 pregnancies per 100 woman years.[3, 4, 5] All studies thus far have been based solely on external observations; there is reason to hope that this effectiveness can be improved through the internal observation that we have previously called "milking the cervix." The possibility of not detecting mucus in time is probably increased when there is a relatively short mucus patch, e.g., less than five days counting the days from its first appearance through the peak day. Thus the other rules for pre-ovulation fertility awareness have been developed.

General Questions about Phase I

• **The beginner couple** should abstain during Phase I during the first 2 or 3 cycles so that the wife can gain experience in detecting the start of her mucus discharge without any interference from seminal residue or the vaginal mucus from sexual excitement.

• *Should couples who end Phase I by the 21 day rule or the guidelines for cycle days 4, 5 and 6 also follow the personal practices necessary for the "last dry day" rule?*

Periodic observation for mucus throughout the day is necessary for any woman who is serious about practicing the sympto-thermal method. In addition, the practices of internal observation, evenings only, and not-on-consecutive days help to give greater accuracy to the detection of early mucus if it should appear before day 7 or before the end of Phase I by the 21 day rule. Thus, we recommend these Phase I practices even when you are using the 21 day rule or the clinical experience rules. They are even more necessary when using the last dry day rule.

• *What if mucus appears on days 4, 5 or 6 or before the end of Phase I as defined by the 21 day rule?*

Such days must be regarded as possibly fertile, and the couple should regard themsleves as being in Phase II, even though the appearance of mucus and fertility on days 4, 5 or 6 is a rare event.

• *Are the days of menstruation infertile?*

In a true menstruation preceded by a sustained thermal shift, the day or days of heavy flow may be regarded as an extension of Phase III of the last cycle. However, see Figure 8.4 on breakthrough bleeding to determine if a bloody discharge is a true menstruation.

Mucus observations must be started right after the days of heavy flow.

After the days of heavy flow, the standard clinical experience and 21 day rules apply during the rest of the menstrual flow. The last dry day rules cannot be applied until you experience post-menstruation dry days.

• *If a woman thinks that a vaginal discharge is simply seminal residue, should she continue to make periodic mucus observations that day?*

Very definitely yes. The mucus flow may also be starting and the regular observations should be made and recorded.

• *Right after menstruation, are days of merely tacky mucus fertile?*

Yes. Though these are days of a less fertile type mucus, a number of pregnancies have been observed from coitus on such days. **The first appearance of mucus marks a positive start of Phase II.**

• *What about days in Phase I that are neither dry nor wet?*

If there are no positive feelings of dryness at the labia but also no feelings of lubrication either, the situation is slightly ambiguous. Dr. Thomas Hilgers believes that a combination of no feelings of lubrication while wiping and no mucus on the tissue paper may be interpreted as a "dry" observation.[6] Additional confidence for the "dry" interpretation is gained by the absence of mucus at the cervical os. On the other hand, if mucus is discovered at the cervical os while the labia still feels dry or "nothing," priority is given to the internal observation, and the couple should consider themselves in Phase II.

● *During very long cycles sometimes mucus appears and disappears. Are any days in this pattern infertile?*

If we are talking about an experienced woman who always notices the definitely more fertile type mucus around the time of ovulation, the dry days between patches of the distinctly less fertile mucus have a high probability of being infertile, especially if such days yield no mucus from the internal observation at the cervical os. We suggest waiting until the evening of the second dry day after such a patch of less fertile mucus before a couple would consider themselves again in Phase I.

However, if the patch of mucus contained any of the characteristics of the more fertile type mucus, then the couple should consider themselves in Phase II fertility until the evening of the 4th or 5th drying up day. If the temperature rises while the mucus dries up, they should wait for the sympto-thermal indication of the start of Phase III. If the mucus dries up without any temperature confirmation of ovulation, then the couple may consider themselves back in a Phase I infertility on the evening of peak day plus 4 (we prefer peak plus 5) and should watch closely for the reappearance of mucus and/or cervix signs of fertility.

In all of this, we are talking about women with a history of long cycles.

II. Guidelines for the presence of Phase II, the fertile time

In this manual, the limits of Phase II, the fertile time, are described chiefly in terms of the end of Phase I and the beginning of Phase III. If, for example, the 21 day rule yielded day 7 as the end of Phase I, couples would regard Phase II as starting on day 8. The start of the mucus sign, as contrasted with the other Phase I rules, actually provides a positive sign of the start of Phase II. Thus, the appearance of mucus takes precedence over the 21 day rule and the clinical experience rules.

The rules for Phase III describe the time of postovulation infertility as beginning on the evening of the day indicated by a particular rule. Thus Phase II, the fertile time, continues until that time.

Couples seeking to achieve pregnancy need to have a way of locating not just overall outer limits of the fertile time but also the time of greatest fertility. Aids for this are provided in conjunction with Figure 8.2 later in this chapter.

III. Rules for the start of Phase III, the time of postovulation infertility

Based on the biological facts and on practical experience, several rules have been developed to be used in different situations. In the basic CCL rules for Phase III, three different temperature patterns are recognized, and all of these are described on page 115:

1. a **full** thermal shift; 2. a **strong** thermal shift; 3. an **overall** thermal shift.

Four rules have been developed to fit the different ways the mucus and temperature signs work together. Rule C is the most conservative rule. The other three rules—A, R, and B—are based on this principle or logic: **the stronger the temperature pattern, the fewer days of dryup are needed as a crosscheck.**

Rules A and **C** require a **full** thermal shift.

Rule R uses a **strong** thermal shift.

Rule B uses an **overall** thermal shift.

In the following examples, the circled temperatures are counted as the thermal shift for that particular rule, and the pre-shift six temperatures are numbered.

With every rule, Phase III begins **on the evening** of the indicated cycle day. Rule C is recommended for beginners, say for the first two or three cycles, and thus it is placed first.

Start of Phase III by Rule C

The most conservative approach requires **both** a full thermal shift for three days **and** four days of drying up. This rule of thumb is labeled Rule C for <u>c</u>autious and <u>c</u>onservative. Rule C is stated thus:

Phase III begins on the evening of
1) the 3rd day (or more) of full thermal shift,
2) crosschecked by 4 or more days of drying up, whichever comes later.

Another way of saying the same thing is as follows: according to Rule C, Phase III begins on the evening of the 4th day (or more) of drying up crosschecked by 3 or more days of full thermal shift, whichever comes later.

Note: On most of the charts in Chapter 8, we have numbered 1) the six pre-shift temperatures, and 2) the temperatures which count as a full thermal shift; and we have circled the temperatures that count for a particular Phase III rule. You will see that using the full thermal shift is excessively conservative in some cases.

When the third day of full thermal shift and the fourth day of drying up are the *same* day, we call it "perfect coinciding"; that's the ideal situation CCL classes usually start with to explain the sympto-thermal method, but real life situations have led to the development of the other rules of thumb.

The cervix symptom has been omitted because it becomes too wordy and too complicated to include it in every rule of thumb. However, it is recognized that some experienced women may find the cervix signs very usable even in the absence of usable mucus signs and thus may use the cervix signs as an adequate substitute for the mucus signs in the rules for both the beginning of Phase II and the beginning of Phase III. The woman who is making the cervix observation is given added confidence when at least three or four days of cervix closing crosscheck the drying up requirements of the four sympto-thermal rules.

Example 1 illustrates a situation of perfect coinciding including the cervix symptom: 3 days of full thermal shift crosschecked by 4 days of drying up past the peak day and 4 days of cervix closing and lowering, all coinciding to indicate the evening of day 18 as the start of Phase III.

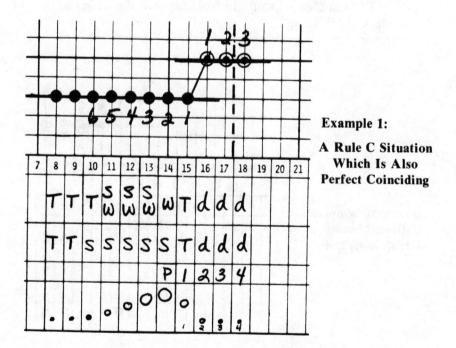

Example 1:

A Rule C Situation Which Is Also Perfect Coinciding

In examples 2 and 3, Phase III would start on day 17 by Rule C. In example 4, Phase III would start on day 21 by Rule C. Rule C is frequently far too conservative except for beginners and couples who have practically a life or death reason to avoid pregnancy.

138

Start of Phase III by Rule A

Sometimes the temperature pattern is very strong and is ahead of the mucus dry-up. Rule A has been developed for this situation and is based on the very wide and successful experience with a three day full thermal shift pattern before much attention was paid to the mucus symptom. *Because of the very strong temperature pattern, this rule can be satisfied with a minimum crosscheck of only two days of drying up.* Rule A is stated thus:

Phase III begins on the evening of
1) the 3rd day (or more) of full thermal shift,
2) simultaneously crosschecked by 2 (or 3) days of drying up past the peak day.

The full thermal shift must be maintained during the days of drying up.

Example 2: Rule A

Strongest Temperature Pattern; Minimum Dryup Required

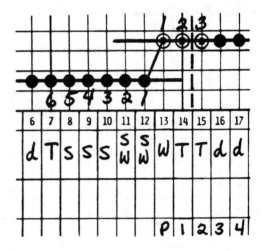

In example 2, the Rule A requirements are met by cycle day 15.

If you have to shave for a Rule A interpretation, you need a stronger combination. With only two days of drying up, you need four days of thermal shift with the last three at the full TSL; with three days of drying up, you can be satisfied with the regular three days of full thermal shift past the peak day.

Example 3: Rule A

Shaved PSB
Needs Stronger
Combination

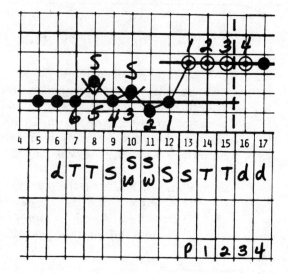

In example 3, the necessity of shaving of days 8 and 10 called for a stronger combination of either an extra day of full thermal shift or an extra day of drying up. In this case, both requirements were met by cycle day 16, but either one or the other would have been sufficient.

•**Rule B and Rule R.** These two rules are for temperature patterns that do not constitute a full thermal shift. Each is for slightly different situations.

You use **Rule R** when you have **three** days of **strong** thermal shift cross-checking **three** days of drying up.

You use **Rule B** when you have the weaker **overall** thermal shift cross-checking **four** days of drying up.

Rule R is a Fahrenheit adaptation of the centigrade rule used for years by Dr. Josef Roetzer. Rule B is basically the four day dryup rule of Dr. Billings with three days of a minimum temperature crosscheck.

••**How to use them.** If your temperature pattern doesn't meet the requirements of a full thermal shift — all three temperatures consecutively at a level 4/10 of 1° above the PSB — then use Rule R or Rule B. On peak day plus 3, you can use Rule R if the temperature pattern is strong enough. On peak day plus 4, you can apply Rule B if an overall thermal shift pattern has also developed.

If you have a temperature pattern that is very difficult to interpret, then wait till "peak day plus 4." At that point, look for some sort of temperature crosscheck, and you'll find the combination of Rule B and shaving extremely helpful.

The principle of "the stronger the temperature pattern, the shorter the mucus dryup required" would ordinarily dictate explaining Rule R before Rule B, but page layout considerations led to the present sequence.

Start of Phase III by Rule B

Frequently the temperature pattern is not as strong or clear as in the Rule A situation and the mucus drying up pattern is very clear and perhaps more helpful. In this situation, *start with the fourth day of drying up and require it to be crosschecked by an* **overall** *thermal shift of at least three days after the peak day.* Rule B is stated thus:

Phase III begins on the evening of
1) the 4th day of drying up past the peak day,
2) crosschecked by 3 (or more) days of overall thermal shift past the peak day.

Rule B has the following requirements for the overall thermal shift:
1. All the temperatures must be at least 1/10 of 1°F. above the PSB;
2. They must be in an overall elevated or rising pattern;
3. At least one of them must reach the normal TSL (thermal shift level) of 4/10 of 1°F. above the pre-shift base level (PSB);
4. Only the temperatures after the peak day are counted among the three necessary to crosscheck the mucus drying-up.

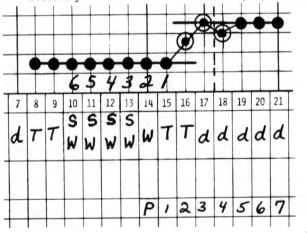

Example 4:

Rule B

In example 4, the third day of *overall* thermal shift coincides with the fourth day of drying up to indicate day 18 as the start of Phase III. In Examples 4, 5, and 6, the circled temperatures are the post-peak temperatures counted as the overall thermal shift pattern for Rule B.

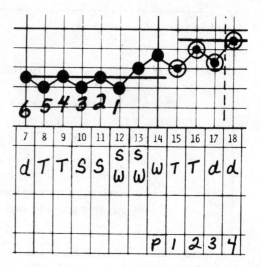

Example 5: Rule B

In Example 5, the *overall* thermal shift starts before the peak day. However, because the temperature pattern does not have the strength of the *full* thermal shift pattern, the start of Phase III is delayed until there are four days of mucus drying up. Rule B yields day 18 as the start of Phase III.

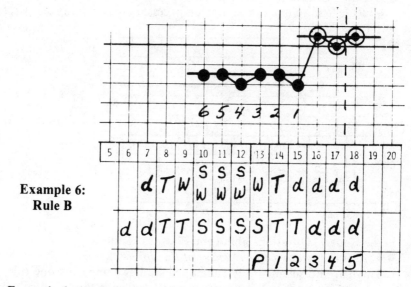

**Example 6:
Rule B**

In Example 6, the drying up starts before the overall thermal shift. This example illustrates that sometimes more than four days of drying up are required while waiting for the crosscheck of three days of thermal shift, and thus in Example 6, Rule B indicates that Phase III starts on the evening of day 18.

Start of Phase III by Rule R

This rule is used with a "three and three" pattern; peak day plus 3 crosschecked by 3 days of strong thermal shift. Rule R is stated thus:

Phase III begins on the evening of
1) the 3rd day of drying up past the peak day,
2) crosschecked by 3 or more consecutive days of strong thermal shift past the peak day.

Rule R is very similar to Rule B, but there are four differences.

1. Rule R requires only 3 days of drying up. (Rule B needs 4).

2. In Rule R all of the thermal shift temperatures must be **at least 2/10** of 1° F. (i.e. 1/10 of 1° Centigrade) above the PSB.

3. Rule R requires **the last day** of the thermal shift to be **a full 4/10** of 1° F. above the PSB. Because of items 2 and 3, we call this a **strong** thermal shift.

4. Rule R should not be used if it is necessary to shave any temperatures to set the PSB.

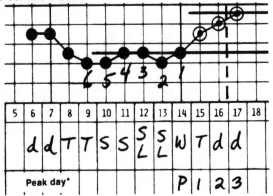

Example 7: Rule R

5	6	7	8	9	10	11	12	13	14	15	16	17	18
d	d	T	T	S	S	S/L	S/L	W	T	d	d		
Peak day*							P	1	2	3			

Some General Questions about the Phase III Rules.

● *What is the relative effectiveness of the different rules?*

There are no scientifically controlled studies comparing one rule with another. However, independent research indicates that each rule has a method effectiveness at the 99% level.

Obviously the effectiveness of all the sympto-thermal guidelines depends upon valid mucus and temperature observations. If the first day of thermal shift pattern is a disturbed temperature (late wake-up, etc.), then it should not be counted as part of the required thermal shift. If a woman is not sure about the first drying up day, she should wait until she is sure.

● *Will strict adherence to the sympto-thermal rules for Phase III guarantee a 100% level of effectiveness in not becoming pregnant?*

No. The evidence shows that a 99% level of effectiveness can be reached (1 surprise pregnancy per 100 women years). We think that the effectiveness of Phase III can be raised closer to the level of 1 per 1000 woman years by requiring a solid four day thermal shift crosschecked by four days of drying up, but the only natural method of birth regulation that can guarantee 100% non-pregnancy is total abstinence from genital contact. We might note that there are only two other 100% methods: 1) male castration (*not* vasectomy) and 2) removal of both a woman's ovaries (*not* tubal ligations).

● *What if there is obviously a temperature shift from a lower level to a higher level but it is less than 4/10 of 1°F.?*

Please review the sections on "shaving the highs" and "thermal shifts of less than the normal amount" in the temperature part of Chapter 7.

Rules for Special Situations

● **Just starting.** Beginners should add at least one day to all rules of thumb as a precaution against their own possible misinterpretation of the signs. This would also hold true in cases where only one sign was being used without a crosscheck from the other signs, a practice we don't recommend.

● **Utmost need to avoid pregnancy.** When the signs do not coincide perfectly, couples having the most serious need to avoid pregnancy are advised to follow the Rule C interpretation of waiting for both four (or more) days of mucus drying up and three (or more) days of full thermal shift. They may also want to follow the beginner's guideline of always adding an additional day as an extra precaution. Based on the Vincent[7] temperature-only study, we estimate that the Rule C interpretation should yield a surprise pregnancy rate no greater than those for sterilization, and that the policy of Rule C plus one day should be even more effective.

● **Temperature-only.** Sometimes a woman finds no indication of fertility or infertility from the mucus or cervix signs. This means that she is unable to recognize mucus, or she has a continuous discharge of tacky mucus which prevents recognition of any changes. Yet she experiences a thermal shift. For such cases, the following temperature-only guideline has been developed:

> Phase III begins in the evening of the 4th day of a rising or elevated temperature pattern in which at least the last 3 temperatures have been at the full thermal shift level.

This guideline uses either a 4 day pattern starting with a day of partial rise and concluding with a 3 day full thermal shift or a pattern where all 4 days are at the full thermal shift level. The extra day is added to the usual 3 day thermal shift to help make up for the lack of a crosscheck from the other symptoms.

● **Mucus-only.** Sometimes for various reasons a couple may decide to use only the drying up of the mucus symptom to determine the beginning of Phase III. We have some reservations about such a practice as noted at the end of Chapter 7, but we cannot ignore the results of a recent W.H.O. study indicating a pure **method** effectiveness at the 98.5% level if and when the rules were understood and followed.[8] (However, the overall **user** surprise pregnancy rates were not at all encouraging.) Couples in that and other studies started Phase III on the evening of the fourth day of drying-up past the peak day. However, because ovulation sometimes occurs as late as the third day past the peak day, we suggest that couples seeking the highest effectiveness with a mucus-only system should interpret Phase III as starting on the evening of the fifth day of drying up past the peak day. (We have added one day to the drying up requirement of Rule B to help make up for the lack of the temperature crosscheck.) We also suggest that they review the guidelines for the mucus-only system at the end of Chapter 7.

● **Just-off-the-Pill.** Women coming off the birth control Pill may have a confusing mucus pattern in the first few cycles off the Pill. In the presence of a very clear and sustained full thermal shift, it is not necessary to wait for a crosscheck from the mucus: it may never come in that cycle. Thus a temperature-only rule has been developed for assistance in cycles just off the Pill. The CCL post-pill rules are stated thus:

> 1. Abstain during Phases I and II during the first three cycles.
> 2. Phase III begins on the evening of the 5th day of an elevated or rising temperature pattern in which at least the last 3 temperatures are consecutively at the full thermal shift level.

The Phase III interpretation assumes the absence of the more fertile type of mucus during the thermal shift. It can be used despite the presence, during the shift, of tacky or sticky mucus due to hormonal residues.

The post-pill 5 day temperature-only rule has taken the 4 day temperature-only rule and added the extra day for beginners. The conservative nature of the above rules is also warranted by the desirability of not becoming pregnant in the first three months after discontinuing the Pill. The manufacturers of the Pill make such recommendations because of a slight possibility of birth defects attributable to the hormonal residues of the Pill during that time. We recommend using these rules for the first three cycles after stopping the Pill even if the mucus dry-up should become helpful during that time.

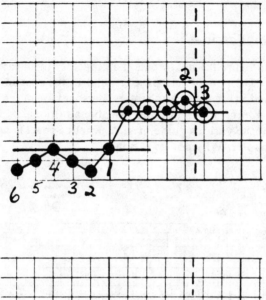

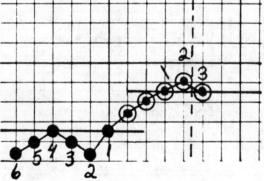

**Example 8: 5 Day Temperature-only
Patterns for Cycles Just-off-the-Pill**

In Example 8, the circled temperatures make up the post-pill thermal shift pattern. In the top graph, all five elevated temperatures are at the full thermal shift level. In the bottom graph the first two days of elevated temperatures are not yet at the full thermal shift level, but they can still be counted as the first part of the five day off-the-pill temperature-only pattern since they are followed immediately by three more temperatures at the full thermal shift level. The last three temperatures consecutively at the full thermal shift level are numbered in each example.

Section B: Practical Applications and Special Situations

Practical Applications

The chart in figure 8.1 below puts it all together in an easily interpreted average cycle. Other applications are found in the remaining sections of this chapter and in the next two chapters. Personal use of the CCL *Practical Applications Workbook* will provide valuable additional experience in the application of the various guidelines. **A practice chart is provided at the end of this chapter. Why not do it now?**

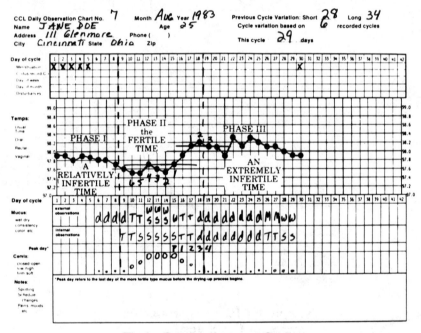

Figure 8.1 An Average Cycle

● **An average cycle.** The mucus is first noticed by the internal observation on day 9 and by external observation on day 10. The drying-up process starts on day 16, and therefore day 15 is the peak day, the last day of the more fertile type mucus.

The rising of the cervix is first detected on day 10. The combination of mucus and cervix symptoms designate days 12 through 16 as the days of maximum fertility, the best days for trying to become pregnant.

The temperature pattern has the typical lower early phase followed by the higher phase after ovulation.

Interpretation: The three different ways to determine the end of Phase I are all illustrated in this example. The clinical experience rules would end Phase I on day 6. The 21 day rule based on the personal history of a 28 day shortest cycle would yield day 7 as the end of Phase I. The last dry-day rule would yield day 8 as the end of Phase I since the mucus was first noticed on day 9.

The first three temperatures above the previous six occur on days 16, 17 and 18, and thus the pre-shift temperatures are established as days 10 through 15. The normal highs among the pre-shift six temperatures are on days 12 and 15, setting the PSB (pre-shift base level) at 97.7 and the TSL (thermal shift level) at 98.1.

The temperature on day 16 is part of an overall thermal shift, but it is not at the full thermal shift level. The first three temperatures at the full TSL occur on days 17, 18 and 19.

The third day of full thermal shift, the fourth day of mucus drying-up, and the fourth day of cervix closing all coincide to indicate the evening of cycle day 19 as the start of Phase III (Rule C, perfect coinciding in this case).

A phase division line was drawn between the temperature lines for days 8 and 9 to indicate day 8 as the last possible day of Phase I by any rule. Another phase division line was drawn between days 18 and 19 to indicate day 19 as the first day of Phase III by any of the A, B, C rules. (A couple using Rule R would have drawn the line between days 17 and 18 to indicate day 18 as the first day of Phase III by Rule R.)

If the mucus and/or cervix symptoms had been of no help, the 4 day temperature-only rule would have yielded day 19 as the start of Phase III. If this had been one of the first two or three cycles just off the pill, the 5 day temperature-only rule would have been used, and it would have yielded day 20 as the start of Phase III. Note that in both of these cases, the mini-rise temperature on day 16 was included as part of the four and five days counts which require that only the last three temperatures be at or above the full TSL.

The post-shift temperatures that dropped slightly below the TSL but which stayed above the PSB (21, 28, 29) are of no concern since they occurred well into Phase III.

The mucus starting on day 26 is likewise of no concern because it has been preceded by a well sustained thermal shift; it is recognized as the pre-menstrual mucus noticed by many women.

● **Note.** The real life charts in the rest of the book were recorded before the space for "internal mucus observation" was printed on the current chart form, and thus that space was left empty on those charts.

Special Situations

There are eight situations that call for special comment:

1. Seeking pregnancy
2. Coming off the pill
. 3. Sickness and delayed ovulation
4. Miscarriage
5. Breakthrough bleeding
6. The anovulatory cycle
7. Pre-menopause
8. The return of fertility after childbirth. This is discussed separately in Chapter 10.

● **Seeking pregnancy.** This refers to the special situation of those who have experienced difficulty in achieving pregnancy, and the guidelines about abstinence for several days prior to coitus are not intended for those who have had no difficulty in becoming pregnant.

Couples who are unable to achieve a pregnancy are said to have a fertility problem. This may be due to one or more male factors such as insufficient sperm or to female factors such as insufficient mucus, excess acidity in the vaginal tract, blocked Fallopian tubes, or failure to ovulate. Some conditions may be corrected by a physician; some cases cannot be corrected and the couple must adjust to the fact that a pregnancy is not possible.

In the general population in the recent past, approximately one out of ten couples have had some sort of fertility problem. However, the current rate of infertility has been raised by a number of factors contributing to female sterility: the IUD, the Pill, abortion, venereal disease, and early and promiscuous sexual relations. It is a current tragedy that these practices, which (except for VD) are touted as new freedoms, can deprive a girl of the freedom to bear a child when as a woman and a wife she truly wants one.

The Couple to Couple League is opposed to any form of artificial insemination, masturbation for seminal analysis or attempted "test tube" conception on the grounds that these depersonalize the sexual act which is meant to be a sacred act, an interpersonal renewal or affirmation of the couple's marriage covenant. The "test tube baby" process has the additional immorality of abortion attached to it because in this process several ova are fertilized, — that is, several new lives are conceived — one is selected for implantation, and the rest are killed.

See Appendix II for data on morally acceptable sperm tests.

Perhaps as high as 80 percent of naturally infertile couples have no apparent impediment to achieve pregnancy but do not. Some couples may be helped by new discoveries, some of which are listed in Appendix II. Others may be called to be adoptive parents, while still others may conceive unexpectedly. To some all we can say is, "Relax;" others may be helped by the following comments about the timing of intercourse to maximize the possibility of conception.

The opening of the cervical os and the presence of cervical mucus indicate the approach of maximum fertility. Couples with a fertility problem should refrain from sexual relations for about 5 days before they try to achieve pregnancy in order to build up a maximum supply of sperm. This means that they will be looking for the time of greatest fertility for their first intercourse after this wait. Indicators that ovulation may be very close at hand include the following:

1. A temperature dip toward the end of the mucus pattern sometimes indicates the day of ovulation.

2. The first drying-up day is frequently the day of ovulation.

3. The first day of temperature rise may be within a few hours of ovulation.

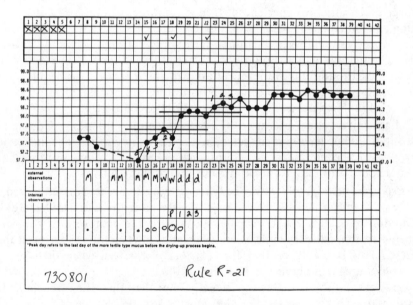

Figure 8.2 Achieving Pregnancy

In the case in fig. 8.2, the couple waited until day 15, the first day up from an apparent dip in temperatures. Day 18 was the second day of a feeling of wetness, and the cervix was more open than the day before.

It is impossible to say which instance of coitus was the one which led to this much desired pregnancy, but from the indications provided, days 18 and 19 appear to be the most fertile days in the cycle. Any time from day 8 to day 20 would have to be considered fertile by a couple of normal fertility and ease of conception.

The achievement of pregnancy is indicated by the temperature pattern remaining elevated for 21 days. To put it another way, when the temperature pattern remains elevated for seven days more than a woman's usual long luteal phase, she has a 99% certainty she has conceived and is carrying a baby.

The pregnancy in fig. 8.2 was achieved about six months after attendance at CCL classes, indicating that even with proper understanding about maximum fertility and optimum timing, it still may take some time for everything to work together to provide the desired pregnancy.

If pregnancy is not achieved in the first month or two by timing coitus according to the ongoing signs of fertility, then a more systematic approach should be used. The couple desiring a pregnancy should carefully chart the signs and symptoms of ovulation and the daily basal body temperature for three cycles. The range of appearance and disappearance of mucus and the thermal shift rise should be observed. Days for coitus in the fourth cycle must be plotted in advance based on the days of maximum fertility of the three cycles already experienced. If in those three cycles the day of ovulation (estimated as the first drying-up day) appeared to be days 13, 17 and 18 respectively, coitus in the fourth cycle should occur on days 14, 16, and 18. The first coital act should occur after at least 5 days of abstinence to maximize the amount of sperm. The day of abstinence between coital acts allows sperm numbers to return to optimum level for fertilization since daily coitus may deplete sperm and contribute to infertility.

The above system was used by fourteen couples attending Couple to Couple League meetings to seek assistance in achieving a pregnancy, and twelve of the couple achieved pregnancy within a few months. See Appendix II for data on making your mucus more fertile.

● *Estimated date of childbirth.* The typical physician has traditionally used a rule of thumb called Naegele's Rule to determine the Estimated Date of Childbirth (EDC). That formula starts with the first day of the last menstruation, adds seven days, and then adds nine months to arrive at the EDC. This is a 19th century formula that works well when the woman becomes pregnant about the 14th day of the cycle.

However, if she ovulates significantly later than that, the Naegele Rule proves to be highly inaccurate. Thus Doctor Konald A. Prem, Professor of Obstetrics and Gynecology at the University of Minnesota Medical School, has developed a modified formula.

"EDC = First day of overall thermal shift minus 7 days plus 9 months."

Because of normal variations in the time of gestation, no formula can be exact. We estimate that the above formula will have the following sort of accuracy.

Actual Date of Delivery	Probability
Within one week before or after EDC:	65%
Within 2 weeks before or after EDC:	90%
Within 3 weeks before or after EDC:	95%
Within 4 weeks before or after EDC:	99%

More accurate than Naegele's Rule, it is still an estimate.

Despite these normal variations the thermal shift provides the single most accurate way of dating the time of conception, gestational age, and thus the estimated time of delivery. It is more accurate than much more elaborate and expensive procedures such as "estimation of uterine size by palpation or measurement, the dates of quickening and engagement of the fetal head and auscultation of the fetal heart tones with the head stethescope..." or "biochemical and biophysical methods such as estriol, ultrasound, and phospholipids ..."[9]

In figure 8.2, the two formulas provide EDCs within 5 days of each other because conception occurred only slightly after day 14. However, we have seen one case where a woman coming off the Pill managed to achieve a much desired pregnancy approximately on cycle day 115 as measured by the thermal shift. In such a case, the Naegele rule would have been erroneous by over three months.

The advantage of Dr. Prem's rule of thumb is illustrated by the following example. A midwest woman using CCL charting took her sympto-thermal pregnancy chart to her physician who refused to give it any credit. Instead, he turned to sonargrams at about seven months. These indicated a headsize about typical for delivery. He wanted to induce labor immediately. However, the woman had delivered other babies with head sizes larger than average, and she still trusted her temperature graph. We were able to send the woman a copy of an article by Dr. Prem.[10] Faced with this and the definite possibility of inducing labor two months prematurely, the physician decided to wait on a week by week basis. The baby came naturally within three days of the temperature based EDC with no signs of being post-mature, a good six weeks after the time originally planned for induced labor.

●**Coming off the pill.** The birth control pills used in the 1960's were generally of a stronger dosage than those used in the 1970's, some of which are called low-dosage pills or the Minipill. By way of review, it should be recalled that the typical birth control pills achieve their effectiveness by a triple mechanism: suppression of ovulation, changes in the cervical mucus to render it hostile to sperm migration, and changes in the endometrium (the lining of the uterus) to make it hostile to the implantation of a newly conceived human being at the blastocyst stage of development.

The high-dosage pills were thought to achieve their effectiveness primarily through suppression of ovulation although it has been reported that ovulation still occurs from two to ten percent of the time in women taking the Pill.[11] Opinion seems to be divided about the lower-dosage Pill, and of course, there are significant differences in the types of Pill, dosage, etc. However, there seems to be a consensus that the lower-dosage pills, especially the progestin-only pills, are less likely to suppress ovulation and thus more likely to rely on one or both of the other mechanisms to prevent pregnancy or its continuation.

Whenever a drug (or a device such as the IUD) prevents the continuation of the newly conceived life by preventing implantation in the uterus, it has not acted as a contraceptive but as an abortifacient. The persons responsible for its use are thus responsible for the killing of a newly conceived human being. Perhaps the realization of this accounts for the many women who want to "get off the Pill" and begin planning their families the natural way.

A woman coming off the Pill may experience some irregularities that she will normally not experience once her body is on a natural cycle again. Sometimes temperatures will be very erratic for one or more cycles. Sometimes the mucus secretion will be quite heavy almost all the time for a few cycles; it may be that her body has stored up excess estrogen from the Pill and that it is taking several months to return to normal. Sometimes the first cycle is fertile; sometimes it isn't. Sometimes the return of fertility is delayed for months or even years. Sometimes a woman will have several more or less "regular" cycles followed by one that is either very short or very long. In short, because of the variety of the drugs used and the variety of effects they have upon different women, it is very difficult to make many generalizations about "typical" experiences of coming off the Pill.

Nevertheless, three charts are included. In the cycles immediately off the Pill, we emphasize the temperature more than the mucus because the mucus might still be affected by residues from the Pill. (See "Just-off-the-Pill" rule in Section A of this chapter.)

The two cycles charted in fig. 8.3a and 8.3b came from the same woman during her first two cycles off the Pill. In the first cycle the mucus pattern is of no help. However, the series of low temperatures from day 22 to day 29 establishes a pre-shift base of 97.2°. The temperature pattern on days 30-32 is ambiguous, but a clear thermal shift is established by the recordings for days 33-35. Thus the 5 day post-pill temperature-only rule yields day 35 as the start of Phase III.

The second cycle shows how both mucus and temperature signs are more normal a month later. The mucus is apparently less abundant and even disappears some days after ovulation. However, it is still of little help in determining the beginning of post-ovulation infertility in this cycle. The pre-shift base is easily set at 97.5°, thus setting the thermal shift level at 97.9°. The five day post-pill temperature-only rule establishes day 25 as the beginning of Phase III.

Figure 8.3 Coming Off the Pill

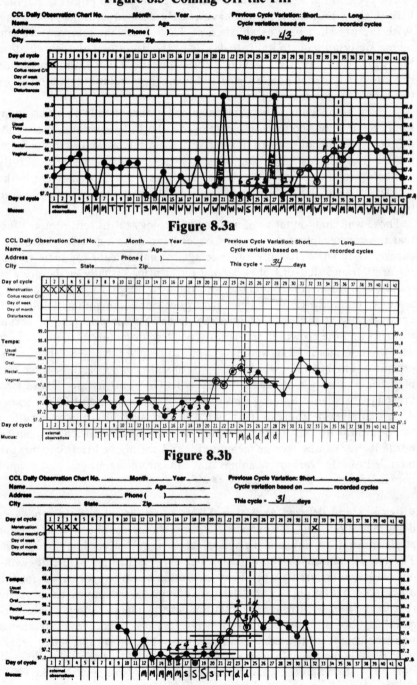

Figure 8.3a

Figure 8.3b

Figure 8.3c

The cycle in fig. 8.3c was likewise a first cycle off the Pill. It is included here to show that some women have clearly defined patterns right away. With the pre-shift base established at 97.1°, both the temperature and mucus signs coincide to indicate day 24 as the beginning of postovulation infertility. However, CCL would still recommend a day 25 interpretation according to the 5 day post-pill rule, following the standard suggestion to use this rule for the first three post-pill cycles.

It is not an uncommon experience among natural family planning counselors to find that couples just coming off the Pill sometimes experience difficulties in the adjustment of their sexual activity as well as in the interpretation of what is happening physiologically. Because sex is so greatly psychological and because our sexual attitudes are so all-important in the regulation of sexual activity, perhaps it might be helpful at this point to review some thoughts that can influence our attitudes.

Those who think in terms of nature and ecology might reflect on the fact that the contraceptive drugs and devices have done a certain violence to nature. They know that any violence against nature calls for some sort of restoration and that this always comes at a price, usually at the price of some form of self-control. Those who think in the psychological terms of maturity certainly know that maturity does not come automatically with age but only at the price of growing pains. This is also true of sexual maturity and the growth in self-control needed for mature sexuality. Those who think in moral terms and have come to regard the practice of contraception as unethical know that their past mistakes or sins call for some sort of penance or work of reconciliation with God and nature. Those who think in Christian religious terms can see in the suffering of Christ something that gives meaning to their own difficulties or sufferings in the effort to be faithful to him. In the last analysis, almost any difficulties can be borne if they can be seen as meaningful, and the above brief thoughts are intended to offer various meanings that can enrich the process and pain of human growth.

●**Sickness and delayed ovulation.** Stress situations of various types can delay ovulation. This stress can be either psychological or physical. It is not at all unusual for sickness, a physical stress situation, to delay ovulation. The mucus and cervix symptoms may give every indication of fertility without ovulation occurring when a pre-ovulation stress temporarily stops the process of ovulation. As the cervix and mucus symptoms temporarily recede, the non-occurrence of ovulation is known by the absence of a thermal shift. Soon after the sickness (or whatever) has ended, the cervix/mucus signs indicate fertility again, frequently for only a short time. After ovulation, there is the typical sympto-thermal crosscheck indicating the start of Phase III. (See fig. 7.3. Charts illustrating this also appear in the CCL *Practical Applications Workbook.*)

● **The return of fertility after miscarriage.** The time after a miscarriage is almost always fertile. Temperature records should be begun immediately after the miscarriage. In some cases, the temperature will remain high for some time (as it was during pregnancy) before it drops to the usual pre-ovulation levels. Couples who desire to postpone another pregnancy should refrain from coitus until postovulation infertility has been definitely indicated by the sympto-thermal signs of mucus and basal temperatures.

Couples who desire another pregnancy immediately may attempt to achieve it during the first post-miscarriage cycle.

● **Breakthrough bleeding.** In long cycles, bleeding may occur that begins like menstruation but really isn't. The endometrium builds up to such a degree that the very top layers cannot be sustained and are sloughed off. However, ovulation can occur at any time. The bleeding may be spotting or appear to be a regular period. If sexual relations occur during this period of bleeding, pregnancy can occur because the apparent menstruation is only breakthrough bleeding and ovulation may occur during it or immediately afterward. It is emphasized that this is an infrequent occurrence during the years of normal fertility.

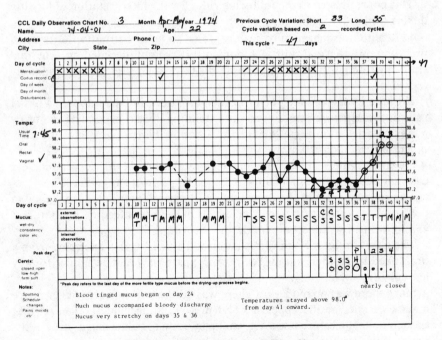

Figure 8.4 Breakthrough Bleeding

The chart in fig. 8.4 is a classic example of breakthrough bleeding occurring near the time of ovulation. The couple, who were in their third cycle of sympto-thermal observations, noticed that there were no indications of being in Phase III when they usually were in their previous cycles, about day 19. On day 24 the woman noticed the appearance of blood-tinged mucus and experienced over a week of mucus and bloody discharge, at the end of which she had clear and stretchy mucus before it began to dry up on day 37.

The pre-shift base is established at 97.4° by the six temperatures on days 31 to 36. Rule R indicates day 39 as the earliest start of Phase III; Rule C yields day 40. The cycle continued through day 47. The coitus on day 38 was too soon by any of the rules, but the couple was planning a pregnancy in a few months and decided to cut down gradually the days of continence.

It is important to realize that in this cycle there are two indications that the bleeding was not menstruation which could be considered infertile. First of all, there was no thermal shift preceding it. It must be emphasized that a bloody discharge cannot be assumed to be menstruation unless it is preceded by a thermal shift, customarily about two weeks previously but sometimes shorter or longer. Secondly, the presence of mucus indicated possible fertility. (This is also illustrated in the CCL *Practical Applications Workbook.*)

This chart illustrates the following rules for the interpretation of fertility during a bloody discharge.

1. A blood discharge may be considered to be menstruation **only** when preceded by a thermal shift. A bloody discharge **not** preceded by a thermal shift **must** be considered as possible breakthrough bleeding and possibly fertile.

2. Phase I starts on day 1 of a true menstruation, and the standard Phase I rules apply. However, we suggest not extending Phase I beyond day 6 during a long menstruation because of the greater possibility of not detecting early mucus during menstruation.

● **The anovulatory cycle** is one in which ovulation did not occur. Such cycles may occur occasionally during the fertile years of any woman. They occur more frequently in the premenopausal period, with some frequency in the first few postpartum menstrual cycles of the breastfeeding mother, and among women with certain endocrine disorders.

The chart in fig. 8.5 shows the pattern. This particular one came from a breastfeeding mother, but the temperature pattern would be similar for any anovulatory cycle.

Since there was no ovulation, there was no thermal shift. However, there may sometimes be the appearance of pre-ovulation mucus. The fact that there is no temperature rise after what may seem to be the mucus usually associated with ovulation indicates that ovulation did not occur.

What about coitus during an anovulatory cycle? Rather obviously, coitus could be engaged in on any day in the cycle without the possibility of conception when there is no ovulation, but such knowledge is of little help

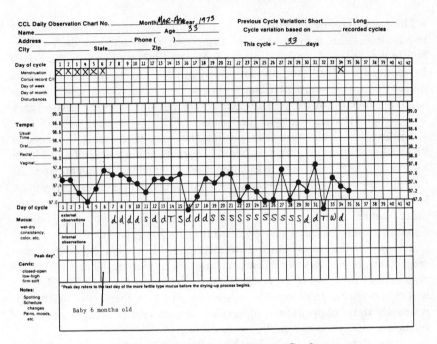

Figure 8.5 An Anovulatory Cycle

because a cycle cannot be determined anovulatory until the next menstrual period. Those who wish to postpone coitus until after the basal temperatures have clearly indicated ovulation and the beginning of postovulation infertility will have no such indication and therefore will not have coitus during that cycle.

The anovulatory cycle points to the definite advantage of observing the pre-ovulation signs of mucus and cervix. According to the standard "absence of mucus" rules, day 10 in fig. 8.5 was the last dry day and thus the end of Phase I. If there had been patches of mucus on and off, the couple might have decided to consider themselves in Phase I after a certain number of dry days after each patch of mucus. (Please review the question, "During very long cycles sometimes mucus appears and disappears. Are any days in this pattern infertile?" This is found in a preceding section of this chapter called *General Questions About Phase I.*)

Most anovulatory cycles would have many more dry days; this chart shows that the return of fertility after childbirth is probably near at hand.

Coitus should be avoided during any vaginal bloody discharge not preceded by a thermal shift because it cannot be determined with certainty whether such discharge is an anovulatory menstruation or the usually lighter breakthrough bleeding discussed previously (fig. 8.4).

● **The premenopausal period.** Menopause refers to the cessation of fertility and is almost always marked by the absence of menstrual periods. The time before menopause is called premenopause, and this is a time characterized by reduced fertility[12] and sometimes by hot flushes, sweatings and other discomforts. It is frequently characterized by cycle irregularity even if the woman has had a history of regular cycles during the more fertile years. This irregularity may be of three types.

1. Length of Cycle. Menstrual periods that may have occurred at regular 28 to 33 day intervals may now begin occurring at both shorter and longer intervals. The irregularity associated with premenopause begins approximately 20 cycles before menopause.[13] However, while variation in cycle length may be greater during this time for many women, there are many other women who go through premenopause having perfectly normal ovulatory cycles without any significant cycle irregularity.

2. Non-fertile Cycles. During premenopause a woman may experience menstruation that has not been preceded by ovulation. These are called anovulatory or non-fertile cycles. Because no ovulation has occurred, there will be no temperature signs of ovulation although there may be the appearance and disappearance of cervical mucus (see preceding pages for further comment on the anovulatory cycle).

In anovulatory cycles there will be no Phase III, just an extended Phase I and/or an "indicated" Phase II, depending upon the mucus and/or cervix symptoms of fertility or infertility.

3. Irregular Shedding. During the premenopausal years there is an increased possibility that a woman will experience the onset of menstruation while the temperature is still elevated (fig. 8.6). The temperature may remain elevated for several days after menstruation begins and drop to pre-ovulatory levels only near or at the end of the menstrual flow. This may cause some problems in using the 21 day rule. When this situation occurs, the first day of the new cycle is the first day of temperature drop rather than the first day of menstruation. Irregular shedding always develops into a menstrual period; it does not leave only to have a menstrual flow appear sometime later.

● *What to do.* In anovulatory cycles, there is no Phase III; in ovulatory cycles during premenopause, Phase III will be about the same length as usual or may be shorter, and the time of real fertility will be about the same or shorter than usual. Most of any significant change in cycle length occurs in Phase I, and thus premenopausal counseling centers around guidelines for Phase I. The following suggestions are offered for couples during premenopause.

1) Review the preceding section on breakthrough bleeding, and do not have coitus during any time of a bloody discharge not immediately preceded by a thermal shift pattern.

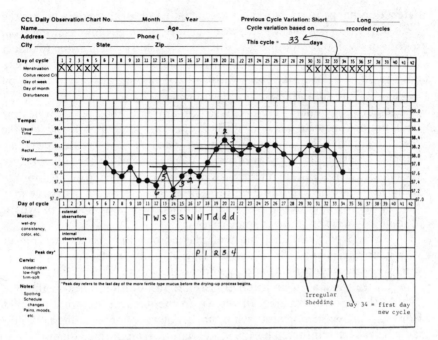

Figure 8.6 Irregular Shedding

2) Do not have coitus beyond days 3 or 4 during a true menstruation, even if allowed by the 21 day rule. The basis for this recommendation is that there is a greater possibility of an unusually short cycle with very early ovulation during premenopause.

3) After menstruation, follow the standard Phase I guidelines of evenings only, not-on-consecutive days, and the internal observation. The cervix observation may be of particular help during premenopause.

4) As soon as any mucus appears, consider yourselves in Phase II.

5) If you experience a patch of mucus (of any type) and/or cervical opening days which are not followed by any sort of rising temperatures, do not consider yourselves back into Phase I infertility until the evening of the fourth or fifth dry day after the disappearance of the mucus patch.

6) If you develop a pattern of continuous less fertile type mucus, we suggest waiting it out during the first one or two cycles to make sure you can detect the change to the more fertile mucus sufficiently before ovulation. If your own experience shows that you are able to detect the onset of the more fertile type mucus or the opening or elevation of the cervix at least five days before the peak mucus day, then you run only an extremely small chance of a surprise pregnancy from coitus during the time of the definitely less fertile mucus providing that there is no coitus after the first show of a more fertile type of mucus or the opening or raising of the cervix. If you can

detect the change to the more fertile type only four or three days before the peak day, there is a slightly increased chance of pregnancy resulting from sperm survival, but we think it is still a small risk. If you are able to detect the change to the more fertile type only two days or one day before the peak day, we believe there may be a significant risk of pregnancy from coitus on the days of the continuous less fertile mucus.

The above comments are not based on any published research dealing with premenopausal women. Rather, they are estimates based on the research showing that ovulation *frequently* occurs on the day after peak day but may occasionally — and very rarely — occur as early as three days before the peak day. In addition, on the basis of charts from women in their normal fertile years, we believe that even the less fertile type mucus discharge may modify the vaginal tract environment sufficiently to allow sperm to live for 72 hours — or even more in some cases.

7) If you experience long and unexplained bleeding, be sure to consult with your physician, and be sure to bring in your sympto-thermal charts.

8) We also suggest that the premenopausal woman be especially careful to eat a well balanced and nutritious diet. In addition, back in the late 1940's, there were a number of reports in the medical literature of relief from various premenopausal symptoms through Vitamin E therapy, and these have been reinforced by anecdotal reports from women themselves.[14] Such therapy has been largely supplanted by estrogen therapy in more recent years, but this is now questioned because of the possible cancer inducing effects of estrogen therapy. And, while many physicians may not recognize the claims of Vitamin E therapy (and we make no universal claims), they acknowledge that at least it is safe.

9) Be sure to keep taking the temperatures on a daily basis during premenopause. In long cycles, the continuation of low temperatures provides an assurance of non-ovulation and non-pregnancy.

10) Become well experienced in the cervix observation and the internal mucus observation well before entering premenopause as these observations may provide you with the most accurate information about your state of infertility or fertility.

● *Pregnancy during premenopause.* From our experience we think it is safe to say that there is an almost universal fear of pregnancy during the premenopausal years. Some of it is based on the fear of being parents again at an age where the couple are already (or could be) grandparents. We share this fear especially since in our case the husband is several years older than the wife. Without knowing the future, we are still committed to using only the natural methods of birth regulation during premenopause and to accepting increased abstinence, if necessary, during those couple of years.

Another huge fear is that of an increased risk of birth defects, especially Down's Syndrome (mongolism). The pessimists say that the risk doubles when the wife is over 35. However, the optimists point out that the risk increases from less than 1% to slightly over 1% and that there is still better than a 98% chance of having a normal baby. In addition, there is some new doubt that the over-35 woman is in the higher risk category for bearing a child with chromosome abnormality. A Danish study considered a woman to be a high risk for birth defects if she was over 35 and if either parent had an abnormality. However, the actual incidence of birth defects was found to be 1.2% in the high risk group, compared with 1.4% in the normal group,[15] The famed geneticist Jerome Lejeune has also questioned the current "risk categories," noting that the oft repeated statement that "older women have a greater chance of bearing a mongoloid child" may not be correct.[16]

Perhaps the best way to allay fears is to listen to Dr. Herbert Ratner who is a good philosopher as well as a physician. We have heard him tell several audiences that he has seen the Down's Syndrome child draw whole families together and that he has seen many cases of a couple being rejuvenated by a premenopausal child.

We don't claim to be able to fathom the ways of Divine Providence, but we believe with St. John that "perfect love casts out fear" (1 John 4:18). Unfortunately, it is probably also true that perfect fear casts out love.

●**Menopause.** When and how does a couple know that the woman has passed menopause and will never ovulate again? The key ingredient is the lack of menstruation for an extended period of time. Dr. Lyn Billings says that she has seen a woman go for more than a year without a period, then have reappearance of a typical fertile mucus pattern followed by menstruation.[17] However, since temperature records were not kept it is not known whether ovulation occurred.

In *The Menstrual Cycle,* Dr. Vollman has graphed the length of the last menstrual cycle before menopause for a group of 32 women[18] (see fig. 8.7). Of these, 24 had a last cycle of 100 days or less, four had last cycles of 100 to 199 days, three had cycles of 200 to 250 days, one just over 300 days and one of 355 days. Thus in this sample, once past six months of amenorrhea (the absence of menstrual periods), there was a 22% chance (7 out of 32) of having another menstrual period. Beyond eight months of amenorrhea, there was a 9% chance (3 out of 32) of having another menstruation; beyond ten months (304 days) there was only a 3% chance (1 out of 32) of having another menstruation. Vollman shows no last cycles of over one year in length.

It must be remembered that this is a time of greatly decreased fertility so the chances of becoming pregnant are much less than the chances of having another menstruation. The general advice traditionally given has been that after six months of amenorrhea a woman has only a very small chance of becoming pregnant, with decreased chances the longer the time of amenorrhea. We would suggest continuing to chart for another year after six months of amenorrhea, and to abstain during any patch of mucus and for 5 days of dryness afterwards. After menopause, the temperature pattern will continue to show variations, sometimes with groups of several days of highs and lows.[19]

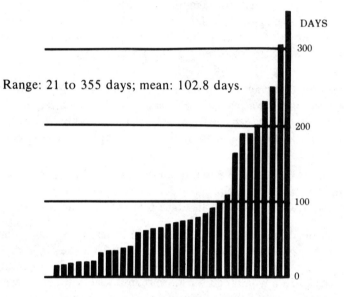

Range: 21 to 355 days; mean: 102.8 days.

Figure 8.7 Distribution of the Length of the Last Menstrual Cycle before Menopause in 32 Women.

From Rudolph F. Vollman, M.D., *The Menstrual Cycle,* 1977 by permission of the author and the publisher, W.B. Saunders, Philadelphia, PA 19105.

Section C: Cycle Variations

In this section are explained a half dozen different temperature patterns and two unusually long cycles. Another twenty charts illustrating a much greater variety of cycles are found in the CCL *Practical Applications Workbook.*

Disturbed Temperatures

Some irregular temperatures are easily explained as due to disturbances and four of these types are illustrated in fig. 8.8.

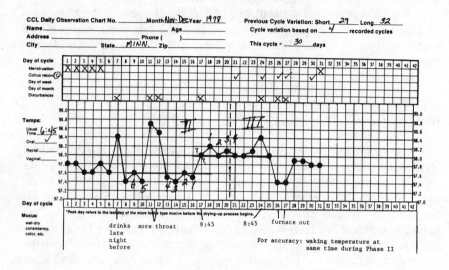

Figure 8.8 Disturbed Temperatures

The most common type of disturbed temperature is due to **late temperature taking.** As mentioned previously, the basal temperature tends to be rising about 1/10 of 1°F. per half hour during the normal waking hours, and thus the temperatures should be taken at the same waking time each day in Phase II. Note the temperature on day 17 in figure 8.8. It appears to be the first day of full thermal shift, but can it be counted? No. It was taken two hours later than usual. It cannot be counted as part of the thermal shift because there is no way of knowing if it is a "false rise" due to late taking or a rise due to progesterone. Thus the temperature on day 17 is ignored and the thermal shift count does not start until day 18. On cycle day 24 the same thing happens again, but at this point in the cycle it makes no difference. The lesson is obvious: during Phase II the temperatures should be taken at the same waking time.

Sickness can cause elevated temperatures as indicated on cycle days 11 and 12. If such temperatures occur among the initial thermal shift temperatures, they cannot be counted. If they occur among the pre-shift six, they are ignored and additional valid earlier temperatures are used for the pre-shift six.

Alcohol still in the bloodstream from drinks the night before can cause a "false rise" for some women. In Phase I and III, no problem. In Phase II, it could complicate interpretations; in addition many people find it prudent to curtail the use of alcohol during Phase II since even moderate drinking frequently makes self-control more difficult.

A big change in environment can also cause changes in the body temperatures. The low temperatures on days 26 and 27 show the effects of two nights without heat in Minnesota during early December. An electric blanket can have an opposite effect and thus should be used at a constant temperature.

Non-disturbed Irregular Temperature Patterns

The greatest aids to the interpretation of temperatures are the natural fertility signs of mucus and cervix, and for most couples the following data on various temperature interpretations may thus be unnecessary. However, in cases where the woman is having difficulty in learning to observe or interpret the mucus and/or cervix signs, this information may be helpful. Each of the cases below is from a real-life chart. We have first interpreted each according to the sympto-thermal rules. Then we have pretended that there were no usable mucus or cervix symptoms and have provided two temperature-only interpretations. One is the standard CCL 4 day temperature-only rule described in Section A. The second temperature-only rule is adapted from that of England's Dr. John Marshall.[20] It is a 5 day rule of thumb as follows: "Phase III starts on the evening of the 5th day of an overall thermal shift where all of the temperatures are a) consecutively above the PSB by at least 1/10 of 1°F., b) in an overall rising or elevated pattern and c) at least one has reached the normal full thermal shift 4/10 of 1°F. above the PSB." Note, however, that Marshall cautions that in some cases of the most serious need to avoid pregnancy, couples should require 3 days of temperatures consecutively at the full thermal shift level as in the standard CCL 4 day temperature-only rule.

Nevertheless, these rules are offered because they are sufficiently conservative to be used in cases of less serious need to avoid pregnancy and may be quite helpful to some couples when the woman is not finding help from the mucus or cervix symptoms.

● **The Slow Rise.** In some cycles (14 percent according to Marshall) a slow rise in temperature occurs that usually reaches the anticipated thermal shift of 4/10 of a degree over several days (see fig. 8.9).

The PSB is easily set at 97.2, and sympto-thermal Rule B yields day 26 as the start of Phase III. The Marshall 5 day temperature-only slow rise rule starts with the first temperature above the PSB, counts 5, and yields day 27 as the start of Phase III. The CCL 4 day temperature-only rule requiring the

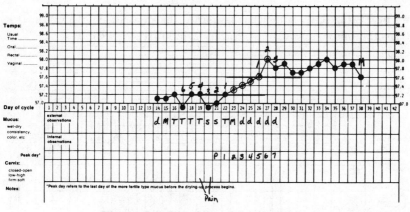

Figure 8.9 The Slow Rise Pattern

last three temperatures at the full thermal shift level yields day 28 as the start of Phase III, which is also a Rule C interpretation.

● **The Step Rise.** A small percentage of charts (3 percent according to Marshall) show a steplike upward progression (see fig. 8.10).

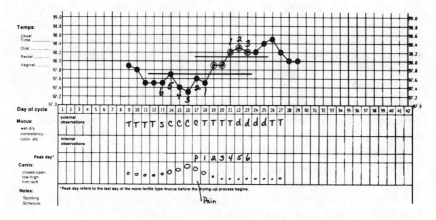

Figure 8.10 The Step Rise Pattern

The PSB is set at 97.7 and the thermal shift level at 98.1. The symptothermal Rule B yields day 21 as the start of Phase III. Assuming no help from either the mucus or the cervix, the Marshall 5 day step rise rule would yield day 23 as the start of Phase III. In this case the last three are all above the full thermal shift level, but if the temperatures on days 21 and 22 had been only at the 98.0 or 97.9 levels, the 5 day step rise rule would still have been fulfilled by day 23.

● The Zigzag Rise. Somewhat similar to the step-rise charts are those patterns that move upward in a zigzag fashion (see fig. 8.11).

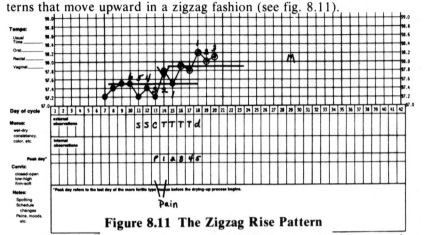

Figure 8.11 The Zigzag Rise Pattern

The PSB is set at 97.5 and the thermal shift level at 97.9. Sympto-thermal Rule B yields day 18 as the start of Phase III.

Assuming no help from the mucus, the 5 day zigzag rule would yield day 20 as the start of Phase III.

In all CCL Phase III rules, all of the thermal shift temperatures must be *consecutively* above the PSB. In fig. 8.11 the rising pattern appeared to start on day 14 but fell back to the PSB on day 15. Thus the Rule B and the 5 day counts had to be restarted on day 16. Note also that the pre-shift six are days 10 through 15 because those are the six temperatures *immediately* before the *sustained* thermal shift. Day 14 was shaved to the next highest level.

●Pre-shift spikes. Some women experience a sharp, unexplained rise in temperature for one or two days, usually right before or including the peak day, and then the sharp rise is followed by a drop back to the previous level. We call these "pre-shift spikes."

The most consistent way to handle these is by applying three principles of chart interpretation that have already been described.

1) If an apparent shift is interrupted by a drop back to the pre-shift base level, the thermal shift count must be restarted;

2) The pre-shift six temperatures are the six temperatures immediately before the start of the *sustained* thermal shift;

3) One or two unexplained normal (undisturbed) temperatures among the pre-shift six may be shaved to the next highest level.

The charts in figures 8.12a and 8.12b are of consecutive cycles from the same woman. In chart 8.12a, by peak day plus 4 the temperature pattern from day 22 onward makes it quite easy to recognize a thermal shift cross-checking the drying up process, and thus it is easy to shave the temperature on day 19 to the next highest level, 97.6.

The chart in figure 8.12b is more difficult to interpret at first glance, but the application of the above principles puts things in order.

1. An apparent shift on days 13 and 14 is interrupted by the fall on day 15 to the level of the six temps before the spike started. Thus the sustained thermal shift does not start until day 16.

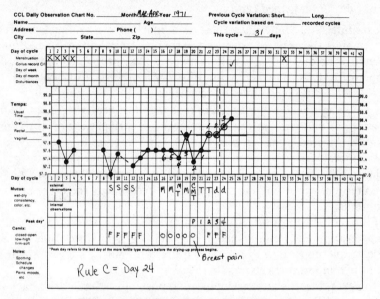

Figure 8.12a Pre-shift Spike of One Day

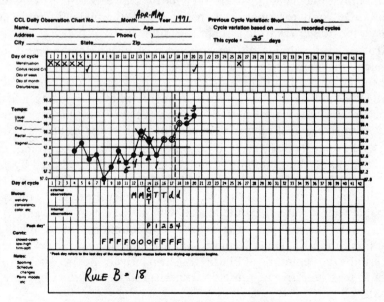

Figure 8.12b Pre-shift Spike of Two Days

2. The pre-shift six temperatures immediately before the start of the sustained rise are days 10 through 15.

3. Days 13 and 14 are shaved. The "next highest level" is 97.7, but the arithmetic average of days 10-15 is 97.75, so the PSB is set at 97.8. The Rule B interpretation yields day 18 as the start of Phase III and is also confirmed by four days of a firmed cervix.

●**Post-shift dip.** Sometimes there is a marked dip in the temperature pattern after the apparent start of the thermal shift. If the dip does not go down to or below the PSB, it offers no particular problem. However, if the temperature falls to or below the PSB *before* the start of Phase III, then the thermal shift count must be restarted.

If a woman is well experienced in mucus and/or cervix signs, and if these indicate postovulation infertility, and if the overall pattern prior to the dip was well elevated or rising, some couples may require for themselves only two temperatures — or even one — beyond the dip to confirm the pre-dip rising trend; but the general rule should be to require three rising or elevated temperatures beyond such a dip to crosscheck the other signs and symptoms.

If the temperatures fall to or below the PSB *after* the start of Phase III has been apparently established, it is most likely a postovulation dip. A dip to or below the PSB in Phase III is quite rare, but we suggest abstinence until the temperatures rise again.

However, there is an extremely small possibility that a drop back to or below the PSB level may indicate that the couple is still in Phase II. We can recall only three incidents of this in over twelve years of reviewing many charts. Our only explanation is that the first "thermal shift" must have been a few false rises from a slight infection, etc.

If it's a postovulation dip after the start of Phase III, the temperature bounces right back, almost always on the next day which is then considered to be in Phase III. But if the temperatures drop and remain at or below the PSB for several days, we simply cannot be sure what's happening, and thus we suggest that this time be considered as Phase II until a later thermal shift, and that's what happened in each of the three cases of this.

These examples illustrate that couples experienced in the sympto-thermal method of natural family planning need not be discouraged by some unexplained temperature elevations. By taking into consideration 1) the previous cycle patterns, 2) the overall pre-shift level excluding the questionable temperature(s), 3) the mucus sign, 4) the cervix sign, and 5) the level of the thermal shift, the experienced couple can make intelligent decisions about shaving the questionable temperatures and can correctly determine the beginning of Phase III. The relatively inexperienced couple should seek help from counselors experienced in the art of interpreting charts.

Irregular Mucus Dry-up Patterns

The classic mucus pattern is a patch of mucus lasting from five to seven days from start through peak day followed by one or two days of the less fertile tacky mucus and then by dry days for the rest of the cycle. However, there are many variations from the typical; some mucus patches are shorter or considerably longer, and sometimes the drying up pattern is interrupted by the return of the more fertile mucus. Three of these latter situations can be classified. In each, the temperature pattern assists the interpretation.

●**The double peak.** When a peak day is followed by four or more days of drying up and then the more fertile mucus reappears, it is called the double peak syndrome. In a true double peak situation, the basal temperature remains low after the first peak, and the couple are made aware of the situation in a timely fashion. See fig. 7.3, "The Double Mucus Patch."

●●**Key elements to remember:**
1. four or more dryup days past a peak day;
2. while the temperature pattern remains low.

●**The split peak.** The split peak refers to dryup patterns in which a peak day is followed by only one to three days of dryup and then by a return of the more fertile mucus.

If the peak day is followed by only a single day of dryup before the recurrence of the more fertile mucus, it is always called a split peak pattern.

If the new mucus patch lasts for two days or longer,·the pattern is always called the split peak pattern. However, if the dryup has been for two or three days and the more fertile mucus reappears for only a single day, the interpretation depends on the temperature pattern. If the temperature pattern has stayed **low,** then this situation is still the split peak pattern. If the temperature pattern is elevated, then see the "split dryup."

With the split peak pattern, the dryup count is restarted after the last peak day.

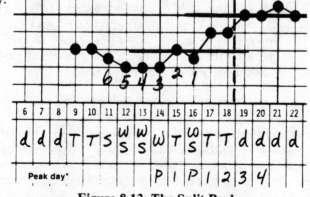

Figure 8.13: The Split Peak

•**The split dryup.** This term refers to a dryup pattern in which the following conditions are met:

1. The peak day is followed by **two or three days of dryup.**

2. The reappearance of the more fertile mucus is **only for a single day** and then is followed by dry days.

3. **An obvious thermal shift pattern** has been established after the peak day.

When all of those conditions are met, we label the day of mucus reappearance with a question mark and continue the dryup count on the next day. We cannot be sure of the cause of this brief reappearance of the more fertile mucus, but it may be due to the slight post-ovulation rise in estrogen illustrated in chapter five, fig. 5.5.

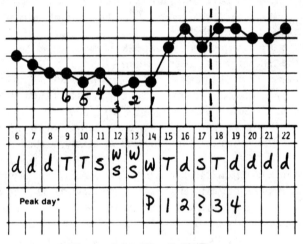

Figure 8.14: The Split Dryup

In fig. 8.13, Rule R would yield day 19 as the start of Phase III. In fig. 8.14, Rule R would yield day 18 as the start of Phase III, and Rule B would yield day 19. However, the mucus-only rules ignore the temperature pattern; thus in fig. 8.14, they require day 17 to be labeled a peak day, so they yield day 21 as the earliest start of Phase III.

Unusually Long Cycles and Calendar Rhythm

The cycle that is illustrated in fig. 8.15 is unusually long compared to the woman's previous cycle variation. This cycle was 59 days long. By the time she reached the limits of her usual cycle length, there was no sign of ovulation. Then on day 41 she began to experience some pain that she associated with ovulation, and on days 44, 45 and 46 she had definite mucus signs.

Peak day was day 46. The PSB was set at 97.9 based on the pre-shift six temperatures on days 42-47, and the TSL was set at 98.3. Rule C, perfect coinciding, yielded day 50 as the start of Phase III.

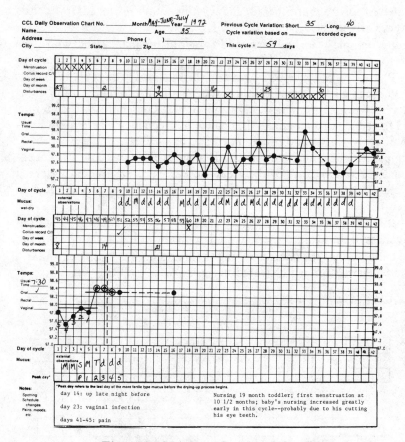

Figure 8.15: A long Cycle and Confidence

This cycle provides an interesting example of why calendar rhythm simply has to fail in certain cases because it cannot adequately handle delayed ovulation. **The formula for calendar rhythm** is very simple: shortest cycle minus 19 = end of Phase I; longest cycle minus 10 = start of Phase III.

Today we would use a modified formula for anyone wanting to use calendar rhythm: shortest cycle minus 21 = end of Phase I; longest cycle minus 10 = start of Phase III.

On that basis the couple would have considered themselves in Phase III by day 30 (40-10). The couple who provided this chart had been using the sympto-thermal method for less than one year and had experienced previous surprise pregnancies with calendar rhythm. They had also previously

172

assumed pregnancy if menstruation had not occurred by the longest previous time (day 41 in this case), and thus they would have begun having coitus by day 41 under their previous practice. In this cycle, by day 41 there was no indication of being in Phase III, so the couple waited. Being strongly motivated to postpone another pregnancy, this couple refrained from coitus from very early in the cycle until day 51.

Another couple who had less need to avoid pregnancy and who were willing to accept the small risk of pregnancy inherent in sexual relations during Phase I might have had coitus on the mucus-dry days between days 9 and 39. Such a couple would follow the standard recommendation of internal observation, evenings only, and not-on-consecutive-days if they wanted to reduce to a minimum the chance of pregnancy due to non-observation of early mucus and/or extended sperm survival.

It should also be noted that the length of the cycle in this case was not entirely unexpected because of the great increase in breast-feeding early in the cycle. This is not at all unusual, and more will be said about it in Chapter 10.

Probably the most important thing about this chart is that it shows the effectiveness of the sympto-thermal method even with unusual cycles if the couple believe what the chart is telling them and do not "think calendar." An opposite situation is illustrated in fig. 8.16.

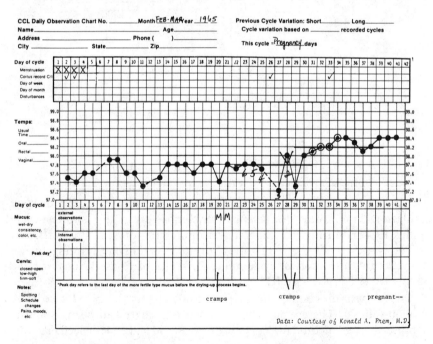

Figure 8.16: A Long Cycle and Lack of Confidence

The woman whose cycle is represented in fig. 8.16 normally had quite regular cycles; she was accustomed to begin her menstruation on day 29 or 30. However, this cycle was going to be much longer than usual for her. She experienced cramps on day 20 and a little mucus on days 20 and 21, but the temperature did not become elevated. By day 28 she convinced herself that she must have ovulated, that the temperatures were wrong. She fully expected menstruation to begin the next day and probably interpreted the cramps on days 28 and 29 as premenstrual. With this reasoning, the couple had coitus on day 28, apparently preferring to rely on past history rather than on the scientifically accurate data on her chart. As subsequent temperatures indicate, coitus occurred very near the time of ovulation, and pregnancy was the result.

This chart illustrates two important facts of life. First, the woman who normally is quite regular may experience an occasional cycle that is significantly different in length from the usual pattern. In this case, with ovulation at about day 28, this cycle would have been about 42 days long instead of her customary 28 or 29.

Secondly, this pregnancy cycle illustrates what can happen if the couple ignore the evidence and instead "think calendar rhythm."

References

1. Josef Roetzer, "The Sympto-Thermal Method: Ten Years of Change," *Linacre Quarterly* 45:4 (November, 1978) 368, 370.

2. John Marshall, *The Infertile Period* (Baltimore: Helicon Press, 1969), 86.

3. Maureen Ball, "A prospective field trial of the 'Ovulation Method' of avoiding conception," *Europ. J. Obstet. Gynec. Reprod. Biol.,* 6:2 (1976) 63-66.

4. Hanna Klaus, et al. "Behavioral Components Influencing Use Effectiveness of Family Planning by Prediction of Ovulation (Billings Method)," *The Family.* 4th Int. Congr. of Psychosomatic Obstetrics and Gynecology, Tel Aviv, 1974 (Basel: Karger, 1975), 218-221.

5. J. A. Johnston and others, "NFP Services and Methods in Australia: A Survey Evaluation," *Int. Rev. of Nat. Fam. Planning.* II:2 (Summer, 1978) 144-145.

6. Hilgers, *op. cit.,* 7.

7. B. Vincent et al., *Methode thermique et contraception: Approaches medicale et psychosociologique* (Paris: Masson, 1967), 52-73. This is the study that found only 1 surprise pregnancy in 17,500 cycles among couples having coitus only in Phase III as indicated by a well defined thermal shift.

8. World Health Organization, "Natural family planning: effectiveness of current methods," *Special Programme of Research, Development and Research Training in Human Reproduction,* Seventh Annual Report, November, 1978, 43-45.

9. Konald A. Prem, "Assessment of Gestational Age," *Minnesota Medicine,* September, 1976, 623.

10. Ibid.

11. John Peel and Malcolm Potts, *Textbook of Contraceptive Practice* (New York: Cambridge University Press, 1969), 99.

12. Dr. Lyn Billings says that there is evidence showing fertility progressively declines so that in the 45-50 age group only 1.3 women per 1000 can become pregnant while the rate is only 1 in 25,000 among the over 50 group. "The Ovulation Method and the Menopause," lecture delivered at Ovulation Method Workshop, Sydney, Australia, 1973.

13. Rudolph F. Vollman M.D., *The Menstrual Cycle* (Philadelphia: W. B. Saunders Co., 1977) 26.

174

14. Richard A. Passwater, "Vitamin E and Menopause (Part VI of a Readers' Survey," *Prevention* (July, 1976), 91-95.

15. John Philip, et al, "Should the indications for prenatal chromosome analysis be changed?", *British Medical Journal,* October 29, 1977, 1117-1119.

16. *Cincinnati Right to Life News,* J. C. Willke, M.D. ed., July, 1978. According to Barbara Willke, R.N., Dr. Lejeune, who is known for his work on Down's Syndrome, is convinced that there is no correlation between the mother's age and Down's Syndrome.

17. E. L. Billings, *op. cit.*

18. R. F. Vollman, *op. cit., 24.*

19. Ibid., fig. 57, 110.

20. J. Marshall, op. cit., 30-35.

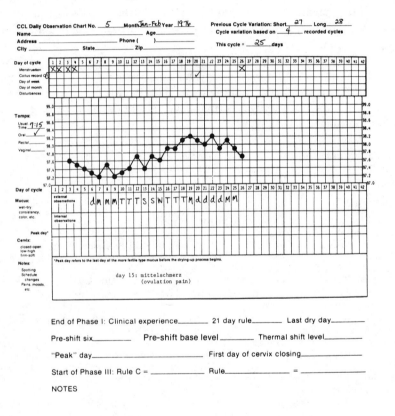

Figure 8.17   Practice Chart

The correct answers are found at the end of Chapter 10.

9

Surprise or Unplanned Pregnancies

Introduction

It would be unfair to the readers of this manual to give the impression that there are no surprise pregnancies among couples who use natural family planning. As we noted previously, there is no such thing as a 100 percent method of conception regulation except 100 percent abstinence or castration, and those are not considered as methods of birth control. At the same time, we noted that natural family planning can be as effective as any method (and more effective than most) if it is properly taught and learned, if there is sufficient motivation, and if it is practiced according to its rules. One study showed only one unplanned pregnancy in 17,500 cycles, a surprise pregnancy rate of about one per 1,458 woman-years of exposure.[1] Let us stress, however, that the couples in that study were well instructed and well motivated; they did not have coitus in Phase I and waited until the temperature shift gave them clear indication of postovulation infertility; where the readings were ambiguous, they did not regard themselves in Phase III, and thus sometimes might not have coitus during the entire cycle.

Surprise pregnancies are of two types: 1) the real surprise and 2) unplanned but no surprise.

1. In the first type, the couple follows the rules properly, but for some reason the wife still becomes pregnant. We analyze the chart to try to determine whether the pregnancy resulted from coitus in late Phase I or early Phase III. The method surprise pregnancy rate for Phase I ranges from well under 1 per 100 woman years to perhaps 7 per 100 woman years depending upon the method used to determine the end of Phase I; evidence indicates that the method surprise pregnancy rate for the sympto-thermal rules for Phase III is not over 1 per 100 woman years of exposure.

2. Most "surprise pregnancies" result from the couple's personal practice.

• Pregnancy can result from coitus using condoms, diaphragms, foams, jellies, and coitus interruptus (withdrawal). All of these are **forms of contraceptive behavior** which have their own pregnancy rates, and they are incompatible with natural family planning. Coitus reservatus (see glossary of terms) and even genital contact likewise must be considered to have the potential of transmitting sufficient sperm for conception.

●Coitus while the signs of fertility indicate the fertile time will obviously be a source of pregnancies. **Taking chances** may result in a pregnancy that was not exactly planned but is certainly no surprise. Most of these pregnancies appear to come from coitus on the days of the less fertile, merely tacky mucus in early Phase II.

●**Improper interpretation** of the signs can result in a couple thinking they are in Phase I or Phase III when they are really in Phase II. The CCL instruction program plus the crosschecking nature of the sympto-thermal method reduces this possibility to a minimum but it cannot be eliminated entirely.

●**Charts wanted.** The Couple to Couple League earnestly asks — literally begs — any couple who experiences a pregnancy that is in any way a "surprise" to send either the original or a photocopy of the conception cycle chart to the CCL National Office, PO Box 111184, Cincinnati, Ohio 45211-1184. Name, address and phone number must be written on the chart. If it is a "user surprise" then we can help you to understand why. If it is a "method surprise" such information is of vital importance to us, for only through such data can we hope to perfect the method even further. We further request any such information as soon as the couple realize they are pregnant (21 days of thermal shift temperatures).

And let us all keep our values straight. A surprise pregnancy is not a failure but a baby, a gift from God — even if an unrequested gift — to be accepted and loved for his or her own sake.

Method Surprise Pregnancies

This section illustrates two surprise pregnancies from late Phase I coitus and one from early Phase III coitus. If a woman was watching consistently for mucus, did not observe any, had coitus on a supposedly "dry" day and became pregnant, we would say that the method failed to provide her with a sufficient indication of fertility. Or if a couple followed the rules for Phase I but became pregnant by reason of extended sperm survival, we would call that a method surprise pregnancy.

●**Apparent dry day.** The cycle in fig. 9.1 illustrates a situation where the cervix and mucus symptoms failed to provide sufficient warning of fertility to the woman. The couple decided to go beyond the limits of the 21 day rule (day 5) and to rely on the mucus to indicate the start of Phase II. In this case, she thought she was still "dry" on day 7, and coitus on that evening resulted in pregnancy.

The woman noted that the cervix still seemed firm and closed. She did not obtain mucus by "milking the cervix" but rather obtained it by a very shallow observation, pretty much at the external labia. This woman

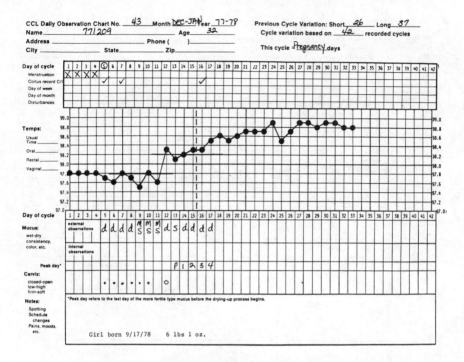

Figure 9.1   Apparent Dry Day Pregnancy

typically had only three or four days of discernible mucus. Her experience appears to validate the belief that relying upon the mucus to indicate the start of Phase II has a higher effectiveness if the woman normally experiences a mucus patch of at least five days from its first appearance through the peak day. And, as mentioned earlier, we likewise recommend obtaining mucus directly from the cervical os for the earliest detection of mucus.

• **Extended sperm survival?** The couple who submitted the chart in fig. 9.2 were not following CCL recommendations for Phase I. That is, the couple were not following the "not-on-consecutive-days" rule, and there should have been mucus recordings from day 4 onwards. Still, even if she had noticed mucus on day 6, extended sperm survival still provides the most plausible explanation. If ovulation occurred on "peak day minus 2" (day 11), pregnancy would have required five day sperm life, the figure assumed in the explanation of the 21 day rule. However, this cycle (March, 1977) was so much like the woman's previous cycle that we think we can make some comparisons. In both the February and March cycles, peak day was on day 13 and the temperature patterns were almost identical with day 16 being the first day of thermal shift in each. In the 27 day February cycle,

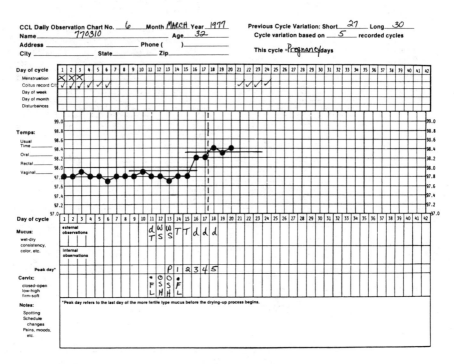

Figure 9.2 Extended Sperm Survival

ovulation as early as peak day minus 2 (day 11) would have required a 16 day luteal phase (days 12 through 27) with the first day of thermal shift coming five days after ovulation. That's not impossible, but it is more likely that ovulation occurred a bit closer to the first day of drying up and the first day of thermal shift. Assuming that ovulation occurred at the same time in the March cycle would require a six to eight day sperm survival to account for the pregnancy.

Assuming that the couple was accurate in saying that there was no genital contact between days 7 and 20, the pregnancy here is really a tremendous surprise. First of all, cycle day 6 is a day of very low fertility; and secondly a sperm life of six to eight days is a very rare occurrence. The odds of this combination occurring? Who can say precisely? Perhaps about 1 in 5,000 woman years — or less.

● **A Phase III pregnancy.** The couple who submitted the chart in fig. 9.3 reported that they had no coitus or genital contact from the beginning of the cycle until day 16. Assuming that to be true, this is an example of a genuine Phase III method surprise pregnancy, an extremely rare occurrence. The PSB is set at 98.0 based on the five temperatures on days 6 through 10. The temperature on day 11 is considered to be part of the overall thermal shift

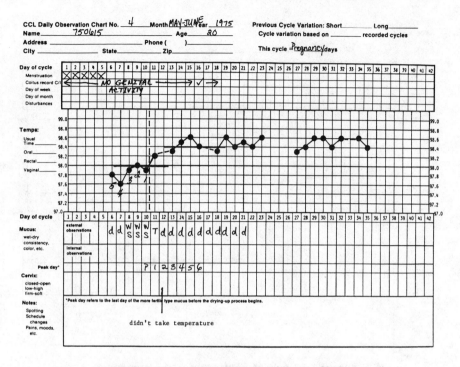

Figure 9.3 A Phase III Surprise Pregnancy

pattern. And even if it was used to set the PSB at 98.2, the requirements for Rule B would still have been met by day 15. All we can say about this is that it shows that we cannot promise 100%; once in a while a pregnancy occurs for which we have no explanation other than that God must have really wanted that child to come into being.

User Surprise Pregnancies

The vast majority of so-called surprise pregnancies result from lack of motivation or erroneous interpretations. A review of some examples of other couples' practices can be very instructive.

180

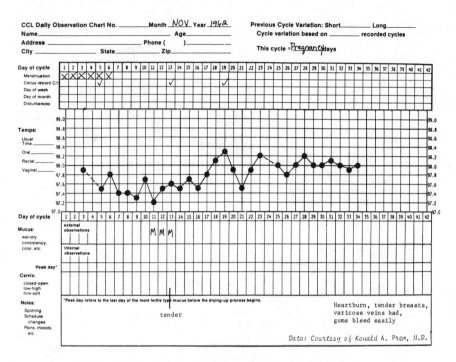

Figure 9.4   Lack of Motivation and Pregnancy

●**Obviously in Phase II.** What is meant by a surprise pregnancy due to a lack of motivation? If a couple have been instructed that pre-ovulation mucus is associated with the time of highest fertility, and if the woman has noticed this mucus, and if they have coitus, can a pregnancy resulting from coitus at that time be called a "surprise pregnancy"? If this is a couple of normal fertility, the greater surprise would be if the woman did not become pregnant. Yet the rules for comparative statistics about birth control methods would have such a pregnancy counted as either a "method failure" or a "user failure." At any rate, the chart in fig. 9.4 illustrates such a case. We don't think of this case as any sort of "failure." Rather it simply illustrates that the presence of cervical mucus indicates fertility. The couple were not motivated to avoid pregnancy.

The chart in fig. 9.5 speaks for itself and illustrates another case where motivation was lacking. Even though the woman was not making mucus observations, this couple had been instructed to consider themselves in Phase II after day 7. While not illustrating a "surprise pregnancy," this chart does point to a difficulty and corresponding challenge of natural family planning. Yes, a little absence does tend to make the heart grow fonder. Yes, in a culture that tends to equate coitus with both "something to remember me

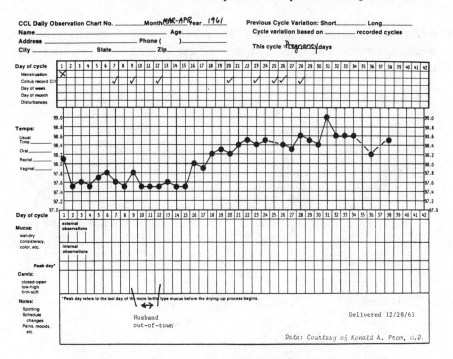

Figure 9.5   Absence, Lack of Motivation, and Pregnancy

by" and a "good way to say hello" there are additional subtle psychological inclinations toward coitus whenever a trip is begun or ended. But no, such coitus is by no means a necessity for a happy marriage. In such situations, the attitudinal stance of both partners, and perhaps the husband in particular, becomes very important. If every night that he has gone to bed alone in his hotel room (or at home if it is the wife who is traveling), he has looked forward to coitus upon their reunion, if perhaps the frequently sexually provocative costuming of airline stewardesses has further turned his thoughts toward the marriage bed, and if this has not been pushed out of the imagination but rather been encouraged by a couple of drinks, then he is hardly engaging in the effort to grow in sexual maturity that is needed to practice natural family planning. Certainly the traveling man is usually going to want to embrace his spouse upon coming together again, but such an embrace need not include coitus. The sexually mature couple will be able to express the warmth, tenderness, and gentleness of marital love in a physical embrace without feeling a necessity to follow their erotic tendencies to their culmination in coitus. The next morning they may well have more satisfaction and self-esteem at having expressed their marital love in nongenital ways than if they had followed the cultural pattern of equating love-making with coitus.

●**Misinterpretations of mucus.** There are three ways to misinterpret the mucus symptom of fertility, and each one is illustrated in the following three charts.

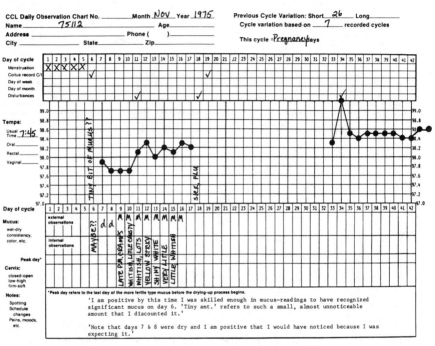

Figure 9.6   Ignoring a Small Amount of Mucus

1. *Ignoring a small amount.* The woman who submitted the chart in fig. 9.6 noticed a small amount of mucus on day 6 but she did not regard it as a sign of fertility. Coitus that evening resulted in pregnancy. The obvious lesson is that the small amount of mucus noticed externally on day 6 indicated the start of Phase II. Day 6 was one day beyond the limits of the 21 day rule. The clinical experience rules for day 6 assume it is still a dry day.

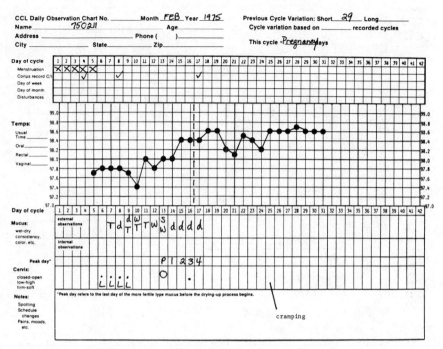

Figure 9.7   Mucus Followed by a Dry Day

2. *Ignoring the start of Phase II.* In fig. 9.7 the mucus started on day 7 but day 8 appeared to be dry, and coitus on the evening of day 8 resulted in pregnancy. When having ordinary cycles, *once the mucus starts,* there is a positive indication of being in Phase II even if there is an occasional dry day after the first mucus day. It is our hunch that milking the cervix would have indicated mucus on day 8, but we were not emphasizing that type of observation back in early 1975.

184

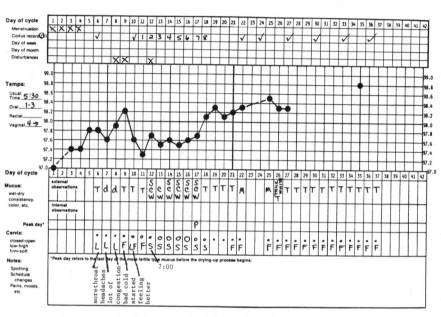

Figure 9.8   Disregard of Less Fertile Type Mucus

3. *Treating less fertile as infertile.* The woman who submitted the chart in fig. 9.8 misunderstood the first edition of this manual and erroneously thought that Phase II didn't start until the appearance of the *more* fertile mucus which started on day 12. The rather obvious lesson is that **the beginning of the less fertile,** merely tacky mucus indicates the start of Phase II. Such mucus started on day 6; coitus on day 10 resulted in pregnancy.

This was the second cycle of sympto-thermal experience for this couple. We strongly recommend that beginners not have coitus during Phase I for the first two or three cycles — even within the first 6 days of the cycle — so that the woman can learn her own pattern of early mucus development without interference from seminal residue or vaginal mucus from sexual excitation.

According to hormonal studies, ovulation can occur as early as Peak day minus 3. On that basis, the sperm life required in figures 9.7 and 9.8 would have been two days and four days respectively.

4. *Only a single observation.* Another fairly good way to insure a "surprise pregnancy" when relying upon the last dry day as the end of Phase I is to wait until the evening to make a single mucus observation for that day. It cannot be overemphasized that the mucus observations **must be made periodically throughout the day in Phase I** if they are to be of any value for detecting the first appearance of mucus which signals the start of Phase II. The most practical solution: make the external observation after each urination during Phase I.

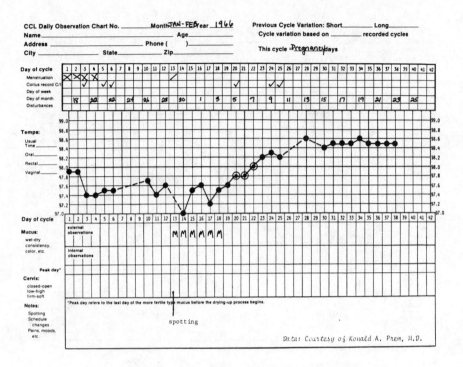

Figure 9.9   Coitus Too Soon for Phase III

● **Misinterpretations of temperature graphs.**

1. *Outsmarting the method?* The chart in fig. 9.9 shows coitus on day 20 prior to any sufficient indication of postovulation infertility. Note that this chart dates back to 1966 when no emphasis was given to the peak of mucus. Thus, there is no indication of any peak or of any changes in quality. This couple would, at that time, have been concerned almost completely with basal temperatures. With the pre-shift base at 97.6°, the full thermal shift level would be 98.0. The day on which this couple had coitus, day 20, was only the first day of any rise above the pre-shift base level. According to the temperature-only rule, day 24 would be the first day of postovulation infertility. If this woman was experienced in making mucus observations and had noted a peak on day 18 with dryness beginning on day 19 and continuing, the pattern of temperatures by day 22 would indicate the start of Phase III by day 22 according to Rule B.

We speculate that the couple may have tried to outsmart the system by guessing that ovulation may have occurred on the dip day, 17, and then counted three days beyond the dip. Thus we stress that the pre-shift base level is set by the *highs* among the pre-shift six and that thermal shift temperatures are only those above the pre-shift base level.

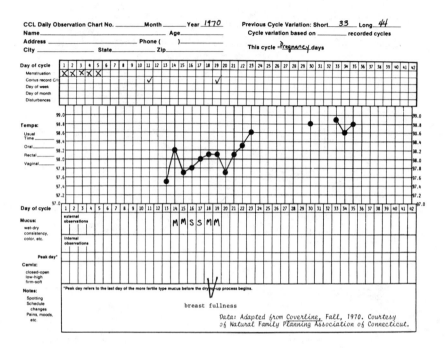

Figure 9.10   Misinterpretation by an Experienced Couple

2. Misinterpretation, experienced couple. The couple who submitted the chart in fig. 9.10 were not instructed by CCL and looked for a thermal shift of only 2/10 of 1°F. Furthermore, back in 1970 the crosschecking requirements of the mucus symptom were not emphasized. In the couple's interpretation, the PSB was set at 97.8 after shaving day 14 because the lady had a history of pre-shift spikes. Day 19 was seen as the third day of thermal shift 2/10 of 1°F. above the PSB. According to those rules of thumb, it was a method surprise pregnancy.

According to the CCL rules of thumb, the temperature graph was misinterpreted. The PSB could still be set at 97.8 after shaving day 14 although another three pre-shift temperatures certainly would have been preferred. The overall thermal shift count started on day 17 but had to be restarted on 21 after the dip below the PSB on day 20. With peak day placed on either 17 or 19, the earliest CCL interpretation indicates the start of Phase III on day 23 by Rule B.

It is a rare occurrence that a thermal shift is only 2/10 of 1°F. above the PSB. The normal shift is at least 4/10 of a degree, and this should be the standard requirement unless a woman has a history of several cycles where the thermal shift is obviously less than the usual requirement.

This page is intentionally blank.

188

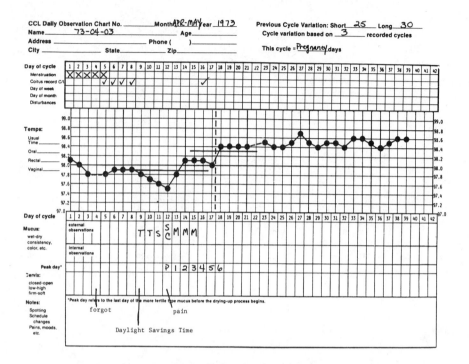

Figure 9.11 Not Following the Rules or Misinterpretation?

3. *Not following the rules or misinterpretation?* Sometimes it is difficult to say that any single factor led to an unplanned pregnancy, and such is the case with the experience expressed on the chart in fig. 9.11. The couple who submitted this chart at first felt that they had acted out of misinterpretation. Upon further reflection, they spoke of lack of motivation. However, at least one thing is clear: the basic rules were not followed as the discussion below will make clear. In addition it is sometimes impossible to determine which coitus caused pregnancy, and that is the case here. It is highly probable that the coitus on day 8 led to the pregnancy, but the coitus on day 16 cannot be ruled out.

• • Disregarding Phase I Rules. It is the policy of the Couple to Couple League to recommend that a couple who are relatively inexperienced in natural family planning should not have coitus during Phase I until they gain sufficient experience with the sympto-thermal method. The 21 day rule should be based on six cycles of experience, and couples should not extend Phase I beyond day 6 until the woman has at least six cycles of experience with mucus observation. The chart in figure 9.11 indicates 1) only three cycles of exprience, 2) going beyond the 21 day rule, 3) going beyond day 6 with inadequate experience and 4) disregarding the rule about not-on-consecutive-days in Phase I.

• • Insufficient Mucus Observation. The sympto-thermal method calls for the recording of mucus observations every day past menstruation until the beginning of Phase III. No observations were recorded on days 6, 7, and 8. Perhaps one reason for this was that the woman thought that any vaginal discharge on these days was simply seminal residue rather than the beginning of the mucus symptom. This illustrates the reason for the not-on-consecutive-days rule; if a couple chooses to have coitus past the time indicated as relatively infertile by the 21 day rule, they should not have coitus on consecutive days.

If the woman's mucus notations are reliable, the rule "Peak + 4" would point toward day 16 as the beginning of Phase III. However, there is an insufficient temperature crosscheck at that point. The sympto-thermal interpretation would indicate day 18 as the first day of Phase III by Rule B.

• • Insufficient Temperature Rise. A significant error in interpretation was caused by regarding the three temperatures at 98.1° as the thermal shift. The pre-shift base level in this chart should be placed at 97.9°, and such a level would make it very apparent that the temperatures at 98.1° were not high enough. It has been said repeatedly that the normal thermal shift is 4/10 to 6/10 of a degree; a rise of only 2/10 of a degree could be regarded as a thermal shift only when there was a long record of such experience. In this case, the history showed regular thermal shifts of 4/10 to 6/10 of a degree. The wife knew that her temperatures were not high enough yet, but the couple was no longer serious about postponing a pregnancy.

The 4 day temperature-only rule with the last three days consecutively at least 4/10 of a degree above the PSB would indicate day 20 as the beginning of Phase III; the sympto-thermal Rule B indicates day 18. Coitus on day 16, as indicated in fig. 9.11, would be too early under any system looking for a basal temperature crosscheck of the start of Phase III.

• • Paying Too Much Attention to Insignificant Details. What allowed this couple to talk themselves into thinking that ovulation had occurred were two things. The wife felt pain on day 12 that she associated with ovulation, and they apparently gave it primary importance, even though it should have been used only to crosscheck other more definite signs. Secondly, they paid attention to the temperature rise from the low dip on day 12 to the higher temperature on day 14. That particular shift is unimportant. What counts is the rise above the high level of the pre-shift six temperatures that determine the pre-shift base level.

Summary Comment on Surprise Pregnancies

We have shown a number of examples of "surprise" or unplanned pregnancies because we believe that honesty is the best policy. We challenge those dealing in Pills, IUD's, sterilization, and the barrier methods to a similar honesty. We cannot promise a 100% effectiveness in family planning; that means that occasionally there will be a true method surprise as well as the user surprise pregnancies. We still believe that when everything is considered from health to morality to effectiveness, the natural methods of conception regulation described in this book are the best methods of birth control the world has ever known. As the author couple who have an over-45 age as the prime reason for wanting to keep our family at its present size, we fully intend to use only the natural methods through the remaining years of our mutual fertility, just as we have used various natural methods — calendar rhythm, breast-feeding, and sympto-thermal — from the beginning of our marriage.

As we mentioned previously, a key element for the happy and successful use of natural family planning is attitude, and the same thing is true in the presence of an unplanned pregnancy. One of the guiding principles of the Couple to Couple League is that every child — whether asked for or not — is a gift from God and is to be loved and respected for his or her own sake. As everyone knows, it has become a deadly custom in this country to kill many of the unplanned babies. We feel this has happened at least partly as a result of absolutizing the idea of the planned family and thus closing the mind and heart to the acceptance of the unplanned child. The acceptance of abortion did not just come upon the scene overnight; it grew out of some other ideas such as absolute personal freedom, absolute family planning, and a confusion of love with the pleasure of genital intercourse. However, many of us know from personal experience and many others know with a deep-down intuition that love is shown much more in the acceptance of adversity and difficulties for a good cause than by being self-willed; we know intuitively or have learned that pleasure and long-range happiness are by no means the same.

Thus, we have thought it appropriate to conclude a brief discussion of surprise pregnancies with a reminder that the value of family planning is only relative. What must be absolutized is the love we must have for all who enter our lives, whether at conception or as adults, whether we really invited that person or not. Planning says something about our anticipated response to an imagined future; our response to the present is the test of our love.

References.
  1. B. Vincent et al.. *Methode thermique et contraception. Approaches medicale et psycho-sociologique* (Paris; Masson, 1967). 52-73.

10
The Return of Fertility
After Childbirth

What is the world's oldest and still most widely used method of spacing babies?

Ecological breast-feeding.

However, this aspect of birth control is given very little attention by most books on natural family planning. To put it more precisely, emphasis has been given to the bottle-feeding mother and the quick return of fertility. Breast-feeding has generally been discouraged, and the general advice has been to wean quickly so as to get back to regular menstrual cycles. Such studies, however, do acknowledge in a backhanded way that there is a real difference in the return of postpartum fertility between the bottle-feeding mother and the breast-feeding mother. What is usually overlooked are the significant differences between the various types of breast-feeding and how these differences affect the return of postpartum fertility. Accordingly, in this chapter we discuss **four distinctly different situations** and how the return of fertility after childbirth is affected by each. By far the greatest emphasis will be given to what we call ecological breast-feeding for several reasons. First of all, we would like to encourage this form of baby care because of all its benefits for both baby and mother; secondly, this form of baby care raises questions in people's minds and we hope to answer a few of them; thirdly, most of the time only this ecological breast-feeding has any significant effect as far as a long period of postpartum natural infertility is concerned.

Preliminary Remarks:
—Abstinence Before and After Childbirth

However, before we discuss the various forms of baby care and the related return of fertility, we think it might be worthwhile to say something about the weeks immediately before and after childbirth. Some husbands become impatient for the resumption of coitus after childbirth because they feel they have gone a long time without it. What has been said previously about attitudes is relevant here, but it is also true that in many cases couples have been advised to refrain from coitus for reasons that have nothing to do with fertility, personal character development, or health. The advice is routinely given by some doctors under the guise of health reasons that couples should refrain from coitus for six weeks or more before the anticipated delivery and for six weeks following childbirth. Add a week or so for the typical late delivery, and there is a routine "doctor's order" to avoid coitus for a quarter of a year. Certainly situations may arise in any marriage where the couple may have a good reason to refrain from coitus for much longer periods. However, the typical routine medical advice about refraining from coitus for a twelve or thirteen week period before and after a normal pregnancy is simply not at all necessary. If the wife is having a normal, healthy pregnancy and the husband has no venereal disease or other infection in the genital area, the advice to refrain from coitus for six weeks prior to the anticipated delivery is unfounded. The more appropriate advice would be to tell such a couple that there are no medical reasons to refrain from coitus prior to the beginning of labor. Their decision to engage in or to refrain from coitus would have to be based on other considerations such as the wife's comfort, personal discipline, and so forth.

After childbirth, the appropriate advice to the medically healthy couple would be to refrain from coitus until the wife would feel comfortable. The idea of waiting until after the six weeks' checkup may be necessary in cases where the woman has difficulty with the healing of the episiotomy, but it is not a universal necessity. A woman can receive individual counseling on this matter from her physician who can tailor his advice to her particular condition. Women who have a prepared and natural childbirth and who completely breast-feed may be in shape weeks before those who participate in the cultural customs of medicated childbirth and bottle-feeding.

We write on the strength of statements made by Konald Prem, M.D., professor of obstetrics and gynecology at the University of Minnesota Medical School. If your doctor disagrees, politely ask him for the medical evidence that contradicts what we have written. We encourage you to read *The Silent Knife* by Nancy Cohen and Lois Estner for valuable information about C-sections and childbirth practices.[1]

Interestingly enough, many of the same doctors who routinely prescribe twelve or thirteen weeks of sexual continence become quite anxious to prescribe a contraceptive or sterilization when the couple have decided to refrain from coitus for two or three weeks for reasons of natural family planning. With increasing frequency we have been hearing of physicians who have introduced the subject of sterilization to their patients. We think that the institution of marriage, the institution of medicine, and society as a whole will be much better off when physicians learn how to help people to live within the natural order and limit their practice of medicine to the attempted cure and prevention of disease. The unnecessary removal and destruction of medically healthy organs for supposedly personalistic and sociological reasons has been followed by the much more grievous evil of the unnecessary removal and destruction of innocent, unborn babies from their mother's womb—for those same supposedly personalistic and sociological reasons.

We intend no polemic against the medical profession; certainly, there are still doctors, hopefully many, who regard the natural as the norm and the goal, who limit their practice of medicine to the cure and prevention of disease, and who do not regard pregnancy, even the unplanned pregnancy, as a disease. However, the tone that is evident in these paragraphs has developed not out of any initial prejudice but rather out of hearing many personal accounts of what is happening today. We hope things will change; we think that a well-informed patient-clientele is one of the best ways of reforming some of the ills in the current practice of medicine. To such persons we would offer this word: simply, politely, but firmly ask for the medical evidence. Do not make the assumption that competence in treating disease in any way carries with it a competence as a moralist or spiritual adviser—or even a special competence in knowing how to foster the natural.

Section I: Bottle-feeding and Cultural Nursing

The Bottle-feeding Mother

Fertility generally returns quite soon after childbirth for the woman who bottle-feeds. As with most things in nature, there is some variation but a general pattern prevails. The earliest ovulation that has been detected after childbirth has been at 27 days postpartum.[2] This would mean that menstruation would occur at approximately 41 days postpartum unless Phase III is short, as sometimes occurs in the first few cycles postpartum. Such cases of ovulatory cycles in the first six weeks postpartum are infrequent; the available evidence indicates that when the first postpartum menstruation occurs at 42 days there is only about a five percent chance that it has been preceded by ovulation.[3] In other words, in about 95 percent of cases when menstruation occurs at six weeks postpartum, it is not preceded by fertility.

During the first three weeks postpartum, as the above evidence suggests, there is almost no possibility of conception. Any coitus during this time would be dependent upon the woman's health and comfort. By the fourth week, we are already within the range of recorded fertility. Thus, the practical advice for avoiding another pregnancy immediately for the bottle-feeding mother would be as follows.

1. Begin taking basal temperatures at least by day 14 after childbirth.

2. Begin mucus and cervix observations as soon as possible. However, the after-childbirth bloody discharge called the **lochia** will obscure the mucus observations for several weeks, and the cervix examination should

not be made until the vaginal tissues are healed from the childbirth experience.

3. After the lochia has disappeared, if the woman has no mucus or cervix signs of fertility, the couple may consider themselves in a Phase I type of infertility. If they have coitus at this time, they should follow the Phase I rules of evenings only and not-on-consecutive-days. The internal observation of the mucus is recommended.

4. If the woman is not experienced with the mucus observation or if there is any confusion, abstinence is recommended until the couple has the sympto-thermal indications of being in Phase III. For the bottle-feeding mother, Phase III will probably not be delayed very long.

5. If a couple decides to have coitus once dry days have been established, the wife should make mucus observations very carefully, and the couple should regard themselves in Phase II at the first appearance of any type of mucus. The couple seeking to postpone another pregnancy should then abstain until they have a sympto-thermal certainty of being in Phase III.

Since the majority of bottle-feeding mothers probably experience six weeks or more of postpartum discharges, the most common practice will be to refrain from coitus until after the first menstruation.

6. Beginning with the first menstruation, the couple should regard themselves as back in the regular fertility cycle. Sometimes the second menstruation will occur without a preceding ovulation, but this would be relatively uncommon in the bottle-feeding mother. Thus, after the first menstruation, the couple should use the regular rules of natural family planning for fertility awareness and the regulation of their practice of coitus or genital contact.

7. The bottle-feeding mother should avoid hormone pills or shots intended to suppress milk production because these drugs may interfere with accurate sympto-thermal observations. Engorgement can be relieved by hand expression, and the milk production will cease in a few days without medication.

Breast-feeding Plus Supplements

Almost all the confusion that exists about breast-feeding and postpartum infertility is due to the practice of partial breast-feeding plus supplements. This is called "cultural breast-feeding." Later in this chapter ecological breast-feeding is explained and contrasted with cultural breast-feeding. It is ecological breast-feeding that is associated with an extended period of postpartum natural infertility.

Therefore, for all practical purposes, the mother who, during the first six months, supplements breast-feeding with formulas, baby foods, cereals or other solids, juices or other liquids including water must regard herself as a bottle-feeding mother as far as the return of fertility is concerned. The same holds true for nursing mothers who use pacifiers, who breast-feed according to a schedule, who go for long periods between nursings and so forth. These are the common forms of cultural breast-feeding that tend to restrict the baby's frequent nursing at the mother's breast.

For anything less than full ecological breast-feeding, it is quite common for fertility to return quickly after childbirth, frequently just as soon as for the mother who does not breast-feed at all. Thus, the guidelines for the bottle-feeding mother should be applied in all the various forms of cultural breast-feeding, i.e., in all cases that do not meet the criteria for full ecological breast-feeding. Quite simply, one cannot expect the natural benefits of any ecological relationship unless the requirements for that relationship are fulfilled. Thus, mothers who use cultural breast-feeding should review the first six guidelines for the bottle-feeding mother.

The greatest difference in the return of fertility between bottle-feeding and cultural breast-feeding is that the latter has a much wider range. Due to big differences in 1) the frequency and amount of nursing and 2) bodily differences among women, the return of fertility in this group may range from four weeks postpartum until after weaning.

Complete Breast-feeding with Deliberate Weaning

By deliberate weaning we mean the stopping of nursing over a very short period of time. The effect on the return of ovulation is the same whether the baby is weaned in a day or over a period of a week. However, weaning in a period of a day or two can be extremely uncomfortable for the mother because her milk supply may continue to be ample for several days, thus giving her engorged breasts. Quick weaning is often hard on babies, and parents who wean the baby off the breast should continue to hold and cuddle the baby often especially during his feeding times.

In his practice, Dr. Konald Prem has successfully used the following guidelines for a ten-day weaning program for the mother who wishes to nurse for only three to four months.

1. The mother should be totally breast-feeding before the ten-day weaning program begins.

2. Beginning with day 1 of weaning, the couple may continue to have coitus until day 10, by which time weaning should be completed. They should begin to take temperatures, if they have not done so already, by day 1 of weaning.

3. On day 11 after they started to wean the baby, the couple should regard themselves as fertile and should refrain from coitus if they do not desire an immediate pregnancy.

4. The couple should continue to refrain from coitus and any genital contact until they have a sympto-thermal indication of being in Phase III.

Of course, if the mucus or cervix signs indicate the return of fertility prior to the beginning of weaning or between days 1 and 10 of the weaning process, such signs should be interpreted as indicating an unexpectedly early return of fertility.

Such a deliberate weaning program may be followed up through the fourth month of total breast-feeding. Beginning with the fifth month, even the ecologically breast-feeding mother may occasionally experience the return of fertility and should be on the lookout for the various signs of fertility.

Furthermore, it should be recognized that such a ten-day weaning program is no assurance of a quick return of fertility. We have seen charts that have indicated a fairly long time between the end of the short weaning period and the return of fertility.

What about the woman who fully breast-feeds for a shorter time, say three to six weeks, and then either weans completely or introduces supplements? In the case where the fully breast-feeding mother weans completely over a ten-day period at any time during the first three or four months, the guidelines in this section would be applicable. However, if she goes from ecological breast-feeding to cultural breast-feeding at any time, then the earlier comments about the bottle-feeding mother and the mother who supplements her breast-feeding are applicable.

Section II: Ecological Breast-feeding

This section deals with what may be the most controversial part of this book for some because the subject of ecological breast-feeding goes far beyond the subject of natural family planning. In fact, because breast-feeding a baby is so much more than "birth control," we would never recommend that a mother breast-feed her baby just for that reason. It is important to do the right things for the right reason, and the right reason for breast-feeding is that it is the best for the baby—nutritionally, dentally, medically, emotionally, and any other way you can think of.

However, when a mother begins to think in terms of what is really best for her baby and realizes that it is ecological breast-feeding, then she has a problem: our society does not expect a mother to experience truly natural mothering. How can she explain to well-meaning relatives and friends that natural, ecological breast-feeding really does space babies? How can she explain to a well-intentioned but poorly informed mother or mother-in-law (or pediatrician for that matter) that her baby is not starving just on breast milk but is getting the best food he can get?

Since breast-feeding is so much more than natural child spacing and there is so much satisfaction in it for the mother, she will very often want to follow the natural pattern of letting the baby wean at his or her own pace which may be months after the return of fertility. Can she find any support for nursing a baby who can walk, even one who can talk, in a culture in which most women do not breast-feed at all and in which it is not common to nurse beyond six months?

It is not within the scope of this book to reply fully to such questions which merely indicate the full context of breast-feeding and natural mothering. Nor is it within the scope of this book to explain in any detail how to achieve the practice of ecological breast-feeding in the face of all our cultural customs to the contrary. The questions we have touched on are among the many related topics that are the subject of another book, a companion to this, *Breast-feeding and Natural Child Spacing: The Ecology of Natural Mothering.*[4] The many letters we have received lead us to believe that men and women who are interested in breast-feeding, child spacing, and natural mothering will enjoy it and benefit from reading it.

In what follows, we treat the baby as a boy to keep the pronouns simple, and we sometimes adopt a question-answer format and address the mother directly.

Definition and Rules of Ecological Breast-feeding

● **Definition.** Ecological breast-feeding is the type of nursing that respects and follows the natural order; it keeps mother and baby physically close and avoids practices that upset the balance of nature between them. In this balance, the baby receives the best nourishment physically and emotionally, and his suckling normally provides his mother with an extended period of natural infertility and absence from menstruation. In addition, his mother receives satisfaction and fulfillment in her womanly role of mothering. Thus, because this pattern of baby care is so much more than feeding, it is called natural mothering.

● **The basic rules.** Simply follow these do's and don'ts. The thing to remember is that frequent suckling at the breast is the key to ecological breast-feeding.

1. **Do** let your baby nurse as often as he wants. **Don't** set up a nursing schedule of so many feedings a day. (The schedule is for the bottle-feeder—to avoid either stuffing or starving.) Don't set a limit for the time at each breast. Since breast milk is so much easier for baby to digest than bottle milk and since the baby enjoys pacification at the breast, it is quite natural for your breast-fed baby to nurse often.

2. **Don't** aim for your baby to sleep all through the night. It is the frequent and regular suckling that suppresses ovulation, and eight to twelve hours without a nursing may be too long. Put your baby to breast before you go to sleep; when he wakes up during the night, bring him to bed with you and let him nurse while you and he sleep. Sleeping with baby, besides its emotional benefits for both mother and baby, is an extremely important factor in natural spacing. It is at these times (during naps or during the

night with mother) that baby will suckle often and contentedly to satisfy his needs.

3. **Don't** use a pacifier. The breast is a wonderful mothering tool and the best pacifier for your baby. Suckling at the breast has a calming effect upon the infant, and a tired baby falls asleep easily at the breast. This mothering aspect of breast-feeding is extremely important to the emotional well being of baby and likewise plays an important part in the natural spacing mechanism.

4. **Don't** give him any solids, liquids, juices, cereals, or water during his early months. His only source of nourishment should be your milk until he's big enough to begin taking food off the table and feeding himself. Some babies will want solids at five months of age, and others are not ready until a few months later.

5. **Don't** force weaning. Natural weaning occurs gradually and usually over a period of many months or a few years at baby's pace—not society's.

6. **Do** be one with your baby. Avoid situations which separate the two of you. Take your baby with you and don't leave him with babysitters. If an occasional separation cannot be avoided, it should not be over a couple of hours.

7. **Do** be prepared to debate with your baby's doctor and some well meaning but misinformed friends and relatives. Let the doctor check your baby's blood if he questions the baby's iron supply at a certain age. Studies and observations show that anemia in the totally breast-fed baby up to six months of age is extremely rare.[5] In the rare case where iron is required, iron drops can be used until the baby is ready for solids. This iron test is very simple, requiring only a drop of blood from baby's finger. It helps to remember that the average doctor learned very little about breast-feeding and child spacing in medical school and that his own wife probably used bottles. Therefore, some doctors are not very helpful when it comes to breast-feeding.

Increasing medical evidence today shows the dangers of overfeeding babies, and research relates the early introduction of solids, liquids, and formulas to the increased amount of allergies and chronic ear infections, increased hospitalization of babies, increased incidence of intestinal diseases and anemia, and so on.[6] Nature's food is still superior. In those early months of life it is good to know that mother alone can provide her baby with the very best.

8. **Do** attend meetings of La Leche League or other nursing mother associations if available in your area, or write the nearest La Leche League representative for any information or questions you would like answered. The best source of information (in addition to their monthly meetings) is their excellent breast-feeding manual, *The Womanly Art of Breastfeeding.*[7] La Leche League has thousands of groups in the United States and in many

foreign countries. This nondenominational "mothering" group offers the expectant or nursing mother proper information and support with regard to breast-feeding and natural mothering. Even mothers with successful nursing experience in the past have benefited from attendance at these meetings.

9. **Do** attend prepared childbirth classes and have your childbirth experience as unmedicated as possible. Problems with breast-feeding can sometimes be traced to the type of childbirth, and these can lead a mother to abandon the attempt, thus losing the typical period of breast-feeding infertility. For example, a medicated delivery can leave the newborn baby drugged and unable to get off to a good nursing start; and a good start can make the difference in some cases. In addition, separation of mother and baby at the hospital can interfere with the early establishment of a satisfactory nursing relationship.

10. **Don't** be discouraged if your relatives and friends think you are an oddball. Instead, reach for the support that you can find in La Leche League, in the Couple to Couple League, and in the previously mentioned book, *Breast-feeding and Natural Child Spacing.*[8]

For more information about full-time mothering, see Appendix IV.

Advantages

●**Health of baby.** The breast-fed baby is normally healthier than the bottle-fed baby. He will have fewer allergies, fewer chronic ear infections, fewer intestinal diseases, and more built-in immunities. The health advantages of breast-feeding led the Committee on Nutrition of the American Academy of Pediatrics to issue a statement promoting a return to breast-feeding to celebrate the 1979 International Year of the Child.[9]

Breast-fed children will typically have fewer dental problems. In areas where prolonged nursing is common, thumbsucking does not seem to be a problem among older children. Likewise, nursing stimulates the growth of the whole facial area; thus, the incidence of orthodontic cases in cultures where women nurse for several years is much lower than the high incidence noted here in the United States.[10] Breast-feeding is recommended as a preventive measure against tongue thrusting, a frequent dental problem associated with bottle-feeding.[11] Studies have showed that the dental decay rate is lower in breast-fed children.[12] Many formulas have sugar added, and this sugar may do serious harm to baby's teeth. In short, nature's plan provides better health for your youngster, and better health means fewer medical and dental expenses.

There is also some evidence that an ecological breast-feeding relationship of over one year may have long term psychosocial benefits for the child in later years.[13]

● **Health of mother.** Breast-feeding that begins right after delivery reduces the possibility of postpartum hemorrhage, and regular breast-feeding helps the uterus to regain its non-pregnant size more quickly. Judging from the experience of countries where prolonged breast-feeding is common, long term nursing offers protection against breast cancer.[14]

● **Money saved.** First of all there is the avoidance of expenses such as bottles, formulas and baby foods; probably $200.00 to $500.00 is saved here in the first six months depending on cost of formulas and foods. One correspondent mother kept a record of all the expenses of bottle-feeding a baby who developed allergies requiring a more expensive diet. The one year total of $1301.31 made her very sorry that she had not learned of the advantages of breast-feeding before the baby was born. Rather obviously, the overall health benefits of breast-feeding can translate into significant dollar savings, both short term and long term.

Ecological Breast-feeding and Infertility

● **Basic principle.** Frequent suckling of the infant at his mother's breast is the basic ingredient that suppresses ovulation.

● **Duration of natural infertility.** Can breast-feeding affect the birth rate? Sometimes a striking example is helpful. Dr. Otto Schaefer, writing in the November-December, 1971 issue of *Nutrition Today,*[15] noted that the Eskimos' birth rate increased 50 percent as they moved into or near towns and adopted the practice of bottle-feeding. The newer crop of babies likewise had more health problems since they have been deprived of their best food—mother's milk. Away from the influence of urbanization, Eskimo mothers breast-fed from two to four years, with babies arriving about three years apart.

In another study (1969-71), Dr. Schaefer and Dr. J.A. Hildes noted that the Igloolik Eskimo mothers who nursed traditionally conceived 20 to 30 months after childbirth, whereas the younger mothers who were now exposed to "cultural" practices were conceiving two to four months after childbirth.[16]

Research done in Rwanda, a country in Central Africa, demonstrates how cultural practices can affect the duration of breast-feeding infertility.[17] Among the rural women at the time of this study, the baby was in constant contact with the mother (on her back) and was given the breast at any time. In the urban areas, the baby had babysitters and therefore had less physical contact with his mother, and he was nursed according to a schedule. In the rural group, 75% of conceptions occurred between 24 and 29 months postpartum, while in the urban areas 75% of conceptions occurred between six and 15 months postpartum. The authors of the Rwanda study believed that the social factor — the difference in breast-feeding patterns — was responsible for this difference.

In a study conducted by the authors, mothers in the United States who followed the natural mothering program outlined in *Breast-feeding and Natural Child Spacing* and in the preceding pages of this chapter averaged 14.6 months without any menstrual bleeding or periods following child-birth. Individuals, of course, varied from that average. We found four mothers who had menses return before nine months postpartun—one as early as six weeks. We also had a few who experienced no periods for two years due to nursing; one experienced her first period 38 months after childbirth. The most frequent return of menstruation occurred within 13 to 16 months following childbirth. Considering the cultural influences in our society today, we feel this study is significant because it shows that American mothers who are serious about breast-feeding can experience a natural infertility similar to that of nursing mothers in other parts of the world which are not so affected by artificial child care practices.[18]

If mothers appreciate the mothering aspects of breast-feeding and follow the guidelines given in this chapter, both they and their babies will generally be healthier, and most of these mothers will experience an extended period of natural infertility. Generally speaking, those couples who desire a spacing of 18 to 30 months between the births of their children will find breast-feeding sufficient for natural family planning. This, of course, is said only with reference to those who follow the "natural mothering" program.

● **A delicate relationship.** For many women this natural spacing process is a delicate matter. For example, the mother who lets her baby sleep in a separate bed and soon finds that he is sleeping all through the night may find her periods returning. The mother who uses the pacifier or who gives her baby early solids or an occasional bottle may find her periods returning.

Sometimes a mother who leaves her baby with sitters or who relies on "mother substitutes" (for example, excessive use of swing chairs, infant seats, playpens, cribs etc.), may find her periods returning early because these have lessened the baby's suckling at the breast. Nature is usually generous to the mother who is generous and unselfish in meeting her child's emotional and nutritional needs. Nature intended that the mother and baby have a close oneness in their relationship. Thus, physical closeness between mother and baby is an important aspect of natural spacing. Mothers who have followed this pattern for the first time and have given nothing but total love to their baby have found joys and rewards that they never experienced with their other children. Mothers who interfere with this oneness or with nature's plan may find menstruation right around the corner.

There are also those mothers at the other end of the scale who require very little stimulation to hold back their menstrual periods. Some may give only two good nursings a day and still not have a return of menstruation. Some mothers may also use a pacifier or leave the baby with sitters occasionally or not encourage night feedings and still experience a lengthy absence of periods. These mothers would probably experience an even lengthier time of amenorrhea if they followed the natural mothering program. Some mothers who desire another baby and who have a long absence of periods become anxious for their cycles to return in anticipation of another desired pregnancy. However, these mothers generally enjoy waiting on nature and would not consider weaning abruptly for their own interests when the child still needs the nursing relationship.

● **Sex of baby.** Some mothers have reported that they felt they had a lengthy absence of periods while nursing because they had a boy baby (they did not have the same experience with their breast-fed girl babies). On the other hand, some mothers have said that they felt the long absence from menstruation was due to the fact that they were nursing a girl baby. *The important factor is how often and how much a baby nurses,* and this is influenced mostly by mothering practices.

● **No periods: is it natural?** Yes, the extended absence of periods for the ecologically breast-feeding mother is a healthy, normal situation. It helps her regain her strength after pregnancy and childbirth by not losing part of her iron supply through periodic menstruation.

Quite a few nursing mothers have gone back to their doctors for a pap smear and have found that the doctor was concerned that they had not had a period for some twenty months. Some doctors suspect pregnancy, tell the mother to wean, and then administer a pill for a few days which will supposedly cause a "period" if she is not pregnant. This is unnecessary and may be dangerous. First of all, under our self-awareness system the woman would know whether she was pregnant or not. Secondly, the pill may not bring on a "period" when the woman is not pregnant. In one such case, the woman followed her doctor's advice. She weaned her baby and took the pill for three days. When she had no "periods" within two weeks of taking the pill, her doctor said on two different occasions that she was pregnant. She disagreed. About six weeks from the date of weaning, she noticed the more fertile type mucus and had a well-defined thermal shift. If she had believed her doctor and resumed relations, this woman possibly could have become pregnant and the approximate time of conception would not have been accurately known. It is an old story that assuming pregnancy results in pregnancy. Thirdly, the use of progestin pills for this test may be harmful to the baby if the mother is pregnant, according to an FDA rule effective December 11, 1978.

The Return of Fertility

● **A Warning Period?** Many women engaged in ecological breast-feeding will experience a menstrual period before the first postpartum ovulation. However, approximately 15% to 20% of such women will ovulate before a warning period. The actual pregnancy rate is much lower than the rate of ovulation.

● **Chances of pregnancy while nursing.** The chances of becoming pregnant while engaged in ecological breast-feeding *prior to the first postpartum menstruation* vary according to two main factors: age of baby and fertility awareness.

During the first 12 weeks, the chances of pregnancy are practically nil.

During the next three months, there is only a slight chance of pregnancy, perhaps about 1% assuming the baby has not begun solids or liquids other than mother's milk. However, if cervix and mucus symptoms should indicate potential fertility, the couple seeking to avoid pregnancy should consider themselves to be in Phase II.

Babies generally start taking solids in a small way around six months, and after that time the chances of a pregnancy before the first postpartum menstruation depend upon the woman's fertility awareness. If a couple practice no fertility awareness or abstinence, three studies by Remfry[19], Prem[20] and Bonte[21] indicate they have a 5 or 6% chance of becoming pregnant prior to the first menstrual period.

The use of the standard sympto-thermal observations and abstinence during the fertile times can reduce this. However, we cannot be precise on this because it depends upon the woman's ability to detect the cervical and mucus signs of fertility. Our general experience is that most women receive an ample indication of fertility from these signs, even more than they have during regular cycles. In fact, there is sometimes a problem with what hindsight shows to be false alarms—patches of the more fertile mucus that come and go without ovulation occurring.

We repeat that the above estimates of postpartum infertility apply only to the time prior to the return of menstruation.

Ecological breast-feeding after six or seven months no longer refers to "total breast-feeding" in which the only food or drink is mother's milk. Rather, it refers to the continuing practice of complete mother-baby togetherness with the baby nursing whenever he desires but also taking slowly increasing amounts of food from the table. This type of breast-feeding generally provides another six months or more of natural infertility after the baby starts solids, but sooner or later fertility returns.

● **Mucus and cervix signs of returning to fertility.** The standard sympto-thermal observations are used to detect the return of fertility. The best results are obtained by the internal mucus and the cervix observations. However, during the first six months or so, it may be satisfactory for most women to rely upon the external mucus observation made after each urination. The mucus observation should be made on a daily basis but it is not really necessary to record these observations during the months of dryness. Daily record keeping should start according to the following recommendations for starting basal temperatures.

● **Basal temperatures** should be taken when any of the following occur:

1. The appearance of cervical mucus and/or cervical opening or elevation.

2. Menstruation or spotting, even if slight.

3. Any sudden decrease in suckling (due to illness of mother or baby, etc.). This is very important.

4. The start of solid foods if this has been followed by an early return of periods with previous nursing babies.

Another benchmark might be the start of the ninth month postpartum — on the basis of the survey which showed that in 72% of the reported nursing experiences, menstruation returned between 9 and 20 months postpartum.[22]

Temperatures started according to the above indications will provide a good history and a good base for the first pre-ovulation level. Also, in the event of a surprise pregnancy, they will indicate when it occurred. Typically, the basal temperatures for the nursing mother tend to be erratic and somewhat lower than usual. Because of the somewhat erratic temperature patterns and our desire not to cause unnecessary concern, it is not a Couple to Couple League policy to make into a natural family planning rule the practice of taking temperatures before any of the above indications.

Ovulation will normally be preceded by a noticeable mucus discharge. (See figure 10.1) (We think we could say "always" but we say "normally" to take into account some medical quirk.) As has been said several times before, observation of this mucus should give ample warning time that fertility is returning. When examination reveals the presence of mucus, especially when its quality ranges from creamy-thick to the stretchy, raw-egg-white type or when it gives a feeling of vaginal wetness or slipperiness, the couple should certainly refrain from genital contact if pregnancy is not desired.

● **Secondary signs.** Some mothers have reported sore nipples before their first postpartum ovulation. This may be due to high pre-ovulation levels of estrogen. This symptom is not universal but it may provide additional fertility awareness for some.

● **Early fertility detection: two examples.** The cycle history in fig. 10.1 came from a *well experienced* woman. In this chart, the smaller letters indicate small quantities of mucus. Note that there was a long period of mucus that was small in quantity and not accompanied by any significant opening of the cervix. Note also that this woman was in her fifteenth month since childbirth and that the chart shows the return of ovulation and her first

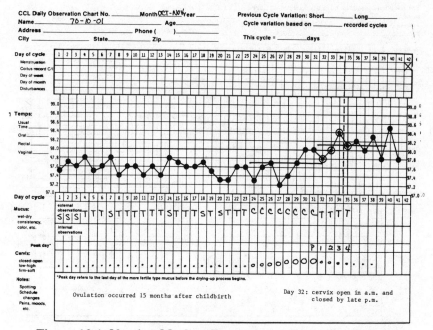

Figure 10.1 Nursing Mother: Detection of Ovulation Before First Menstruation After Childbirth.

menstruation. It is not unusual for nursing mothers to have an extended period of some form of mucus prior to the return of their first ovulation. Some women may even experience mucus during one or more anovulatory cycles before ovulation eventually resumes.

Note also, however, that the mucus that is clear and with threads (indicated by the large C's) is accompanied by a very definite opening of the cervix.

In this chart, the pre-shift base level (PSB) is 97.7 and the thermal shift level is set at 98.1. An overall thermal shift pattern begins on day 30. The post-peak temperatures on days 32-35 qualify as a very strong crosscheck on a 4 day drying-up pattern, thus yielding the evening of day 35 as the start of Phase III by Rule B. Rule C would indicate day 36.

206

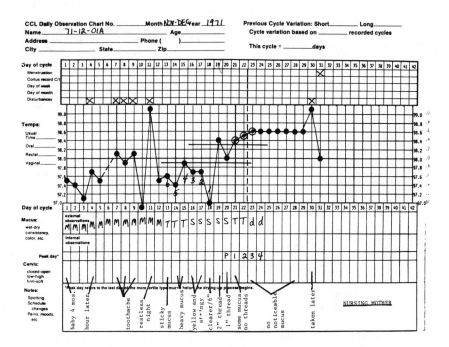

**Figure 10.2 Fertile First Menstrual Period Postpartum:
Detection by an Inexperienced Woman
Practicing Ecological Breast-feeding**

The cycle history in fig. 10.2 came from a *very inexperienced* woman who had learned about NFP and CCL just a few weeks before the first temperature recorded here. She had no previous experience in mucus observation. In fact, she questioned whether she would be able to use this sign, as she felt she had mucus all the time during regular cycles. However, women who have a difficult time observing mucus in later cycles generally find this observation very easy to observe prior to the first menstrual period. Some women may note much wetness instead of clear, stretchy mucus, and this too is an important sign of possible approaching fertility or menstruation.

When her baby was four months old (day 13 on the chart), she observed what she thought was the presence of mucus. She wondered if this was the kind of mucus she was looking for and had a knowledgeable physician examine her. The doctor helped her to identify the thick and sticky mucus then present and advised her to refrain from coitus. Five days later the mucus was clear and would stretch six inches. The next day her temperature rose and two days later (day 21) the mucus began to disappear. Eleven days after the "peak day" (20), menstruation returned.

For interpreting the start of Phase III, the PSB is set at 97.9 and the TSL at 98.3. The first two temperatures above the PSB — 19 and 20 — are ambiguous (as were the temperatures on days 30-32 in fig. 10.1) and are not yet crosschecked by the drying-up of the mucus. Three days of full thermal shift — 21-23 — are crosschecked by the drying up and disappearance of mucus on those same three days to yield the start of Phase III on the evening of day 23 according to Rule A. This chart shows the importance of recording mucus and temperature observations as soon as the mucus begins to appear even while fully breast-feeding day and night. By observing the mucus she became aware that fertility might be approaching, and by taking her temperature she was assured that ovulation had definitely occurred. The importance of temperature recording is stressed in this case because a breast-feeding mother may experience a long period of mucus before her first menstrual period.

While we cannot state that *every* inexperienced woman will observe the symptoms of fertility prior to the first postpartum ovulation, we certainly have evidence that inexperienced women *can* detect them.

● **Ambiguous signs — transition phase.** With both the bottle-feeding mother and the breast-feeding mother, there is a period of transition from postpartum infertility to the return of more or less regular cycles of fertility and infertility. This transition phase is frequently characterized by some ambiguous symptoms of fertility. The difference between bottle-feeding and ecological breast-feeding in this regard is that the transition phase will occur much earlier and may be shorter with bottle-feeding.

For some couples, these ambiguities may entail additional abstinence if they have a most serious need to avoid pregnancy and are concerned about the woman's ability to detect the real beginning of fertility. For both bottle-feeding and breast-feeding couples, it is important to keep in mind that the transition phase is temporary and that the normal fertility patterns will soon return. Because this time can be more extended for the breast-feeding couple, the following comments are directed to them although certain aspects may likewise be applicable to the bottle-feeders. Furthermore, these comments assume that the mother is engaged in ecological breast-feeding.

1. *Time of first appearance.* For all practical purposes, mucus of any kind that appears in the first 12 weeks postpartum can be ignored assuming the presence of ecological breast-feeding and the absence of menstruation or spotting. We assume that there will be an occasional exception, but we have no reason to believe that a couple have over a 1% chance of becoming pregnant during this time under these circumstances.

Beginning with the 13th week, the first appearance of mucus must be treated as the start of Phase II — at least for a while. If it is the more fertile type, the couple must consider themselves in Phase II. If it remains the less fertile type, the situation can change.

208

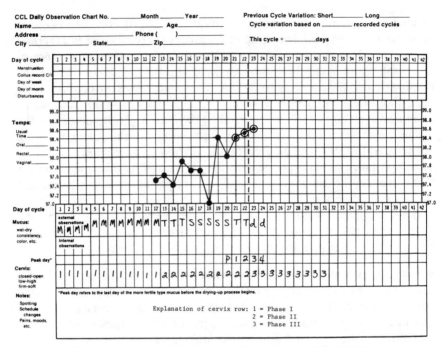

Figure 10.3 Application of "Continuous" Guidelines to Figure 10.2

2. *Continuous less-fertile mucus.* Some women will develop a basic pattern of breast-feeding infertility that is characterized by the continuous presence of the less fertile, merely tacky mucus. As mentioned above, when such a mucus discharge first appears, it must be treated as a symptom of fertility. However, after it has remained as a constant situation for three weeks, then many couples come to regard it as simply a characteristic of her pattern of breast-feeding infertility, and they treat such a time as if it were all dry days. These couples recognize that they are in an extended Phase I type of infertility. By following the standard rules and recommendations for Phase I (not-on-consecutive days and evenings only; internal observation if possible) and by abstaining as soon as the mucus changes towards a more fertile type, such couples continue to run a very low risk of a surprise pregnancy, probably not over 2 or 3%.

This does not apply once menstruation has returned or during regular cycles. That is, during regular cycles, the start of the less fertile mucus must be regarded as the start of Phase II.

For the purposes of illustration in fig. 10.3, let us assume that the woman who gave us the cycle data for fig. 10.2 had been noticing an all-the-time discharge for three weeks prior to the start of this chart and that she and her husband had decided to treat the days of the constant less fertile mucus as if they were "dry days". Thus they considered themselves to be in a Phase I infertility from day 1 through 12 of this charted time. Beginning on day 13, they considered themselves in Phase II because the mucus distinctly changed. This is very important. Even though the mucus on day 13 was not yet the "more fertile type," it was a definite change from the continuous discharge she had experienced for weeks. That change signaled some sort of change in estrogen activity, and thus the change had to be considered the start of Phase II. The mucus soon changed again to the more fertile type. After a few more days, it dried up in conjunction with a thermal shift, and there was a sympto-thermal start of Phase III by day 23.

3. *Patches of mucus.* The breast-feeding mother may also experience patches of mucus that come and go. Sometimes the pattern may consist of patches of the less fertile type mucus interspersed with dry days, and at other times the pattern will consist of days of the more fertile type mucus interspersed with dry days or days of the less fertile type mucus.

For ovulation to occur, there must be several days of higher estrogen activity, and this is normally reflected by the days of the more fertile mucus and by the opening and rising of the cervix. When the more fertile mucus is followed by "drying up" and a thermal shift, the couple are assured that ovulation has occurred. However, when a mucus patch is not followed by a sustained thermal shift, then the couple know that they are still in Phase I or Phase II. The following guidelines refer to patches of less fertile mucus as well as to patches of the more fertile mucus because patches of even the less fertile type mucus against a background of overall dryness indicate a possible change in estrogen activity.

• • *Patches of three days or more.* Abstinence begins with the start of the mucus. If the temperature has begun to rise during the drying-up process, the couple should wait for a sympto-thermal start of Phase III. If the temperature remains low, then Phase I is restarted on the evening of the fourth drying-up day after the end of the mucus patch.

• • *Patches of one or two days.* The more conservative course is to treat these as above. However, if a woman knows from her own past experience that she always experiences at least three or four days of continuous mucus discharge when ovulation occurs during normal cycles, then there is a heavy presumption that a mucus patch of only one or two days during ecological breast-feeding is not associated with ovulation. Abstinence must start when the mucus begins because no one can say at the outset how long it will last. When the drying-up starts, if the temperature should start a thermal shift pattern — very unlikely after such a short patch of mucus — the couple should wait for a sympto-thermal start of Phase III. With the temperature remaining low, the couple may consider themselves back into Phase I on the evening of the second day of drying up.

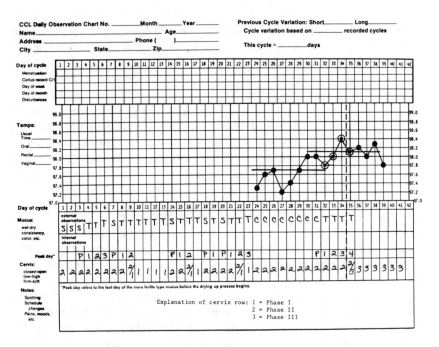

Figure 10.4 Application of Patch Guidelines to Figure 10.1

These guidelines are applied in fig. 10.4 to the mucus pattern of fig. 10.1. The 3 day more fertile mucus patch on days 1, 2 and 3 is followed by three days of "drying up". However, on what would have been the 4th day (day 7), the more fertile mucus returns for a one day patch. Phase I starts on the evening of day 9 indicated here by 2/1. Day 14 is a one day patch and Phase I restarts on 16. Day 18 is a one day patch but is not followed by two days of drying up. The one day patch on day 20 is followed by a restart of Phase I on the evening of day 22, and then Phase II finally begins on day 24.

The obvious concern to couples following such guidelines is that they may have coitus on the day before it is obvious that Phase II has started. Because of the usually ample warning given prior to the first postpartum ovulation, the risk of pregnancy from such an occurrence is small. Assuming that ovulation occurs no earlier than Peak day minus 2, in fig. 10.3 ovulation would occur no earlier than day 18. In this case, coitus on the last day of Phase I (12) would require a sperm survival of more than five days for conception. While not impossible, it is very unusual. In fig. 10.4, the last day of any Phase I infertility was day 23. Again, a sperm survival of over five days would have been required for conception.

4. *Help from the cervix.* The woman who has learned the cervix signs of fertility and infertility can be greatly assisted during times of ambiguous or on-and-off mucus symptoms. The cervix that remains low, firm and closed gives her a considerable boost in confidence in recognizing the infertility of a continuous less fertile type mucus discharge and in applying the patch guidelines described above. Referring to fig. 10.1, with hindsight it can be seen that the cervix symptom provided a better indicator of infertility than the mucus, but the patches of the more fertile type mucus could not be ignored.

5. *Color of vaginal walls.* Additional help in the clarification of postpartum fertility and infertility may be gained from the color of the vaginal walls. During deep infertility, they are ruby red in color. When fertility returns, they are more pinkish. While this is physiologically the case, we are not sure how helpful it will be in any given case that is otherwise ambiguous. We pass it on for whatever help it may give to an occasional couple.

• **Summary comment.** The above discussion has been intended to alleviate unnecessary worry caused by sometimes ambiguous signals from the mucus symptom. Couples should keep all of this in a proper perspective. If other couples who practice no fertility awareness and no abstinence have only about a 6% chance of becoming pregnant before the first postpartum menstruation, then certainly the couple practicing fertility awareness and periodic abstinence can be reassured that they are significantly reducing that possibility. We have not yet been able to run a controlled study of couples following these guidelines, but we doubt very much that couples following them have over a 3% chance of becoming pregnant prior to the first menstruation. After the first postpartum true menstruation, the couple must assume they are back into regular cycles and treat all the less fertile type mucus as indicating the beginning of Phase II.

A continued low temperature pattern after a mucus patch indicates that ovulation did not occur and thus that conception has not occurred.

The Return of Menstruation

As a general rule, the return of menstruation signals the return of fertility and the couple are advised to consider themselves back in a cyclical pattern of fertility and infertility. However, this is not always or immediately the case.

• **Suppression of menstruation.** Sometimes after an initial menstruation, further menstrual periods are suppressed or delayed for a considerable time, especially if the first menstruation occurs in the first six months. Cases of menstruation being suppressed from one month postpartum to 16 months have been reported. In other cases, ovulation may be delayed within a cycle; this long cycle may give the appearance of having missed a period. These situations occur for different reasons such as (1) a child's illness with resulting increased nursing, (2) a mother's change in mothering which increased the nursing, or (3) special circumstances which increase or decrease the nursing.

An example of one such circumstance might be a family's move from one place to another. The effect upon the child may be such that he increases his nursing for a few days or weeks. In another special circumstance, family gatherings on holidays or a vacation away from home can result in decreased nursing. In these situations, the mother may feel restricted when being around those who do not have favorable attitudes toward breast-feeding. Her period may return within a few weeks due to limited nursing during the time spent with relatives or friends. (This latter situation is unfortunate because normally trips to strange places and among strange people should continue to suppress cycles since babies usually require more nursing for emotional reasons when exposed to a new situation.) Once the mother reestablishes her old nursing pattern, she may find her periods are suppressed once again.

Some mothers have a bleeding episode at about six weeks postpartum but then have no periods for many months. Such a one-time "period" may not be a true menstruation but a form of bleeding due to changing hormonal patterns. In some cases, a hospital environment which greatly restricts nursing immediately from birth could be a factor for an early return of menstruation before the cycles are once again inhibited.

There are mothers, however, who will experience their first period soon after childbirth and will attempt to suppress their cycles once again by nursing more often but will still continue to have their periods.

After an initial menstruation or spotting, the sympto-thermal observations should be charted for six weeks. If there are no further signs of fertility, notations on the chart may be discontinued, but the observation for the start of mucus should continue to be made several times a day.

● **Transition cycles.** The first few cycles after the first menstruation are frequently part of an overall transition and are characterized by patterns that would be considered irregular under normal circumstances.

Delayed ovulation, longer cycles with an extended Phase II, and a short luteal phase are rather common at first. In fig. 10.5, the start of the less fertile mucus on day 14 indicates the beginning of Phase II. (This chart is the continuation of the cycle history shown in fig. 10.2.)

The breast-feeding mother in this case had an early return of fertility, and the baby continued a very heavy pattern of ecological breast-feeding. It would appear that the extended Phase II is a result of conflicting signals — the ovulation supression signals from the breast-feeding versus other ovulation stimulus signals. Ovulation finally occurred, probably between

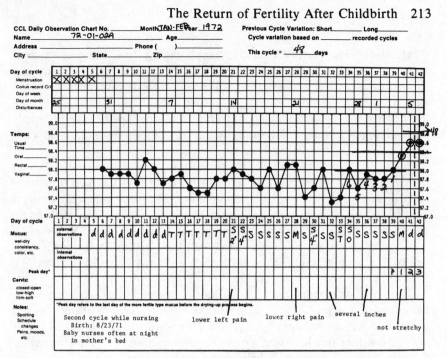

Figure 10.5 A Transition Cycle

days 38 and 40. With a PSB of 98.0, Rule R indicates the start of Phase III on the evening of day 42. The nine day luteal phase as measured by elevated temperatures (days 40-48) is a bit on the short side, but many women will experience an even shorter luteal phase in the first one or two postpartum cycles.

The length of the transition phase will vary; during this time Phases I and II will become shorter, and Phase III will become longer as the cycle pattern shortens to its normal range.

Do not use the length of the immediate postpartum cycles for applying the 21 day rule, since each cycle may be shorter than the previous ones. If using the 21 day rule, base it on your pre-pregnancy cycles.

● **Infertile cycles.** The twelve charts comprising fig. 10.6 illustrate a case of early menstruation followed by several infertile cycles. The first menstruation occurred at four and a half months postpartum despite the fact that the woman was very definitely engaged in ecological breast-feeding.

The first two cycles (January-March and March-April) were definitely anovulatory (without ovulation) as indicated by the absence of any thermal shift.

In the third cycle (April-May), ovulation may have occurred, followed by a very short thermal shift pattern. Such a cycle may have been infertile since it is believed that implantation does not take place unless the lining is maintained for at least nine days after ovulation. Thus cycles with luteal phases of less than nine days are sometimes called infertile. However, if conception should occur, it is possible that the HCG from the newly conceived life can maintain the corpus luteum and thus the endometrium. We evaluate cycle 3 as possibly fertile.

Cycle 4 postpartum was anovulatory; cycle 5 was also probably anovulatory. Cycles 6 and 7 seem to indicate infertile ovulations; cycle 8 indicates a fertile ovulatory cycle; cycle 9 is questionable; and cycles 10, 11 and 12 indicate fertile ovulatory cycles. Throughout the year covered by this sequence of charts, the baby continued to nurse regularly day and night.

In this sequence, the cycles beginning with cycle 4 were of typical length with a relatively short luteal phase when ovulation occurred. In the ensuing months, as the baby nursed less, Phase II shortened and the luteal phase gradually lengthened while the overall cycle length remained about the same.

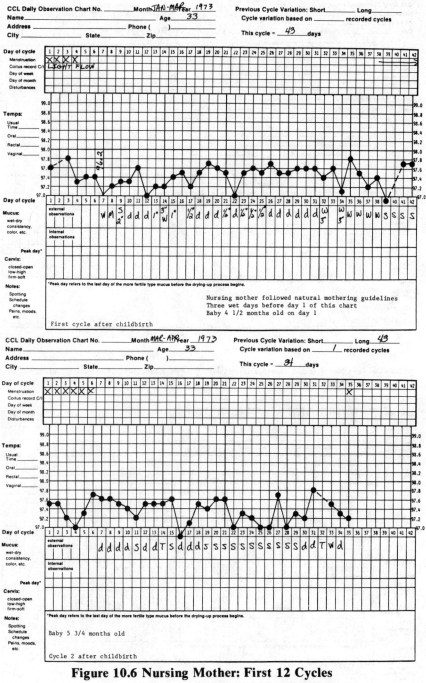

**Figure 10.6 Nursing Mother: First 12 Cycles
after the Return of Menstruation
(page 1 of 6)**

216

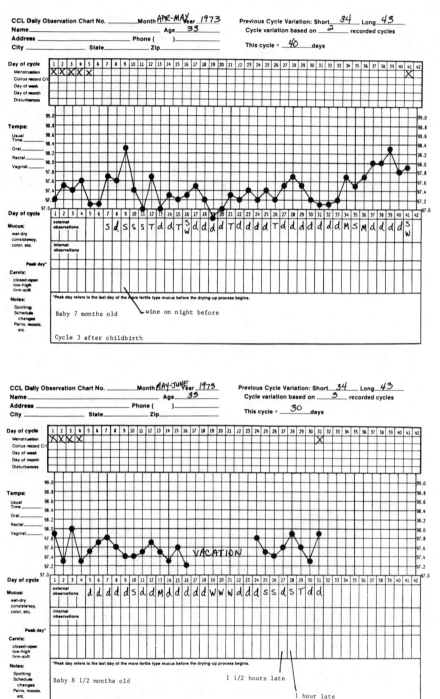

Figure 10.6 (page 2 of 6)

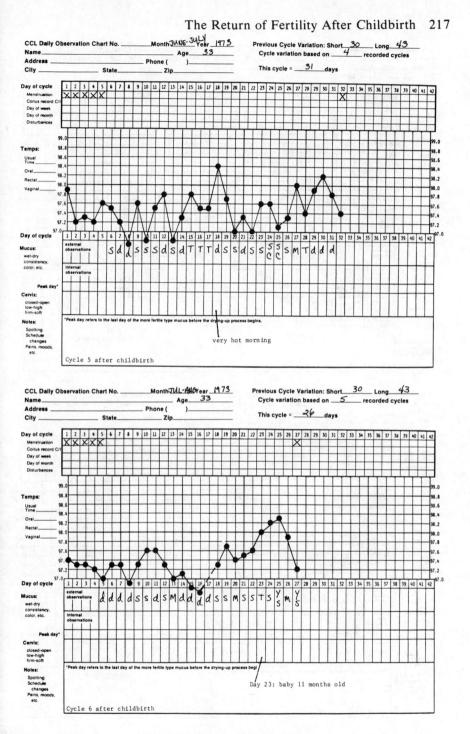

Figure 10.6 (page 3 of 6)

218

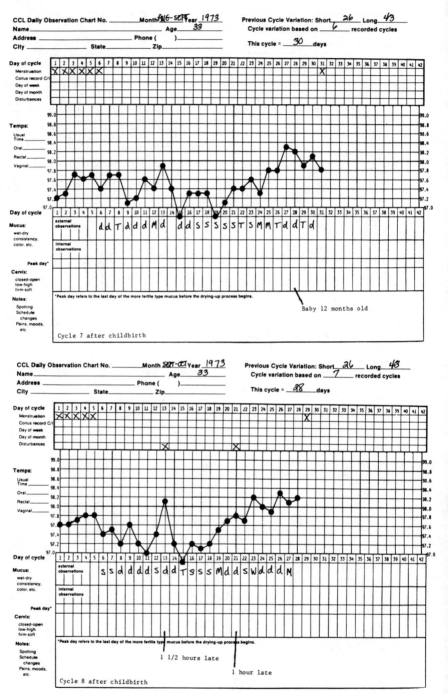

Cycle 7 after childbirth

Baby 12 months old

1 1/2 hours late

1 hour late

Cycle 8 after childbirth

Figure 10.6 (page 4 of 6)

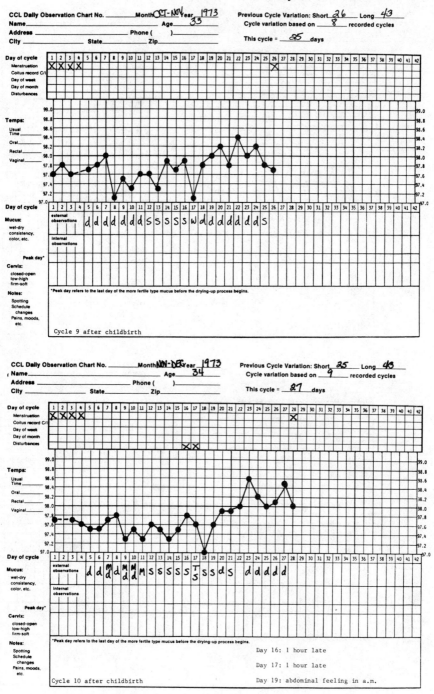

Figure 10.6 (page 5 of 6)

220

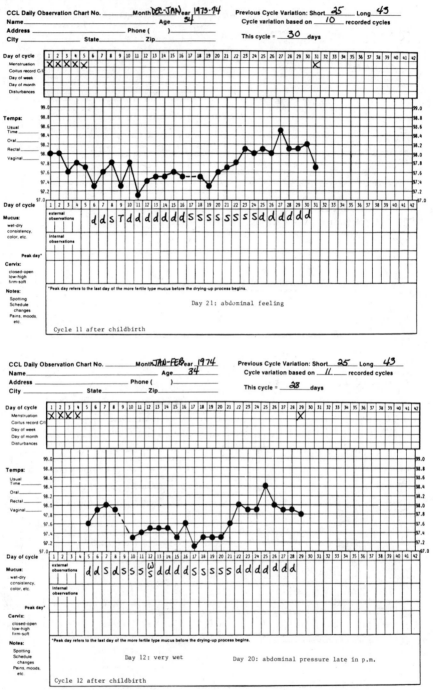

Figure 10.6 (page 6 of 6)

Some General Questions

- *Can any mother nurse?*

In the briefest terms, yes; any normal woman can nurse. However, the ignorance and misinformation about breast-feeding in a bottle-feeding culture have led many women to think that they could not nurse successfully.

One of the most common reasons for an unsuccessful nursing experience may be a fear of an inadequate milk supply, a fear sometimes caused by a belief that a baby should nurse only every four hours. Rarely will a nursing baby go that long between nursings. The uninformed mother may believe that the baby wants to nurse more frequently because it didn't get enough milk. However, breast-fed babies nurse frequently because breast milk is so much more readily digested and absorbed. Nature intends the baby to nurse frequently, and it is frequent suckling that normally provides the side effect of extended natural infertility.

We suggest that mothers interested in breast-feeding attend the classes of La Leche League (LLL) or other responsible nursing mother associations. We know of individual mothers who were told by their doctors that they couldn't nurse because of their milk, their blood, their medication, or their physical condition and who have gone on to nurse their babies with success after gaining the support of such organizations. We always recommend that any mother who is told to wean — no matter what the reason — should contact a LLL representative or the LLL medical advisory board first, if she still desires to continue a nursing relationship with her child.

Any woman can nurse, but no woman should nurse while taking any form of the birth control Pill, including the minipill. The Pill may decrease or dry up the mother's milk supply, the artificial hormones may affect the baby through the mother's milk, and the Pill can significantly reduce the protein content of breastmilk.

- *Can a mother nurse during menstruation or throughout pregnancy?*

Yes; menstruation and pregnancy are not reasons to wean. Mothers have nursed through an entire pregnancy and have given birth to healthy babies. In our culture, it is commonly thought that a woman should wean during early pregnancy. We know of women who have weaned due to a pregnancy but then later had a miscarriage or a stillborn baby; they sadly regretted their decision to wean. One mother noted the difference between the child that had been weaned during pregnancy and the child that nursed throughout pregnancy. The weaned child was very hostile towards the new baby, but the nursing child accepted the baby and remained a very happy toddler after being displaced from the breast. She felt this was an added bonus to prolonged nursing.

Sometimes weaning occurs naturally during pregnancy; the mother finds nursing uncomfortable due to tender breasts or hormonal changes in her body, or the child appears not to like the taste of milk during pregnancy or the colostrum which develops in the latter months of pregnancy.

- *What causes spotting?*

Any treatment such as a pap smear or cauterization may cause spotting or slight bleeding for a few days. This is related to the treatment and not to the menstrual cycle.

The normal type of spotting seems to indicate that ovulation and regular menstruation may be just around the corner. The spotting may occur for only one or two days, or it may occur on and off for one or two weeks.

We know of a few women who have become pregnant within a short time after the first spotting. Therefore, any spotting — no matter how slight — may be a sign that fertility or menstruation is returning. If the woman is not already doing so, she should begin making mucus observations and recording temperatures for six weeks as with an initial early menstruation.

A woman who has extensive, prolonged spotting should see her doctor.

- *With so much emphasis placed on natural mothering and breastfeeding, where does the husband fit in?*

The husband is of particular value to the nursing relationship in providing support and love to both wife and baby. In addition, while the wife is experiencing a deeply satisfying relationship with the baby, she must also remember that her husband still needs to know that he's very special. Deepened communication and extra signs of marital love and affection should be present between husband and wife so that the husband does not feel neglected and does not feel that time his wife spends with the baby is time taken away from him.

A mature husband will appreciate the benefits of the nursing relationship and will be proud that his wife is giving their baby the very best care. Furthermore, he should be sharing in parenthood by cuddling and holding the baby. Such caring for his child's needs will help to make him more aware both of the time involved and the satisfaction that can be gained by relating to and enjoying his baby.

- *What happens to a nursing mother's sexual desire?*

The nursing literature indicates that many nursing mothers experience an increase in sexual desire, but that is by no means universal. Other nursing mothers experience a reduced sexual drive, and fatigue can further reduce sexual interest or response.

Rare is the husband who will complain if his breast-feeding wife has an increased sexual desire, but the case of reduced desire requires mutual understanding. On his part, he will be understanding, not demanding, and he will assist her with the baby and around the house to reduce fatigue. On

her part, she will recognize that she is still his wife and that he is most likely
not experiencing a similar reduction in sexual desires. In a marriage
characterized by caring love, the couple will still be able to experience the
coital expression of mutual love under these circumstances.

• *Are there sometimes fairly long periods of refraining from coitus when the
wife is following the program of ecological breast-feeding and baby-led
weaning?*

For the couple who are extremely serious about avoiding another pregnancy, there can be some fairly long periods of refraining from coitus
because of uncertainty about possible fertility, especially during the time of
transition from breast-feeding amenorrhea and infertility to the resumption
of regular cycles. For example, a breast-feeding mother may have a
menstrual period and then go for well over a month before ovulating. If a
couple had decided to wait until the beginning of Phase III, they may have
an extended period of coital abstinence.

Or, for another example, a woman may have extended periods of mucus.
It may not be the more fertile type associated with ovulation, but the couple
may not be willing to risk a mistake in judgment about the type of mucus,
especially if she is inexperienced in this observation.

Some couples may choose to accept the slight risk of pregnancy inherent
in using the dry day rules during Phase I; they may learn to make use of the
dry days between patches of mucus as explained previously. Other couples
may choose to refrain from coitus until there are definite signs of being in
Phase III.

• *If the couple choose the more conservative course, will such coital
abstinence affect their marriage?*

Some people think that any extended abstinence will adversely affect a
marriage, and some think that other couples will refuse a course of action
that entails some sexual self-control even if they themselves will accept it.
Thus, some have routinely encouraged early weaning in the hopes of establishing regular cycles soon after childbirth.

It is our opinion and experience that couples are willing and able to
accept some lengthy periods of coital continence if they have sufficient
motivation (e.g., putting the baby's needs before theirs) and keep up their
noncoital means of communicating love and affection. In fact, the marital
relationship, far from being adversely affected, can actually be improved
during periods of extended coital continence, as is indicated by the following letter from a reader.

> The baby had a bout of pneumonia in early December. She had to be put
> in the hospital for a time. My good doctor got us a private room so I could
> stay with her. Molly, however, went on a nursing strike and after we got
> home things began to happen. We noticed all sorts of signs pointing to
> menstruation, and although Molly started breast-feeding when we got home

I got my period about six weeks later. We did pretty well though — Molly was then 11-3/4 months old. We are following the manual like a bible. We are now in a cycle and no signs of anything! Temps show nothing and there has been very little mucus. Thus far we have abstained for ten weeks — I do hope I get that second period! Actually all is going very well and I am wondering if we are abnormal: it isn't bothering us. In fact, we are closer than ever before.

• *Can sexual satiation be a problem during pregnancy and extended breast-feeding infertility?*

Sometimes yes. The periodic abstinence in normal cycles for couples postponing pregnancy is psychologically healthy but is lost as a "necessity" during pregnancy and postpartum infertility. Some couples will mutually agree upon periodic abstinence during these times in order to avoid sexual satiety.

Rather obviously, these last three questions point up that the sexual relationship during the time of breast-feeding infertility varies from couple to couple and according to the clarity of fertility and infertility.

• *Are there any general recommendations for nursing mothers who are interested in the natural mothering program that haven't been mentioned yet?*

Yes. The nursing mother should eat nutritionally balanced meals and get sufficient rest during the night (which she can do if she is sleeping with the baby) and a good nap during the day. A woman who does excessive work around the house or continues to have a heavy, demanding schedule may find her milk supply decreasing. This influence on the milk supply may mean a return of her periods.

Summary of Natural Mothering, Breast-feeding and Child Spacing Program

● Basic Principles

1) The suckling stimulation by the baby at the breast when repetitious and frequent inhibits the return of fertility.

2) Natural mothering almost always provides this adequate stimulation. By natural mothering we mean that type of baby care which follows the natural ecology of the mother-baby relationship. It is characterized by mother-baby togetherness, avoids the use of artifacts, and follows the baby initiated patterns. It is characterized by the items in Part I and II below.

● Part I of Natural Mothering: MOTHER ONLY

This phase usually produces infertility as long as the package is complete. What's in the package?

—Use of the breast for pacification

—Frequent nursing

—Sleeping with or near baby (night feedings)

—Absence of schedules

—Absence of bottles or pacifiers or early cups

—Absence of any practice which tends to restrict nursing or to separate mother and baby

—Total breast-feeding in the early months

● **Part II of Natural Mothering: MOTHER PLUS OTHER SOURCES**

—Begins when baby starts solids from the regular meal table. Liquids are begun later, again when baby begins on his own.

—Continues over a period of a year or two or more until baby gradually loses interest in nursing.

—Includes what may be a long period when the baby will be nursing as much for emotional reasons as for nutrition.

Part II is a very gradual program in which the amount of nursing is 1) not decreased at all at first and 2) lessened only gradually at baby's pace. For the majority of mothers, Part II will be longer than Part I with regard to natural infertility if the natural mothering program is followed. Our survey indicated an average of 14.6 months of amenorrhea for mothers following this form of mothering.

● **Risk of Pregnancy.** Under the natural mothering program there is about a 1% chance of pregnancy occurring before the first menstruation during the "mother-only" phase assuming regular coitus and no form of birth control. Once the baby begins solids and other liquids, there is about a 6% chance of pregnancy occurring before the first menstruation without any fertility awareness or abstinence. The Couple to Couple League helps mothers to reduce this risk by teaching them to observe the mucus and cervical signs which occur before ovulation.

● **Natural Spacing by Breast-feeding Alone.** For those couples who desire 18-30 months between the births of their children, "natural mothering" should be sufficient.

References

1. Nancy M. Cohen and Lois J. Estner, *Silent Knife: Cesarean Prevention and Vaginal Birth After Cesarean,* (Bergin & Harvey Publishers, Inc., 1983, soft cover). Available through CCL.

2. T.J. Cronin, "Influence of Lactation upon Ovulation," *Lancet* (1968), 422.

3. Konald Prem, "Post-Partum Ovulation." Unpublished paper presented at La Leche League International Convention, Chicago, July 1971.

4. Sheila Kippley, *Breast-feeding and Natural Child Spacing: The Ecology of Natural Mothering* (New York: Harper & Row, 1974; Penguin paperback, 1975). Available through CCL as well as at most bookstores.

5. "Anemia: Rare in Breast-fed Babies." This pamphlet is available from the La Leche League, Franklin Park, Illinois.

6. For the lay person we recommend Dr. Richard Applebaum's book, *Abreast of the Times,* which is available only through the La Leche League and the International Childbirth Education Association. For the medical professional we recommend the following booklet:

226

D.B. Jelliffe and E.F.P. Jelliffe, "The Uniqueness of Human Milk," reprinted from *The American Journal of Clinical Nutrition,* 24 (August 1971).

7. This breast-feeding manual is available through the Couple to Couple League as well as from La Leche League.

8. Kippley, op.cit.

9. "Breast-feeding: A Commentary in Celebration of the International Year of the Child," *Pediatrics* 62:4 (October, 1978).

10. Mary White, "Breast-feeding: First Step Toward Preventive Dentistry," *La Leche League News,* (July-August, 1972), 57.

11. Daniel Garliner, *"Your Swallow: An Aid to Dental Health,"* pamphlet. The Gulf Building, Suite 715, 95 Merrick Way, Coral Gables, Florida.

12. White, op. cit.

13. Niles Newton, "Psychologic differences between breast and bottle-feeding," *The American Journal of Clinical Nutrition,* 24 (August, 1971), 993-1004.

14. Newton, "Mammary Effects," op.cit., 989.

15. Otto Schaefer, "When the Eskimo Comes to Town," *Nutrition Today,* (November-December, 1971), 15-16.

16. J.A. Hildes and O. Schaefer, "Health of Igloolik Eskimos and Changes with Urbanization." Paper presented at the Circumpolar Health Symposium, Oulu, Finland, June, 1971.

17. Monique Bonte, Emmanuel Akingeneye, Mathias Gashakamba, Etienne Mbarutso and Marc Nolens, "Influence of the Socio-economic Level on the Conception Rate during Lactation," *International Journal of Fertility,* (1974), 97-102.

18. S.K. Kippley and J.F. Kippley, "The Relation Between Breast-feeding and Amenorrhea: Report of a Survey," *JOGN Nursing,* (November-December, 1972), 15-21.

19. Leonard Remfry, "The Effects of Lactation on Menstruation and Pregnation," *Transactions of the Obstetrical Society of London,* 38 (1897) 22-27. Found a pregnancy rate of 5% prior to the first period among breast-feeding mothers.

20. Prem, op. cit. Found a pregnancy rate of 6% prior to the first period among fully breast-feeding mothers.

21. Monique Bonte and H. van Balem, "Prolonged Lactation and Family Spacing in Rwanda," *Journal of Biosocial Science,* 1:2 (April, 1969), 97-100. Conceptions during breast-feeding prior to the first period were on the order of 5.4%.

22. Kippley and Kippley, op. cit.

Analysis of practice chart at end of Chapter 8 (fig. 8.17).

End of Phase I:

Clinical experience: day 6

21 day rule: not applicable (less than six cycles of experience)

Last dry day: not applicable (less than six cycles of experience)

Pre-shift six temperatures: days 10 to 15

Pre-shift base level: 97.7

Thermal shift level: 98.1

First three days consecutively at full thermal shift level:

18, 19, and 20

"Peak" day: 15

First day of cervix closing: not applicable

Start of Phase III:

Rule C: day 20   Rule B: day 19   Rule R: 18

This same chart appears as Chart 4 in the CCL *Practical Applications Workbook* where it is analyzed in greater detail.

11

Putting NFP Into Practice

Let's assume you have just finished the first CCL class (or have just browsed through this book). How do you get started? Whether you are seeking to achieve or avoid pregnancy, the starting procedure is the same: abstain until you know you are in Phase III, the time of post-ovulation infertility.

The First Steps

1. Mrs. A., figure out where you are in your cycle, that is, how many days it has been since the start of your last period. If it's been 20 days, then start your recordings on day 20 of the CCL daily observation chart. Start making your mucus observations, at least externally, today—after each urination. If you are ready to start the cervix observation, then record those observations too; and while you are doing that, you might as well try the internal mucus observation.

2. Mr. A. Tonight, shake down the thermometer over the bed; tomorrow morning, give it to your wife when the alarm goes off. After 5 to 7 minutes, take it back, record it on the temperature graph, and store it someplace out of sight and out of reach of little people's hands. A top dresser drawer usually is best.

Important Reminders

1. Keep loving each other regardless of whether you are having coitus or not. Periods of sexual restraint can be periods of care and consideration; they need not be periods of restraint from all physical embracing. Keep up the marital courtship and enjoy the honeymoon later on.

2. Keep your attitudes positive and work together as a team. With the proper attitudes you can go for extended periods without coitus, and your marriage will grow rather than weaken.

3. Keep good records on a daily basis. Incomplete records greatly complicate the process of interpretation.

4. Feel free to seek technical or personal support from members of the Couple to Couple League or other natural family planning groups.

A Brief Review

●**Mucus.** Review pages 97-105.

Remember that the mucus observations must be made periodically throughout the day. The beginning of the mucus discharge, even the less fertile type, signals the start of the fertile time. The internal observation will sometimes reveal the appearance of mucus a day or more before it is noticed externally.

Record your observations at the end of each day. Be sure to mark "D" when you are "dry." Use the symbols at the bottom of the chart for the other recordings. The more fertile mucus is described in various ways: clear or cloudy, stretchy, being like raw egg white, producing sensations of vaginal lubrication or wetness.

The **peak day** is simply the last day of the more fertile type mucus, and it can be labeled after 2 to 4 days of drying up that follow it. The Rule C rule of thumb recommended for beginners requires 4 days of drying up past the peak day to cross check the temperature rise for the start of Phase III, the time of postovulation infertility.

●**Cervix.** Review pages 106-110.

Examine the cervix several times daily but not the first thing in the morning. Use the same position. During the infertile phases, the cervix is easier to reach and firm. As ovulation approaches, the cervix becomes more difficult to reach and becomes softer; the end of it opens a little, usually enough to accept a finger tip.

Record the cervix changes by using the symbols given on the chart.

Both the mucus and the cervix observations may take between 2 and 6 cycles to develop skill in observation and confidence in interpretation.

●**Ovulation Pain.** Review page 110.

This is a secondary but still sometimes useful symptom.

●**Temperature.** Review pages 111-121.

Use a basal thermometer and take your temperatures either orally, rectally or vaginally. Take the temperature for 5 to 7 minutes upon awakening, and take it at the same time each day during Phase II. In case of a variation of 1/2 hour or more, indicate the time on the chart.

Read the thermometer and mark the reading on the chart. If the temperature is right between 2 lines on the thermometer, consistently use the lower reading. Also record any disturbances that might have affected the temperature such as a cold or a fever.

To determine the postovulation thermal shift, ask yourselves two questions:

1. Are there at least 3 temperatures above the previous 6 temperatures?

2. Are those 3 temperatures **enough** above the pre-shift six to fulfill the requirements for a Phase III rule of thumb?

After you find 3 temperatures above the previous 6 temperatures, the following terms are used. The 6 temperatures immediately before the upward shift begins are called the **pre-shift six**. The normal high temperatures among the pre-shift six set the **pre-shift base level (PSB)**.

The Rule C recommended for beginners in the first two or three cycles requires three temperatures that are consecutively at least 4/10 of 1°F. above the PSB to crosscheck at least 4 days of drying up past the peak day.

●**Phase I: Pre-ovulation infertility.** Review pages 128-135.

We strongly suggest that you abstain from all genital contact during Phase I for the first 2 or 3 cycles when just starting on natural family planning even if you want to become pregnant very soon. In this way, Mrs. A. will be able to become familiar with the onset of her mucus pattern without any interference from seminal residue or vaginal mucus from sexual excitement. With the experience gained at this time, the woman who achieves pregnancy soon will know what she is looking for when fertility returns after childbirth.

When you are ready to start having coitus in Phase I, be sure to review the rules on the pages listed above. There you will find 3 different ways to determine an end of Phase I. We suggest not going beyond day 5 or day 6 until you have at least 6 cycles of experience and Mrs. A. is confident about her mucus and cervix observations. The day 5 rule assumes short cycles in the 23-25 day range; the day 6 rule assumes short cycles of 26 days and longer.

●**Phase II: The Fertile Time.** Review page 135.

If you have had difficulty in achieving pregnancy, be sure to review the appropriate section in connection with figure 8.2 in Chapter Eight and also Appendix II. If you are seeking to avoid or postpone pregnancy, the fertile time calls for creative continence. Review Chapter 4 on marriage building to help make this time one of growth in your marital relationship.

●**Phase III: Postovulation Infertility.** Review pages 136-143.

When you are just beginning the sympto-thermal method, we suggest that you use the most conservative rule of thumb, Rule C, for the first 2 or 3 cycles. That means waiting for the third day of full thermal shift and the fourth day of drying up, whichever comes later. We also suggest that beginners add an extra day to the beginning of Phase III for the first couple of cycles as a precaution against possible misinterpretations. If your temperature pattern doesn't seem to form the **full** thermal shift pattern called for by Rule C (and Rule A too), get in touch with your local CCL teacher or with us at CCL Central for assistance with interpretation when just getting started. After those first 2 or 3 cycles, you may be ready to apply Rules A, R and B where applicable. Remember that Phase III begins in the **evening** of the day indicated by a particular rule of thumb.

The First Few Cycles

Experience is of great help in natural family planning, and we suggest the following steps while you gain that experience.

● **Your First Incomplete Cycle**

If you start the sympto-thermal method early enough in your cycle to establish a pre-shift six and a thermal shift, you should be able to determine clearly the start of Phase III by one of the rules mentioned in the next section below. If you start observations too late to establish a pre-shift six and a subsequent thermal shift, we recommend abstinence during the first incomplete cycle.

● **Your First Complete Cycle**

Begin a new chart with the first day of menstruation. Begin your mucus observation right after menstruation or by day 6 at the latest. Abstain during Phase I and Phase II during the first 2 or 3 cycles.

Use **Rule C** to determine the start of Phase III and add 1 day as a precaution against misinterpretation due to inexperience. The evening of the day indicated by Rule C plus 1 day should be well into postovulation infertility with almost no chance of pregnancy.

Or, if the mucus is of little or no help in the first cycle, you may want to use the **4-day temperature-only** rule (see page 141) and add the extra day for beginners.

If you are **coming off the pill,** be sure to review the special 5 day temperature-only rule (pages 142-143). This rule already has the extra day for beginners built into it.

Thus, it is apparent that if you have a good indication of being in Phase III by one of the above rules, it is not necessary to abstain during Phase III of the first complete cycle.

● **Your 2nd and 3rd Cycles**

We recommend abstinence during Phases I and II during your first 2 or 3 complete cycles. As Mrs. A. gains skill in her mucus and/or cervix observations and as you both gain confidence in the interpretation of your temperatures, you can drop the "extra day for beginners," but you may still want to use the conservative Rule C to determine the start of Phase III.

● **Cycles Four Through Six**

If Mrs. A. has not had cycles shorter than 26 days in the last two years, you can consider yourselves to have a 99% probability of being in Phase I up through day 6. Depending upon the strength of the temperature shift and the clarity of the drying-up of the mucus, you might start using Rule A, Rule R and Rule B interpretations for the start of Phase III.

● **After Six Cycles**

Six cycles of experience should be sufficient for most couples to use either the 21 day rule or the "last dry day" to determine the end of Phase I. Be sure to review the details on the pages given above for Phase I.

In the Swing of Things: Various Examples

Once a couple gain sufficient experience, their practice of NFP will most likely fall into a fairly regular pattern. The following examples may help to give the beginner a good idea of what the practice of NFP will be like for experienced couples depending upon various circumstances.

Couple A (minimum Phase I abstinence)

You are a couple who have two children. You are planning on having more but want to delay the start of pregnancy for another year. Mrs. A's shortest cycle has been 27 days.

As Mrs. A. you will begin making and recording mucus observations (and probably cervix observations, too) as soon as your period ends or by day 6 at the latest. You have noted that both the 21 day rule and clinical experience rules have indicated day 6 as the end of Phase I. Confident in your mucus and cervix observations, you go beyond day 6 but do not have coitus before evening or on consecutive days.

As soon as you notice the beginning of a mucus discharge or some changes in the cervix, you call your husband's attention to it. You both decide whether to accept pregnancy now or to limit your display of love and affection to non-genital ways. You discuss the matter long before going to bed. If you choose to avoid pregnancy, you avoid genital contact beginning with the first day of the show of cervical mucus. You notice that in a few days the mucus has become clear and stretchy, and then it begins to thicken and dry up again. You perhaps notice a little "ovulation pain" about this same time. Then, your temperature records show that your basal temperature is going up. You experience several "dry" days that coincide with a sustained higher temperature level. When the sympto-thermal signs indicate the beginning of Phase III, you resume coital relations with confidence that you are in the phase of postovulation infertility. On the chart, you mark down the first day of your next period.

Aside from differences in family size, this will be the typical family planning process for many couples.

Couple B (using the 21 day rule or clinical experience rules)

You have serious reasons for wanting to avoid pregnancy at this time. You do not want to run the slight risk of not noticing the start of the mucus pattern and therefore you want to be more conservative than Couple A. For at least six months you have been limiting coitus to Phase III. During this six-month period, your shortest cycle has been 25 days and your longest cycle has been 30 days.

According to the 21 day rule, Phase I ends on day 4 (25-21 =4) and thus you, as Mr. and Mrs. B., may decide not to have coitus beyond day 4. Or, you may decide to consider Phase I as ending on day 5 or day 6 according to the clinical experience guidelines based on the very low fertility potential of those days. However, in any case you consider yourselves in Phase II beginning at least by day 7 and do not have genital contact after day 6 until the start of Phase III.

You continue to record carefully all your sympto-thermal observations, and you will use a combination of at least 3 days of thermal shift and 2 to 4 days of drying up (according to Rules A, R, B, or C) to determine the start of Phase III.

Couple C (very cautious)

You have what you consider the most serious reasons for avoiding pregnancy. Unless and until you are very experienced in observing, recording and interpreting the mucus and cervix signs of fertility, you will refrain from genital contact from the beginning of menstruation until the beginning of Phase III. If you decide to have coitus in Phase I, you will follow the more conservative guidelines and will not have coitus beyond days 5 or 6. The chances of becoming pregnant using conservative guidelines for the end of Phase I and the beginning of Phase III are very low and are described in the appropriate sections of Chapter Eight. Some couples with the most serious reasons for avoiding pregnancy may decide to have coitus only in Phase III and to abstain in Phases I and II.

Couple D (great irregularity)

No one is perfectly regular, having a built-in 28-day menstrual clock. Almost all women vary one to five days each month. But when a woman varies from 20 days in one cycle to 45 days in the next cycle, she's irregular—and also an exceptional case. A few of these women may occasionally go for three months between menses. When a woman is highly irregular, it may be advisable to have a doctor check her endocrine functions.

Couple D, if they are serious about avoiding pregnancy, should refrain from genital contact until Phase III begins while Mrs. D. learns how to observe the signs of mucus and cervix. If you are this couple, you will not have coitus during the menstrual flow for at least the first six months of charting. (In a very short cycle, ovulation might occur at or near the end of the menstrual flow.) In the next few cycles, while Mrs. D. is becoming more experienced in detecting and recording the mucus and cervix signs of ovulation, you will refrain from genital contact until Phase III begins (as indicated by mucus, cervix, and the thermal shift sustained into the third day). Once Mrs. D. has become experienced in detecting the mucus and cervix signs of fertility, you may decide to apply the clinical experience rules up through cycle day 6 but should not have coitus beyond day 4 if the menstrual flow or spotting continue on day 5 and beyond. Once menstruation is over and dry days have been established, you can consider yourselves in Phase I infertility, applying the standard Phase I rules of having coitus only in the evening, not on consecutive days, and preference for the internal observation. At the first sign of mucus or the opening or rising of the cervix, you will recognize Phase II and will refrain from genital contact until the beginning of Phase III.

It should be apparent that one of the biggest advantages of the mucus and cervix signs is that they indicate the approach of ovulation. In a long cycle, sexual continence is normally not required for an extended period using these signs, while the couple who rely solely on the thermal shift that comes *after* ovulation may have a rather long period without coital relations.

Although it has been emphasized in previous chapters, we probably should repeat again that coitus prior to ovulation carries with it an inherently higher possibility of conception than coitus in the postovulation infertile stage for two reasons: (1) the possibility of not detecting the mucus or cervix signs, and (2) the possibility of extended sperm survival. For the experienced couple, the first possibility may be extremely small, but some couples with severe irregularity may find the guidelines for Couple C appropriate for them.

Couple E (premenopause) Review pages 158-162.

Mrs. E. is approaching menopause. Her cycles are becoming more irregular. Because of increased motivation to avoid pregnancy at this stage in life, Couple E may adopt a more conservative pattern of interpretation. They decide to end Phase I on day 3 because of the possibility of a very short cycle, although some couples will consider themselves back in Phase I after menstruation and during the days of no mucus or cervix indications of fertility. They also begin requiring a four-day thermal shift pattern for the start of Phase III. If the temperature drops to or below the PSB just before menstruation, they will count the first day of such low temperatures as day 1 of the new cycle. Aside from these changes, Couple E will probably follow a pattern very similar to that of Couple D.

Couple F (nursing mother)

This couple are new parents, and Mrs. F. is nursing her baby according to the natural plan described briefly in this manual. Thus, her menstrual periods may not return for 6, 12, 20, or even 30 months.

Many couples who want only natural spacing between babies will ignore all signs of fertility and look forward to the next pregnancy. Others will decide to use the signs and temperature observation techniques only after the first menstruation.

In most cases, menstruation will occur before the first postpartum ovulation. However, many couples may not want to take the risk of being in that approximately 6 percent of cases in which the woman becomes pregnant before the first period. To reduce that risk, Mrs. F. will begin looking for the pre-ovulation signs of mucus and opening and/or rising of the cervix, especially after the baby has reached six months of age and is eating some solids. She may also begin temperature recordings. When she detects mucus, they will refrain from genital contact. If this is the true pre-ovulatory mucus, she will soon register a sustained rise on the temperature chart (see Chapter 10 for actual cases).

It should be noted that a mother's experience with one baby and postpartum menstruation is no guarantee of the same experience with the next baby and postpartum menstruation. For example, with baby 1 the mother may not ovulate until *after* her first postpartum menstruation, but with baby 2 she could ovulate *before* the first menstruation.

Concluding Remarks

Several things are necessary for successful natural family planning, including motivation, proper instruction, adequate understanding, and cooperative attitudes. Through this manual and through its regular classes, the Couple to Couple League tries to assure proper instruction and adequate understanding. In several chapters and sprinkled throughout other sections are some ideas that can be used by a couple for their own motivation and attitude formation, but it is obvious that couples have to agree with these ideas and make them their own before they can be really helpful.

Undoubtedly, many couples experience occasional difficulties in the practice of natural family planning. However, with the proper attitudes, any such difficulties remain small ones and are turned into stepping stones toward increased marital maturity, mutual self-respect, and true sexual freedom.

In summary, the practice of natural family planning provides an extremely effective method of birth regulation. It does this not only without any harmful physical or psychological side effects but also provides its own benefits of developing the whole person and fostering marital maturity. With almost everybody recognizing the need for some form of birth regulation, and with almost everybody who commented upon Watergate recognizing the need for character development and acting on principle, what's the world waiting for?

The authors hope this manual will serve your needs and prove helpful at every level.

Appendix I: Possible Helps for Irregular Cycles and Pre-Menstrual Tension

This discussion about efforts to reduce cycle irregularity is placed in an appendix to emphasize its speculative nature. In other words, the data about NFP is founded on much experience and research, but the same cannot be said for what is in this section. However, because some of these things apparently work for some people and because none of them appear to have any medically adverse side effects, we have thought it worthwhile to share our thoughts on a couple of efforts to achieve greater cycle regularity.

Nutrition

In one sense, it is definitely established that very poor nutrition affects fertility. Women imprisoned and starved in concentration camps stop menstruating and presumably stop ovulating. The same is true of young women afflicted with anorexia nervosa, the semi-starvation experience in which girls, fearing to add an ounce of weight, stop eating or deliberately vomit up their meals and stay very skinny, sometimes dying of malnutrition. At the other end of the spectrum, it has been reported to us by more than one physician that truly obese women have more cycle irregularity and generally more menstrual problems. One physician noted that the ovarian hormones are fat soluble and that an excess of fat may absorb the ovulation inducing hormones sufficiently to delay ovulation.

We have seen some articles about women athletes indicating that when a strenuous exercise program significantly reduces the normal percentage of body fat, menstruation may be delayed more or less indefinitely. We have also seen anovulatory cycle charts from women who lost about 15 pounds in a month while on a weight reduction program.

● **Overall Diet.** It appears that the overall diet may influence the menstrual cycle since it is well known that it is possible to eat and drink much and still be poorly nourished. In an article that appeared in *the CCL News* (November-December, 1976), Pierre Slightam, M.D., noted that "people who are insulting themselves nutritionally . . . with a diet high in empty refined calories (nutritionless — without vitamins and minerals) will find it is impossible for their bodies to function in a healthy manner . . . (and) to have good balance and control of their nervous systems." In his opinion, "many women would have more regularly spaced natural periods and menstrual

235

cycles if they would eat better. The woman who avoids caffeine and cuts down on sugar, (white) flour and refined or 'factory foods' might not have B-complex deficiencies resulting in a chronic vaginal discharge . . ." which complicates the mucus observation.

● **Some basic nutrition suggestions.** Most of the following ideas are adapted from the article of Dr. Slightam, and variations of these can be found in almost any health book or magazine.

1. Eat "natural" foods, e.g., lean meat, fish, fowl, eggs, cheese, lean non-sweetened dairy products, vegetables, fruits and nuts.

2. Eat vegetables raw or as lightly cooked as possible, and use the cooking juices.

3. Drink pure water (if you can get it), milk, and unsweetened fruit juices.

4. Avoid refined flour and sugar and factory foods containing these because most of the nutrition has been refined away.

5. Avoid artificial preservatives and dyes.

6. Avoid caffeine. This comes in coffee, tea, chocolate and cocoa, and cola drinks.

7. Avoid the empty calories of soft drinks and alcohol.

In the real world, it may be impossible to avoid these things entirely, but all of us can at least eat properly and sharply limit our intake of caffeine, soft drinks and alcohol, and we can use more whole wheat than white breads.

● **Dietary supplements.** This part is admittedly controversial. According to Dr. Slightam and others, "a balanced vitamin and mineral program *may* be of some help to make up any deficiencies that have occurred due to agricultural methods or processing or preparing. Basically, a once per day preparation with perhaps extra Vitamin C and Vitamin E to be taken at the main meal seems to help most people. There are many variables here, and vitamin and mineral supplementation is an individual thing and very controversial."

Some women have reported a significant reduction in cycle irregularity when an already good diet was supplemented by additional vitamins and minerals. Other women have reported no such changes. Some people find that a B-complex supplement reduces feelings of stress or fatigue. The health magazines regularly carry anecdotal reports that various women find significantly better relief from menstrual cramps with a variety of dietary supplements than with aspirin or other pain relievers.

The wide range of experience suggests two things. First of all, some cycle irregularity or other menstrual cycle problems may be alleviated by proper nutrition including a prudent use of dietary supplements. Secondly, because of individual differences, what helps one woman may not help another. In addition, some problems of cycle irregularity may be entirely unrelated to nutrition. (See summary of this section.)

We suggest that, if you decide to use vitamins and minerals, you purchase products from companies whose primary business is dietary supplements rather than the products of pharmaceutical companies involved in the manufacture of abortifacient and contraceptive devices and drugs. For example, the Upjohn Company manufactures a prostaglandin product whose only government approved use is for abortions. Why buy their vitamins (Unicaps)?

Light and Ovulation

Ever since the publication by Dewan[1], speculation has continued about the possible connection between light and ovulation. This was started by the observation that in lower forms of life there is sometimes a marked connection between light and fertility and by the fact that in some primitive tribes there was some evidence indicating that all the women (or nearly all) were ovulating at about the same time — during the full moon. One woman built this speculation into a book, claiming that a small amount of light in the bedroom on nights 14-17 of the cycle produces very regular cycle patterns.[2] However, she did not start with women who had already recorded cycles with significant cycle variation.

The most recently reported research indicated excellent success in "regulating" irregular mucus patterns through the combination of total darkness in the sleeping room for most of the cycle and the Dewan light regimen at the appropriate time.[3]

We have repeated some of this research in an informal way, and the results are somewhat similar to those of dietary supplements — mixed. One couple swears that this system has induced an almost clockwork regularity of typical cycle length after previous experience with much greater irregularity of cycle length including much longer cycles than they now experience with the light bulb stimulation. Other women have had no such results. A preliminary analysis has indicated that there was some reduction in cycle range for approximately half of the women. The advocates of this practice make an educated guess that light acts upon the pineal gland which in turn influences the hypothalamic-pituitary interactions.

For those who want to try this, the following guidelines are being used by others. 1. Beginning with menstruation, the bedroom should be very dark, not lit up by streetlights. 2. A light is turned on all night long on cycle days 14 through 17. Dewan first used a 100 watt bulb in a lamp placed on the floor at the base of the bed, but we don't think that such brightness is necessary. After all, the idea is to duplicate the light of the moon. Thus all that is needed is enough light so that a woman is conscious of light in the room with her eyelids closed.

●**Summary.** Some amount of cycle irregularity may be due to inadequate nutrition, whether from an inadequate diet or insufficient absorption, and some of this cycle irregularity may be reduced by an improved diet and/or the use of dietary supplements. Some other cycle irregularity may be reduced by the "Silvery Moon" experiment described above.

Other cycle irregularity may be due to an imbalance or improper functioning of the endocrine system. Sometimes a thyroid deficiency, for example, is reflected by very low basal body temperatures and significant cycle variation. Thus, a woman who experiences wide cycle variation, say a range of 14 days or more, may be well advised to have an endocrine checkup by a competent physician.

●**Pre-Menstrual Tension.** Various symptoms ranging from anxiety and mood swings to cravings for sweets, from depression to unusual weight gain have been reported as characteristics of pre-menstrual tension syndrome (PMTS).

When women have some of these symptoms in a severe way, they suffer, and Phase III becomes something less than a honeymoon.

Only in recent years has much attention been paid to this situation; both causes and treatments are still being worked on. Some physicians have been using natural progesterone vaginal suppositories during the luteal phase of the cycle, but the value of that treatment is very questionable, and it is certainly expensive.

There is some indication that PMTS is sometimes associated with short or scanty mucus patches and/or weak thermal shift patterns. At the time of this writing, there was a growing agreement that a combination of proper nutrition and exercise was by far the best treatment for pre-menstrual tension.

Water retention during the luteal phase is blamed for part of the PMTS; elimination or greatly reduced consumption of both sugar and salt are recommended for reducing water retention. However, if a woman completely reduces her consumption of iodized salt, she may need alternative sources of iodine lest she experience a thyroid deficiency and increased cycle irregularity. Seafood and kelp tablets are such sources.

References:

1. E.M. Dewan, "On the Possibility of a Perfect Rhythm Method of Birth Control by Periodic Light Stimulation," *American Journal of Obstetrics and Gynecology,* 99:7 (1967), 1016-1019.

2. Louise Lacey, *Lunaception: A Feminine Odyssey into Fertility and Contraception* (New York: Coward, McCann & Geoghegan, Inc., 1974).

3. Joy De Felice, "The Effects of Light on Cervical Mucus Patterns in the Menstrual Cycle: A Clinical Study." Sacred Heart Medical Center, Spokane, Washington, 1979.

Appendix II: Possible Helps for Seeking Pregnancy

●**The Sims-Huhner Test.** As mentioned in the section on "Seeking Pregnancy," the Couple to Couple League "is opposed to any form of artificial insemination, masturbation for seminal analysis or attempted "test tube" conception on the grounds that these depersonalize the sexual act . . ." (page 148).

Because so many physicians dealing with relatively infertile couples almost routinely tell the husband to masturbate for seminal analysis, the moral objection to this practice has raised the practical question, "Are there any morally acceptable methods of semen collection that are also medically useful?" The answer is "Yes."

The Sims-Huhner test is a sperm gathering process that is morally and medically acceptable because it simply involves gathering a sample of semen from the vagina after normal intercourse. For the Sims-Huhner test to be valid, intercourse must take place during the flow of the most fertile mucus because this is the time most favorable to sperm life. If the test is performed during the infertile time, the vaginal environment is hostile to sperm life, and a false count will most likely occur.

The Sims-Huhner test has the additional advantage of showing how the sperm and cervical mucus interact. In a few cases of infertility, there may be a normal sperm count, but the sperm are somehow clumped or immobilized by contact with the cervical mucus.

●**The perforated condom.** Another medically and morally acceptable method of gathering sperm may be used if the physician needs a sample of semen that has not been in contact with cervical mucus. A condom with a small hole at the end may be used during normal intercourse. After ejaculation, some of the semen will be deposited in the vagina, and some will remain in the condom from which it may be taken for analysis. The process respects the requirements of the natural law that deliberately sought orgasm (as contrasted with nocturnal emission) occur only in connection with sexual intercourse and that ejaculation result in the depositing of semen in his spouse's vagina.

This may sound like hair splitting to some, but an understanding of the history of the contraception movement among Catholics shows that this is not the case. In fact, the theologizing to justify contraception started with the acceptance of masturbation for seminal analysis by a few moral theologians. Then they said, "See, for the good purpose of achieving pregnancy, we have 'justified' masturbation (which had previously always been condemned) and **therefore** we have justified departing from the natural law if there is a sufficient reason. The conclusion is that we can accept contraception, oral sodomy, etc. which likewise violate the natural law if the couple think they have a sufficient reason for avoiding pregnancy." This is not a prediction of a theological domino theory; this is what has already happened, and the first step was ridicule of the perforated condom and the acceptance of masturbation for seminal analysis.

●**Sperm Motility.** When sperm cells become sticky and clump together, it is called sperm agglutination. According to Earl B. Dawson, a research professor at the University of Texas at Galveston, when more than 25% of a man's sperm clumps together, his sperm cannot fertilize the ovum.[1] Dawson tested Vitamin C with a group of such men against a control group receiving placebo pills. Within a few months, the wives of the Vitamin C group were all pregnant, but none of the control group had conceived. Dawson's study group took 1 gram of Vitamin C daily, but he believes that drinking just one glass of orange juice daily should be sufficient.

●**Boxer Shorts.** Even the type of underwear can be critical for some men. Nature intends the testicles to hang down from the body, and in this way they are kept a bit cooler. Tight fitting underwear presses them into the rest of the body where the higher heat causes reduced fertility. A number of couples have solved their "infertility" problem by the husband switching from tight fitting underpants to the boxer type.

●**More fluid mucus.** Cervical mucus that impedes sperm migration or tends to immobilize sperm can be a cause of infertility. The expectorant drug guaifenesin has been found to liquefy cervical mucus and appears to have aided a number of couples seeking pregnancy. The drug is found in various expectorant cough syrups; Robitussin plain expectorant syrup is mentioned the most frequently.

A friend of ours who had been trying to get pregnant for thirteen years and had adopted five children heard about this and tried Robitussin for a month; the couple achieved their desired pregnancy. Coincidence or partial causality — who can say? However, the bottle of cough syrup was much less expensive than the battery of infertility tests she had taken ten years previously.

Vitamin A can also increase the quantity and quality of cervical mucus. Another friend mentioned a very scanty mucus discharge; we suggested eating more foods rich in Vitamin A. She began eating lots of carrots and reported mucus with a five inch stretch! Vitamin A is necessary for the proper functioning of all the mucus membranes in your body. Once again, the importance of proper nutrition is evident.

References

1. Earl B. Dawson. Reported at the 1983 annual meeting of the Federation of American Societies of Experimental Biology. "New Claim for Vitamin C," *The Cincinnati Enquirer,* April 17, 1983, page D-2.

Appendix III: Daylight Savings Time and Temperature Changes

In the spring of the year, the change to daylight savings time has the effect of getting you up an hour EARLIER. Temperatures taken for the first 2 or 3 days after the start of daylight savings time might be lower than they would be otherwise, but this offers no problem as far as false high readings are concerned.

However in the fall of the year, the change back to standard time has the effect of getting you up an hour LATER, so the temperatures may be higher for 2 or 3 days. If you are in Phase I or Phase III, there's no problem. If you are in Phase II and want the most accurate temperatures for the transition, follow this plan:

> First day of standard time: take it 40 minutes early
> Second day of standard time: take it 20 minutes early
> Third day of standard time: take it at your usual time.

Appendix IV: Support For Full-Time Mothering

Ecological breast-feeding or natural mothering involves full-time mothering. However, in Western culture, questions about being a full-time mother are raised from two different directions—career and money.

Rest assured, there is no more important or challenging career than mothering. You are helping to form the attitudes, convictions, moral values and emotional attachments of your offspring who in turn will have the same responsibilities with their children. Pope John Paul II has noted the importance of full-time mothering when he wrote in *Familiaris Consortio:*

"...society must be structured in such a way that wives and mothers are not in practice compelled to work outside the home, and that their families can live and prosper in a dignified way even when they themselves devote their full time to their own family.

Furthermore, the mentality which honors women more for their work outside the home than for work within the family must be overcome. This requires that men should truly esteem and love women with total respect for their personal dignity, and that society should create and develop conditions favoring work in the home."[1]

For continued support along these lines, we suggest that you read *Breastfeeding and Natural Child Spacing*[2] and keep reading *The CCL News*, the bi-monthly membership newsletter of the League.

Is it impossible to get by on just your husband's income? Read *The Heart Has Its Own Reasons*[3] by Mary Ann Cahill, and you may find the way. This book was written to show couples how to manage on one income, sometimes well below the national average, and the author offers many real life examples of how mothers can produce some income while remaining with their children. An added benefit of this practical book is that the many suggestions for a simpler lifestyle can strengthen family life.

All the above mentioned books are available through the CCL National Office. Write and ask for the CCL Basic Materials List.

References.
1. Pope John Paul II, *Familiaris Consortio*, n.23.
2. Sheila Kippley, *Breastfeeding and Natural Child Spacing: The Ecology of Natural Mothering* (New York: Harper & Row, 1974; Penguin paperback, 1975).
3. Mary Ann Cahill, *The Heart Has Its Own Reasons* (La Leche League International, Inc., 1983).

Glossary of Terms

abortion. The destruction of a human life at any time between fertilization/conception and birth. An abortion is called spontaneous when it occurs solely from natural causes; it is called induced when it results from human interference with the normal development of the unborn baby through the use of procedures, drugs, or devices designed to kill it.

abortifacient. A device or drug that causes an abortion.

absolutely infertile. Unable to become pregnant; refers to the infertility beginning several days after ovulation. However, this term does not mean that it is absolutely impossible to become pregnant when having coitus only in the time designated as post-ovulation infertility by any given guideline.

amenorrhea. Prolonged absence of menstrual periods.

anovulatory. Without ovulation; a menstrual cycle in which no ovulation occurs is anovulatory.

basal temperatures. The temperature of the human body at rest, unaffected by activity, food, or drink.

cervical mucus. A fluid secreted by glands in the cervix; it becomes watery and stretchy before and at the time of ovulation.

cervix. The lower, narrow part of the uterus.

coitus. Sexual intercourse.

coitus interruptus. Withdrawal from intercourse resulting in ejaculation outside the vagina.

coitus reservatus. Sexual intercourse controlled so that neither party experiences orgasm.

conception. The term applied to the creation of a new human life through the union of sperm and ovum; the process of becoming pregnant; fertilization.

condom. A contraceptive device put over the penis to prevent sperm from entering the vagina.

contraception. The practice of using procedures, devices, or drugs intended to prevent conception by interfering with the natural development or survival of ova and/or sperm either before or after ejaculation; artificial birth control.

contraceptives. Devices and drugs used in the practice of contraception.

corpus luteum. The name given to an ovarian follicle after it has released its ovum; as a gland, it secretes progesterone for about ten to fourteen days after ovulation.

diaphragm. A contraceptive device inserted into the vagina to cover the cervix to prevent sperm from entering it; called a cervical cap in England.

douche. A stream of water directed into the vagina to wash it out.

ecological breast-feeding. The type of nursing that fosters the natural relationship of mother and baby; characterized by (1) nursing as often as the baby wants; (2) no supplements or solids before the baby takes them from the family table; and (3) baby-led weaning.

ectopic pregnancy. See tubal pregnancy.

ejaculation. The spasmodic expulsion of semen from the penis.

endocrine glands. Glands that secrete substances into the bloodstream for the purpose of controlling metabolism and other bodily functions.

endometrium. The inner lining of the uterus that builds up in each cycle and then is discharged in menstruation if pregnancy has not occurred.

episiotomy. An incision made to enlarge the vaginal opening for birth.

estrogen. A hormone that causes the cervix to secrete mucus.

fallopian tubes. The pair of tubes that conduct the egg from either ovary to the uterus.

fertile, fertility. In human reproduction, the state of the woman being able to conceive or of the man's sperm being able to fertilize the ovum.

follicle. Any one of thousands of tiny ovarian containers which each hold one ovum; upon release of its ovum, it becomes a gland called the corpus luteum.

FSH. Abbreviation for follicle stimulating hormone, a substance secreted by the pituitary gland to stimulate the maturation of ovarian follicles.

full thermal shift. Three or more temperatures *consecutively* at a level .4 (4/10) of 1°F. above the pre-shift base level.

gynecologist. A medical doctor who specializes in the treatment of the female reproductive organs.

hormone. A glandular secretion that influences the action of cells in another part of the body.

implantation. The process of a newly conceived life at the blastocyst stage of development embedding in the lining of the uterus.

impotence. The inability to sustain an erection for coitus.

infertility. The state of a woman being unable to conceive or of a man being unable to fertilize an ovum.

IUD. Abbreviation for intrauterine device, a device placed within the uterus to destroy human life prior to implantation.

labia. The lips, both inner and outer, of the vulva; the outermost parts of the female sexual organs.

lactation. The process of producing and yielding milk from the mammary glands.

lochia. A postpartum discharge, usually bloody and usually lasting several weeks.

luteal phase. The postovulation phase of the menstrual cycle under the influence of progesterone secreted from the corpus luteum.

mammary glands. The breasts; more exactly, the glands in the breasts that secrete milk.

masturbation. Self-stimulation for carnal pleasure and orgasm.

menopause. The cessation of menstruation and ovarian activity.

menses. Synonym for menstruation.

menstruation. A vaginal bloody discharge caused by the sloughing off of the outer layers of the endometrium.

minipill. A low-dosage oral contraceptive; a less powerful version of the Pill. It probably acts more as an abortifacient than as a contraceptive.

miscarriage. A spontaneous or natural abortion.

mittelschmerz. A German term meaning "pain in the middle" and used to describe a pain sometimes associated with ovulation.

mucorrhea. The state of producing cervical mucus.

mucus. A watery, slippery substance secreted by various mucus glands.

NFP. Abbreviation for natural family planning.

nocturnal emission. An involuntary and unconscious night-time ejaculation of excess semen.

obstetrician. A medical doctor who specializes in the delivery of babies and in pre- and postnatal care of the mother.

os. The Latin word for mouth; the opening of the cervix.

ovary. The female reproductive organ containing the ova, or eggs.

overall thermal shift. A thermal shift pattern in which there are at least three temperatures consecutively above the PSB, in an overall rising or elevated pattern, with at least one reaching a level 4/10 (or more) of 1°F. above the PSB.

ovulation. The process of an ovarian follicle releasing its ovum, thus making the woman fertile and able to become pregnant.

ovum (plural: ova). The woman's egg.

pediatrician. A medical doctor who specializes in the treatment of children.

penis. The male sexual organ used for coitus.

Phase I. The time of pre-ovulation infertility.

Phase II. The fertile time.

Phase III. The time of postovulation infertility.

Pill. Capitalized, it refers to all the various birth control pills whether they act as abortifacients or contraceptives.

pituitary gland. A gland located at the base of the brain that controls many bodily functions through various secretions.

POB. Abbreviation for pre-ovulation base, another term for pre-shift base.

postovulation infertility. The infertile time starting several days after ovulation and continuing until the next menstruation.

postpartum. After childbirth.

premenopause. The transition stage in life between the years of normal fertility and menopause.

pre-ovulation infertility. The infertile time starting with menstruation. The end of this infertile time is determined in several ways.

pre-shift base. The level from which the thermal shift is measured; usually determined by the normal highs among the pre-shift six temperatures.

pre-shift six. The six temperatures immediately before the beginning of the rising temperatures that make up the thermal shift.

progesterone. A female hormone secreted by the corpus luteum.

prostate gland. A male sexual organ that provides a fluid which mixes with sperm to produce semen.

PSB. Abbreviation for pre-shift base level.

rhythm method. A term used to describe calendar ryhthm, a system of estimating fertility based on previous cycle lengths.

rule of thumb. See Chapter 8, Section A for a description of the basic rules of thumb.

scrotum. The sac below the penis that contains the testicles.

sperm. The male cells that unite with the female ovum to cause conception.

sterilization. The process of rendering either male or female sterile, i.e., incapable of becoming pregnant or causing pregnancy.

strong thermal shift. A thermal shift pattern in which there are at least three temperatures that are all consecutively at least 2/10 of 1°F. above the PSB with the last one at least 4/10 of 1°F. above the PSB.

sympto-thermal method. A natural family planning system making use of all the signs of fertility.

testicles. The male sexual organs contained in the scrotum and producing sperm.

thermal shift. The postovulation rise in temperatures sustained in an overall rising or elevated pattern for at least three days, reaching and staying at a level usually .4 (4/10) of 1°F. above the pre-shift base level. See also "full thermal shift" and "overall thermal shift," and "strong thermal shift."

tubal ligation. A sterilization procedure consisting of tying the Fallopian tubes to prevent sperm from meeting ova.

tubal pregnancy. Ectopic pregnancy; a pregnancy in which implantation occurs within the Fallopian tube rather than in the uterus.

uterus. The female organ in which the baby grows during the nine months of pregnancy; frequently called the womb.

vagina. The female sexual organ used in coitus.

vaginal foams and jellies. Chemical contraceptive products made to be inserted in the vagina before coitus to kill sperm.

vasectomy. A male sterilization procedure that prevents sperm from becoming part of the semen.

vulva. The external parts of the female sexual organs, including the labia.

womb. The uterus.

Additional Materials

Daily Observation Charts. A booklet of 14 CCL Daily Observation Charts.

Practical Applications Booklet. A workbook of 20 different charted cases including explanatory interpretations. It is intended for use with **The Art of Natural Family Planning** and is really a *must* for self-instruction.

CCL Family Foundations is sent six times a year to all members as a benefit of an annual contribution of $15.00 or more. New pamphlets usually are printed in **CCL Family Foundations,** and each issue carries articles of value to those practicing or promoting natural family planning.

A series of inexpensive pamphlets and brochures on special subjects have been published by the Couple to Couple League. Couples using natural family planning inevitably get questions about all forms of birth control and related issues, and the following publications have been designed to inform NFP users and others about these subjects.

Breastfeeding: Does It Really Space Babies? Yes, it can, if it's done the right way. This brochure describes the type of nursing (ecological breastfeeding) that spaces babies usually 18 to 30 months apart, and it also tells how to detect the return of fertility. 5 references.

The Case for Natural Family Planning. Eight reasons modern couples are choosing NFP.

The CCL Story. An explanation of the origin, principles and methods of the Couple to Couple League.

From Contraception to Abortion. Father Paul Marx explains the importance of sound sexuality and how contraception has lead to the contraceptive mentality and then to abortion; how to change this.

Holy Communion: Eucharistic and Marital. A five-fold analogy showing that marital union must not be closed to the transmission of life.

The Legacy of Margaret Sanger. Explains the legacy of Margaret Sanger's contraceptive philosophy in terms of fornication, adultery and abortion, the role of Planned Parenthood in transmitting this legacy, and the counter philosophy of CCL.

247

The Natural Way of Planning Your Family. Some basic questions and answers about NFP.

Not in the Public Interest: the Planned Parenthood Version of Sex Education. The results and an analysis of the Planned Parenthood approach to sex education with suggestions for a better plan.

A Physician's Reference to Natural Family Planning. Especially for physicians, a description of the Sympto-Thermal (ST) method, the relation of the ST method to other forms of NFP and the endocrinology and physiology that forms the basis for the ST method. The scientific explanation in this brochure is more detailed than in **The Art of Natural Family Planning.** 22 references.

The Pill and the IUD: Some Facts for an informed Choice. Documentation on the abortifacient properties and health hazards of the Pill and the IUD. 25 references.

Sexual Sterilization: Some Questions and Answers. The medical and psychological aspects of vasectomy and tubal ligation. 32 references.

The Sympto-Thermal Method and the Ovulation Method. A thirteen point comparison of two methods of natural family planning.

What Can the Couple to Couple League do for My Community? How a CCL chapter can help families, clergy and physicians, and how to get one started.

What Does the Catholic Church Teach About Birth Control? A review of the Catholic teaching on birth control and finding a solution in natural family planning. 18 references.

What Others are Saying about NFP and CCL. Endorsements from prominent Americans for CCL and statements by NFP users.

Birth Control and Christian Discipleship. A 36-page pamphlet detailing the Protestant rejection of contraception before 1930, the connection between contraception and abortion, what the Bible says about birth control, and the whole issue in the light of Christian discipleship.

AUDIO-VISUAL

A New Dawn: Christian Marriage and Birth Control. A slide/sound program introducing NFP to engaged couples. Also has sections on the Pill, IUD, and conscience. Designed especially for Catholic pre-marriage instructions, it can also be used in a variety of other places. 131 color frames; 29 minutes. Complete with slide carousel or filmstrip, tape cassette and program booklet. Please specify slides or filmstrip.

Looking Ahead: Marriage and Family Planning introduces the concept of natural family planning to high school students. It uses some of the material from **A New Dawn** (sections on the Pill, IUD, and conscience), but it also contains additional information showing how sexually active teenage girls can contract diseases that will make them sterile and unable to have babies when they want them. 129 color frames; 27 minutes; slides or filmstrip; complete with carrousel for slides, script, and 2 tapes for both audible and automatic, inaudible operation.

The Springtime of Your Life. This pro-chastity AV program describes 17 practical reasons not to get sexually involved before marriage, using a framework of 12 "freedoms from" and 5 "freedoms to." **Springtime** also provides meaning to sex by its affirmation that sex is meant to symbolize marital commitment and love. **Springtime** is acceptable to parents concerned about sex education in the schools. Aside from one slide illustrating the union of ovum and sperm, it has no physiology. Its emphasis is on the chaste use of sexuality — postponing sexual involvement until marriage. 140 color frames; 26.5 minutes; slides or filmstrip; complete with carrousel, script booklet, and 2 tapes for both audible and automatic, inaudible operation.

For a complete materials list with prices and for information on these and other programs in the planning stages as this book went to press, contact the Couple to Couple League, P.O. Box 111184, Cincinnati, OH 45211-1184. Phone: (513) 661-7612.

This index will be fairly useful, but no effort was made to be complete in the sense of listing each page where mucus or temperature, etc., is mentioned.

Many readers have said that this book should be entitled
Natural Mothering: Its Beauty and How it Relates to Baby Spacing
because it is principally about natural mothering.

This book has helped thousands of mothers to recognize the real
needs of their babies and to free themselves from some of the fears
and prejudices of our culture. Response by mothers seeking to provide nurturing care to their babies has been overwhelmingly
enthusiastic.

Available at general bookstores in cloth or paper. Also available
through the CCL National Office for $3.95 (paperback). Please add
$1.25 shipping and handling for one item and $.20 for each
additional item.